The University of Leeds

Nuffield Institute for
Health Service Studies

INFORMATION RESOURCE CENTRE

Advances in Selection
and Assessment

Advances in Selection and Assessment

MIKE SMITH

and

IVAN T. ROBERTSON

Manchester School of Management
University of Manchester Institute of
Science and Technology

JOHN WILEY & SONS
Chichester · New York · Brisbane · Toronto · Singapore

Library of Congress Cataloging-in-Publication Data:
Advances in selection and assessment/[edited by Mike Smith & Ivan, T. Robertson.
   p.   cm.
   Bibliography: p.
   Includes index.
   ISBN 0 471 92099 1
   1. Employee selection. 2. Employee selection—Case studies.
I. Smith, Mike (J. Mike) II. Robertson, Ivan, T.
HF5549.5.S38A38 1988
658.3'112—dc19   88–20727
                                                          CIP

British Library Cataloguing in Publication Data
Advances in selection and assessment.
   1. Personnel selection
   I. Smith, Mike,   *1945–* II. Robertson,
   Ivan, T.
   658.3'112
   ISBN 0 471 92099 1

Phototypeset by Input Typesetting Ltd., London SW19 8DR
Printed in Great Britain by St Edmundsbury Press Ltd, Bury St Edmunds

Contents

FAIRNESS IN SELECTION

SELECTION AS A SOCIAL PROCESS

META-ANALYSIS

UTILITY ANALYSIS

List of Contributors

Professor J. A. Algera   *Technische Hogeschool, Afdeling der Bedrijkskude, Vakgroep Organisatiepsychologie, Postbus 13, 5600 MB Eindhoven, Netherlands*

Dr A. E. Akkerman   *LTP, Vossius Straat 54, 1071 AK, Amsterdam, Netherlands*

Lt Col R. D. Ballentine   *4518 Meredith Woods, San Antonio, TX 78249, USA*

Professor J. W. Boudreau   *New York State School of Industrial & Labor Relations, Cornell University, Ithaca, NY 14851, USA*

Mr T. D. Coggin   *4720 Carberry Court, Matthews, NC 28105, USA*

Dr M. A. M. Greuter   *Psychologisch Laboritorium, Vakgroep Arbeids-en Organisatiepsychologie, Weesperplien 8, 1018 XA Amsterdam, Netherlands*

Professor R. M. Guion   *Department of Psychology, Bowling Green State University, Ohio OH 43403, USA*

Professor P. Herriot   *Department of Occupational Psychology, Birkbeck College, Malet Street, London WC1E 7HX, UK*

Professor J. E. Hunter   *Department of Psychology, Michigan State University, 133 Snyder Hall, East Lansing, Michigan, USA*

Dr T. Janz   *Faculty of Management, The University of Calgary, Calgary, Alberta, CANADA*

Dr R. S. Kandola   *Pearn Kandola Downs, Occupational Psychologists, Windsor House, 12 High Street, Kidlington, Oxford, OX5 2DH, UK*

Professor F. J. Landy   *Department of Psychology, Pennsylvania State University, University Park, PA 16802, USA*

Professor Claude Levy-Leboyer   *Université René Descartes, 12 Rue d'ecole de medicine, Paris, France*

Mr D. McLeod   *25 Riverside Close, Wheatsheaf Lane, Staines, Middlesex, TW18 2LW, UK*

Dr M. A. Pearn   *Pearn Kandola Downs, Occupational Psychologists, Windsor House, 12 High Street, Kidlington, Oxford, OX5 2DH, UK*

Dr H. Rastegary   *Department of Psychology, Pennsylvania State University, University Park, PA 16802, USA*

Dr I. T. Robertson   *Manchester School of Management, UMIST, PO Box 88, Sackville Street, Manchester, M60 1QD, UK*

Professor P. R. Sackett   *Industrial Relations Center, University of Minnesota, Minneapolis, Minnesota, USA*

Professor N. Schmitt   *Department of Psychology, Psychology Research Building, Michigan State University, East Lansing, Michigan, USA*

Professor H. Schuler   *Universitat Hohenheim, Institut 430, Postfach 70 05 62, D-7000 Stuttgart, Federal Republic of Germany*

Professor F. L. Schmidt   *Department of Industrial Relations and Human Resources, University of Iowa, Iowa, USA*

Dr J. M. Smith   *Manchester School of Management, UMIST, PO Box 88, Sackville Street, Manchester, M60 1QD, UK*

Dr M. Tenopyr   *AT&T, Room JK 3D123, 150 JFK Parkway, Short Hills, NJ 07078, USA*

Dr R. J. Tissen   *Management Studiecontrum, Stichtig de Baak, Konigin Astridboulevard, Noordwijk ZH, Netherlands*

Dr R. S. Williams   *The Management College, Henley-on-Thames, UK*

1

Perspectives

MIKE SMITH and IVAN T. ROBERTSON
University of Manchester Institute of Science and Technology

HISTORICAL TRENDS IN SELECTION AND ASSESSMENT

Early days to mid century

Academic subjects rarely develop at an even pace, for reasons which would, by themselves merit a major study, they seem to proceed in a series of phases of immense activity interspersed by longer periods of lower activity. Within our own subject area of selection and assessment there have undoubtedly been two previous peaks of activity: one during the early years of the century when Münsterberg and others were pioneering the subject: one during the middle years of this century as organizations and governments attempted to cope with the problems of war and greater mechanization. This book is founded on the belief that we are, as the century draws to a close, in the middle of another of these periods of intense development.

Mid century and decline

By the mid 1950s selection and assessment seemed to have reached its zenith and seemed to be heading for a period of consolidation if not decline. In these years of high employment and even labour shortages employers were often grateful to accept any additional staff. From an academic viewpoint the laws of diminishing returns had started to set in and most of the 'easy' academic prizes had already been gained and by the early 1960s the centre stage was clearly shifting to other areas such as motivation, organizational structuring

Advances in Selection and Assessment. Edited by M. Smith and I. T. Robertson

and the quality of working life. The conceptual developments of the middle years seemed to contain the seeds of destruction. Emphasis and greater awareness of psychometric properties such as reliability and validity led to more extensive and formalized collection and collation of data. This, in turn, seemed to reveal that the advantages of good selection were apparently minimal. The work of people such as Ghiselli was interpreted by some to show that the going rate for the validity of a selection device was a measly correlation of 0.2 or 0.3. To make matters worse, the evidence also seemed to show that even these low correlations could not be relied upon—a lot depended upon the circumstances in a specific organization and so methods needed to be revalidated in every organization where they were used. To many practitioners the efforts involved seemed disproportionate to the rewards. By the mid 1960s, the issue of equal opportunities was making an impact because it seemed that many of the measures favoured by occupational psychologists had an adverse impact against women and minority groups. The cumulative effect of these influences was to lead many academics, practitioners and organizations to pay less attention to the development of new approaches to selection and assessment and rely on traditional methods, and the subject area seemed set for a long period of decline.

Renaissance

Less than two decades later a very different scene had emerged. Organizations were paying far greater attention to the selection process. The reasons are a matter of speculation but a greater emphasis on productivity and efficiency, often engendered by a climate of intense international competition, has played a part. With the rise in living standards throughout the developed world, labour costs are now the largest single cost in many organizations. Part of the proper management of these resources lies in proper selection. Higher rates of unemployment and with them a greater pool of available applicants have been another factor. In many countries legislation concerning security of employment has also added to the pressure to select staff as accurately as possible. Despite the early reactions of some organizations, the process of complying with equal opportunities legislation has produced a greater understanding of the selection process.

There has been an academic renaissance too. Many of the earlier views have been challenged by more recent work: it now seems that validities are higher than the depressing figures gathered by Ghiselli and it seems that these validities are fairly stable across similar occupations. Furthermore, it seems that many methods of selection have little or no adverse impact upon women and minority groups. The academic advances have not been restricted to overturning earlier views; there have been further developments of existing lines of thought such as the way in which utility theory has built upon work started in the 1940s so that now we can arrive at reasonably precise estimates of the costs and benefits of various methods of selection. Indeed, this line of enquiry has arrived at the point where it is contributing to conceptual developments by modelling the selection and assessment processes in a way that provides direct links to mainstream human resource management.

The recent renaissance of interest in selection and assessment has also involved advances with few antecedents in the 1950s or 1960s—probably the prime example of this has been the advances in meta analysis.

ORIGINS AND PLAN OF THIS BOOK

This book takes the view that the renaissance of activity in selection and assessment has occurred and that its further vigour will be aided by taking stock of what has already been achieved and then identifying avenues where further work is both needed and likely to bear fruit. To this end, a small international conference was convened at Buxton in the UK in 1987. The aim was to achieve a small critical mass of expertise which would provide both synthesis and stimulation. This book is largely the result of that conference.

Rather than produce an unintegrated catalogue of chapters on interesting topics a clear scheme was adopted which was based upon the general selection paradigm. Of course this paradigm is a simplification and in reality the process is iterative with interaction between the stages but it serves as a useful structure. In essence, this book focusses upon the seven stages enclosed in thick boxes, in Figure 1.1, and a section of three chapters is devoted to each. The first chapter is the largest in each section and attempts to summarize and codify recent developments in that area. In addition, the first chapters in each section also identify lucunae in our knowledge and suggest avenues of future investigation which might be fruitful. The second chapter in each section presents a further, shorter, view of the topic. The authors of the 'comment' chapters had the benefit of both the 'state of the art' chapters and the comments of participants at the Buxton Conference. The final, very short, chapter in each section presents a case study to give the flavour of the issues contained in the previous two chapters.

Gaps

Many seasoned strategists will affirm the axiom that identifying what is absent from a situation is just as important in understanding a problem as knowing what is present. If it is accepted that the contents of this book and, less directly, the issues raised at the Buxton Conference are a reasonable reflection of the present activity in selection and assessment, the paradigm can be used to identify those areas which have been given scant attention and three main 'orphans' emerge: production of personnel specifications; attraction of candi-

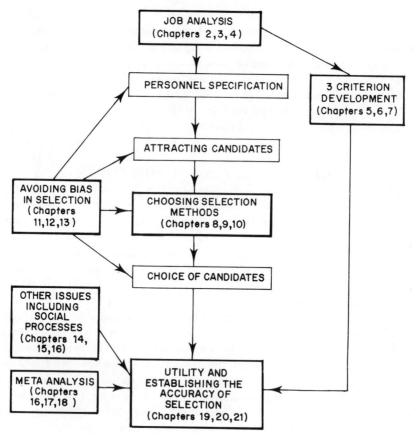

Figure 1.1   The selection paradigm

dates; and the choice of candidates. These areas could well represent gaps in our knowledge.

Personnel specifications

The case for the production of personnel specifications being a major gap in our knowledge is the hardest to sustain. Some methods of deriving scientifically based personnel descriptions already exist. Indeed, some are identified in Algera and Greuter's chapter on Job Analysis. Yet there is nowhere near the research base on the production of personnel specifications as there is on, say, utility or bias in selection. Certainly, we could not find enough material to justify a substantive chapter in its own right. This absence may not be too significant if the selector chooses the 'job sampling' path to the selection of employees. But probably most selection is based on attribute requirements or dimensions. Thus in many situations the inferential leap from the relative objectivity facts of a job analysis to the attributes set out in a personnel specification is an important link in the chain yet there is precious little systematic evidence on how this leap is made or on the reliability and validity of the final result.

Attracting candidates

There is an even larger dearth of systematic knowledge concerning the various methods of attracting candidates. The few studies that have been conducted suggest that this would be a fruitful avenue to follow since some methods seem to attract 'better' candidates than others. The first step in filling this lacuna is more comparative studies of the effectiveness of various media or methods in terms of the cost and the quantity and quality of applicants produced. The second stage is probably a more analytical one of establishing why various methods produce the results they do. The third step would be to link this knowledge with other areas of the selection paradigm. To an extent tentative links have already been formed. The media used to attract candidates are an aspect of the dialogue between the individual and the organization which is highlighted in Herriot's chapter (Ch. 14). In addition, one of the studies quoted by Boudreau (Ch. 20) contrasts the utility of improving selection (i.e. using a more valid predictor) with the utility of improving attraction of candidates by employing an agency which is able to obtain a better pool of candidates.

Choice of candidates

Although academic validity studies and case studies in organizations using 'best practice' methods give us some information on how organizations should select employees, much less information is available about how selection is carried out in the average organization. Even the basic descriptive statistics on which methods or which combination of methods is used under which circumstances is sparse and largely anecdotal—although as noted in Robertson and Smith's chapter a start has been made in this process. Most of the academic work is conducted in an environment of scientific rigour where selectors are presumed to follow a simple rule (e.g. hire on a top-down policy using interview impressions or hire on a meets-the-pass-mark basis using test scores). In reality there are usually individuals making decisions on the basis of many, and often contradictory, pieces of information. How is this process achieved? Which sources of information are given the greatest weight? What factors such as age, education or training of the selector determine his or her choice of predictors and his or her choice of candidates? Another series of questions asks about organizational characteristics such as size, industry or structure which may mediate these relationships. Again some information is available, possibly from the literature on interviewing or decision-making but it is patchy and certainly insufficient to support a major chapter in a volume such as this.

Links to other human resource interventions

Perhaps the biggest lacuna is not even evident from Figure 1.1—the depth of knowledge concerning the links between selection and other human resource interventions. For example, exactly how does an improvement in selection influence training? Undoubtedly, as Hunter's chapter on meta analysis implies, better selection should produce candidates who are easier to train but the relationship is probably more complex and needs more explicit statement. In a similar vein it is possible to ask how does better selection affect the motivation, well-being and health of employees, how does it affect organizational structure? How does it affect the introduction of information technology? We simply have little data on these questions other than an intuitive response that poor selection may inhibit the effectiveness of other human resource interventions or may indeed provide the original problems which give rise to the need for other interventions.

2

Job Analysis for Personnel Selection

Jen A. Algera
Eindhoven University of Technology, Eindhoven

and

Martin A. M. Greuter
University of Amsterdam

1 INTRODUCTION

Job analysis is used for many different purposes in personnel management. Levine (1983) mentions no less than 11 purposes of job analysis in work organizations. Given this many purposes, it is not surprising that a very great number of job analysis methods have been developed in the past. These methods vary in the kind of job data, the method of data collection, the information sources and the method of data analysis. The range of possible options is so big that Brinkman (1983) devised a classification system for job analysis methods. Using this schema, it becomes possible to compare existing job analysis methods, so that the choice of an optimal (combination of) job analysis method(s) in an actual situation is facilitated.

Although some existing methods and instruments pretend to be suited for many purposes, it turns out (see e.g. Algera, in press) that for purposes such as training, selection and job evaluation often very specific requirements are relevant, which a job analysis method should measure up to. It seems very un-likely that one job analysis method or instrument is appropriate for all purposes.

This chapter focuses on job analysis for personnel selection. We therefore will restrict ourselves to methods and instruments that are relevant within this area. The chapter is aimed at giving a 'state of the art' review of the role

Advances in Selection and Assessment. Edited by M. Smith and I. T. Robertson

of job analysis within different frameworks for the prediction of future job performance. Furthermore we will review some recent developments with regard to content-based selection devices, validity generalization and synthetic validity as far as the role of job analysis is concerned.

2 THE ROLE OF JOB ANALYSIS IN PREDICTING WORK PERFORMANCE

By applying job analysis to personnel selection problems a specific goal is intended: as a result of job analysis, characteristics (behavior and ability requirements) must be laid down, which are typical of effective job performance. In addition, these characteristics must be appropriate as predictors of future work performance. Or, to underline the selection-specific nature of this last purpose more precisely: job analysis should contribute to the development and evaluation of prediction models in order to predict job performance.

In this paragraph it is explained how this contribution can be achieved. At first, we concentrate on a general definition of models, thereby highlighting the various benefits of using models in the context of personnel selection. Subsequently the role of job analysis is discussed in constructing prediction models.

2.1 Performance modelling

Models are simplified representations of reality. The notion of 'simplification' is crucial in developing models.

Deletion of some aspects and elements is deliberate and premeditated for the sake of reducing the scope of information. In this manner phenomena and relations can be revealed which would have remained unnoticed otherwise. In this respect selective omission or abstraction can be more fruitful than complete representation.

Several types of models can be identified (In 't Veldt, 1981; Bosman, 1977). In increasing degrees of complexity iconic, analogue and symbolic models can be distinguished, depending on how reality is portrayed by means of a model. With iconic models, portrayal is being achieved by constructing a concrete or realistic symbol system: in the symbol system the same attributes are used as in reality. The only difference may pertain to a difference in scale, although real size models may also be applied (for example: an airflight simulator).

In the case of analogue models reality and symbolic system have comparable structures but in the symbolic system actual circumstances and objects are replaced by symbols. For example: drawing of an electric installation, road maps with divers symbols for main roads, bridges, junctions. In the context of personnel selection a well known example is provided by a work sample for selecting tram crews, developed by Münsterberg in 1911. In this work sample traffic situations were simulated on a map by using figures and letters to represent various traffic participants as pedestrians, cars and horsed vehicles. By moving the map behind a little window, applicants could be confronted with alternative traffic situations.

In symbolic models reality is modeled by means of an abstract or ideal symbolic system, i.e. by abstract concepts which cannot be observed in reality in a direct sense. These concepts are made meaningful in explaining reality by incorporating them in (psychological) theories or hypotheses concerning the phenomena being studied.

System characteristics are represented by mathematical and logical symbols and formulas. The existence of usable theories or hypotheses is a prerequisite for using symbolic models. Note that this last point distinguishes symbolic models from analogue models. Analogue models are not necessarily anchored in psychological theory.

In building prediction models several activities need to be undertaken. In addition to self-evident matters such as problem formulating and specifying model requirements it is also necessary to define (1) content, (2) structure, (3) form and (4) parameters of the model. Finally the model should be (5) evaluated in terms of the *a priori* formulated design criteria. How steps (1) to (5) are worked out in practice, depends on the intended context of application. In the case of personnel selection the following elaboration is advised (Roe, 1984, 1986):

(1) Specifying content: what should be predicted and how? The variables that tend to be included in a selection-oriented performance model are (a) criterion variables that refer to job performance aspects, and (b) predictor variables usually referring to individual characteristics like abilities, skills, interests, temperaments. These characteristics should be sufficiently stable to allow predictions over some time interval.

(2) Structure: once the elements for the model have been chosen, their relationships must be made explicit: how are criterion variables interrelated and how do the prediction variables interrelate? How are both sets related to each other?

(3) Form: in defining the form of the model, an important choice is whether one should choose an incomplete representation specifying regressive functions only or a complete representation, specifying density functions as well.

(4) Estimating parameters: parameters may be estimated in several ways, empirically or rationally. From the empirical methods the classical solution calls for applying unbiased regression methods. In addition, biased regression methods can be applied (for example Stein- and Ridge-regression: cf. Darlington, 1978). Also one might prefer non-empirical

solutions (rational methods including equal or unequal weighting schemes) or a combination of non-empirical and empirical strategies (cf. the J-coefficient of Primoff, 1955).

Job analysis is of special importance for the first of the above steps.

2.2 Signs vs samples

In principle two different ways of representing reality have been elaborated that might be labeled as 'signs' vs 'samples' (Wernimont and Campbell, 1968). These strategies can be conceived as symbolic and iconic (possibly analogue) representations, respectively.

SIGNS	SAMPLES
— representation by means of an abstract symbolic system (symbolic model)	— representation by means of a concrete symbolic system (iconic or analogue system)
— symbols refer to theoretical concepts	— symbols refer to empirical concepts
— predictions are based on performance theory	— predictions are based on point-to-point correspondence between predictor and criterion

Figure 2.1   Signs vs samples

In building models according to the principle referred to as 'signs', work performance is modeled in an abstract manner. The model is based on empirical or theoretical hypotheses (sometimes 'educated guesses') with regard to relatively stable person characteristics.

Because work performance and individual traits are interconnected by hypotheses, individual characteristics measured by tests can be regarded as 'signs' or 'indicators' of future work performance. In constructing predictors according to the sampling approach stable traits are not included explicitly in the prediction model, but this method is based on the behavioral consistency between test performance and job performance.

In this approach, prediction is accomplished by statistically generalizing from a sample to a population. Generally the following steps must be taken. At first, a comprehensive inventory of task and performance requirements is made. From this 'task universum' a sample of tasks is selected and reformulated as exercises or tests that might be used in selection procedures. These exercises can be performed *in vivo* as in work samples and situational tests; one can inspect past performances on the appearance of critical behaviors (question-naires tapping biographical information, cf. Pannone, 1984) or one might elicit descriptions of possible courses of action when one is confronted with certain types of situations ('what would you do if you were . . .?') as is done in the situational interview (Latham *et al.*, 1980; Latham and Saari, 1984). These performances can be conceived as predictors of future behavior on the condition that behavioral consistency prevails in similar circumstances. Due to the content similarity of predictor and criterion, these predictors are referred to as content-based selection devices (see also paragraph 3.1, this chapter).

2.3 Specifying model content by job analysis

As was noted before, job analysis comes primarily into play in the first stage of model building, i.e. in specifying the content elements of the model: criteria and predictors. Before proceeding with this question, it should be emphasized that job analysis does not form the sole basis for identifying conceptual criteria and predictors. One can also rely on results of meta-analysis or on explorative validation studies (cf. Roe, 1983). Nevertheless job analysis is the predominant method in our opinion. Also, it must be realized that meta-analysis and explorative validation studies each imply some sort of use of job analysis methods.

1 Identifying criteria

If predictions are to be based on signs, more abstract and general conceptual criteria should be chosen, so they can be applied to a broader category of jobs than the job under study. It must also be possible to relate these criteria to existing psychological theory. If this last pre-requirement is not met, it becomes almost impossible to generate plausible hypotheses concerning relevant capacities and personality traits. Viewed in this light, the best results can be obtained from a worker-oriented job analysis. Despite various critics the Position Analysis Questionnaire (PAQ) still seems to be the most promising candidate. The job dimensions of the PAQ can be encompassed in a more comprehensive theory and relations with relevant individual characteristics (called 'attributes') can be laid down, at least in principle (cf. McCormick *et al.*, 1979).

Job-oriented methods often result in a specific and detailed description of jobs that is not easily fitted to more abstract performance theories. A noticeable exception is the Occupation Analysis Inventory (OAI) of Cunningham *et al.* (1983). Research shows that the factor analytic structures of job elements data and attribute data are similar (as judged on a subjective basis; no numerical evidence is available). This lends some support to the notion that the OAI job dimensions can be meaningfully related to underlying characteristics.

In applying the sampling approach (work sample, situational test, biographical questionnaires, situational interview) very detailed job information is needed. Job content must be defined exhaustively so that no parts are missed in simulating the job. There is some evidence that job information pertaining to the development of content-oriented selection devices is more and more scrutinized by the courts in terms of completeness and relevance (Hogan and Quigley, 1986). Moreover, the predictive qualities of samples derive from point-to-point correspondence between predictor and criterion. Another reason is that job content must be copied on a very concrete and realistic level, thereby enhancing the face validity of the instrument. All in all, a job-oriented analysis seems to be necessary in order to acquire a complete understanding of the job. Preferably, different information gathering techniques should be used (observation, interviews, questionnaires) and various job experts (job incumbent, supervisors) should be consulted.

The Critical Incidents Technique (CIT) of Flanagan (1954), including subsequent methodologies such as BARS/BOS, seems to be the most frequently mentioned method for constructing predictors following the sampling approach in more or less homogeneous job families (cf. Dunnette, 1976; Landy and Farr, 1983). The CIT produces detailed and more abstract job information simultaneously, by grouping behavioral incidents into more encompassing behavioral dimensions. It also offers good prospects for operationalizing performance dimensions in relation to performance appraisal systems (cf. Carroll and Schneier, 1982; Latham and Wexley, 1981). Last but not least, behavioral dimensions are formulated on a level that can be connected to the world of abilities and personality characteristics.

2 Identifying predictors

The choice of predictors must be based on the content of criteria as defined in an earlier stage. Thus, criteria serve a dual purpose: making explicit what should be predicted and pointing out potentially relevant predictors.

It seems not to require much effort to derive sample type predictors, because criteria and predictors are conceptually similar and belong to the same domain. However, the population of tasks should be defined in relevant terms and a sampling procedure must be laid down in which criteria are specified (among others) for judging the representativeness (content validity) of the resulting predictor. For example, representativeness of the predictor can be judged in terms of adequateness of time sampling (are the most time-consuming tasks represented in the predictor instrument?), task relevance (are all relevant tasks included?), criticalness of suboptimal performance (are those tasks included that lead to deleterious effects if performed incorrectly?) etc.

Things become more complicated in the case of sign type predictors. Now, criteria and predictors are not conceptually similar; they relate to different conceptual systems. Criteria refer to performance behavior and predictors refer to individual characteristics. The problem to be solved is to find a way to link those two different systems, to paraphrase Dunnette (1976). This linkage process can be accomplished by:

1. rational methods (abilities-oriented job analysis, rational validity, J-coefficient, etc.);
2. meta-analysis (validity generalization);
3. explorative validation studies.

These methods vary along the dimension 'rational vs empirical deduction of predictors', and the unit of analysis: job aspects or job-as-a-whole.

From the aforementioned methods for identifying predictors we will concentrate below on the use of rational methods. Because of the voluminous recent research on validity generalization, this topic will be treated separately in paragraph 3.2.

The third method for choosing predictors, conducting an explorative validation study, is not treated in detail, because in this type of study the role of job analysis is rather restricted.

Rational methods for identifying sign type predictors

A common characteristic of all rational methods is that expert judges are asked to pass judgement on the relevance of a given predictor with regard to the job as a whole or in relation to separate aspects of the job. This approach can be recognized in the well-known J-coefficient of Primoff (1955). This method results in an estimated validity coefficient of a predictor based on (1) estimated beta-weights and validity of this predictor for relevant subcriteria, and (2) estimated beta-weights and correlations between these subcriteria and overall job performance. The resulting validity coefficient has been labeled as J-coefficient.

The components that define the J-coefficient (beta-weights, validities etc.) can be estimated in several ways, for example by policy capturing, the judgement of the incumbent's supervisor, test experts, etc. (cf. Hamilton and Dickinson, 1987; see also p. 22, this chapter).

A comparable method has recently been proposed by Schmidt et al. (1983). This time, 'normal' validity coefficients are estimated instead of beta-weights. Furthermore, judgement is based on the job as a whole, not on subcriteria. The resulting validity coefficient is termed rational validity (Schmidt and Hunter, 1980). According to Schmidt et al. (1983) the procedure seems to work well when experts in the field of selection research are asked to estimate validities. Real validity is underestimated only with a small fraction and the combined judgements of twenty experts are as reliable as a local validation study with an N of 981. Less experienced judges but still 'trained professionals in the field of personnel selection' are not as well equipped to perform this judgement task. Nevertheless, the aggregated judgement of twenty experts is still as adequate as the result of a validation study with an N of 217 (Hirsch *et al.*, 1986). Apparently, selection of qualified judges is highly critical. Schmidt *et al.* (1983) note that even individuals holding a doctorate in industrial psychology may not be suitably experienced to make accurate estimates.

A third category of rational methods can be identified in relation to the PAQ and OAI, instruments which are highly similar with regard to research design and results. In developing these job analyses, arrangements are made for obtaining ratings of attribute requirements. As a construct, an attribute is somewhat akin to the concept of worker trait (McCormick *et al.*, 1972, p 394). Some of the attributes can be referred to as aptitudes or abilities. Others are referred to as situational attributes (i.e. working alone, time pressure, complexity of duties, etc.). The various attributes are rated in terms of their relevance to each job element in the PAQ or OAI. This rating process ends up with an 'attribute profile' for each job element.

Conceptually, the gap between job content and predictors can also be bridged by ability-oriented job analysis. The Task Abilities Scales (TAS) of Fleishman of which a modified version has recently appeared (cf. Fleishman and Quaintance, 1984) can be viewed as the most rigorously constructed questionnaire among ability-oriented job analysis methods. Ratings have to be made for a total of 52 abilities and aptitudes of a cognitive, sensory, physical and psychomotor nature. Ratings are made on a seven-point scale of which three points (low–middle–high) are anchored by concrete examples. For some of the abilities decision flow diagrams have been developed. By making a series of dichotomeous yes/no decisions, the relative importance of an ability can be confirmed.

3 RECENT DEVELOPMENTS IN JOB ANALYSIS

The state of the art in job and task analysis for application to problems of personnel selection seems to develop along several lines. On the one hand, an interest in *content-oriented* methodologies can be observed. On the other hand, within the framework of *validity generalization* the crucial question is what job classification techniques are most appropriate, i.e. how to investigate similarities and differences between jobs and how to establish job groupings. A third line seems to be the renewed interest in the *synthetic validity* approach, both in Europe (e.g. Algera and Groenendijk, 1985) and the United States (Mossholder and Arvey, 1984; Trattner, 1982; Hamilton, 1981). We will discuss each of these developments in more detail.

3.1 Content-based selection devices

Since the early 1970s in the United States a strong emphasis has been put on selection instruments constructed along the lines of the sampling method: content-based selection devices. Content-based selection devices were credited with many advantages that could be summarized under the qualifications: valid, practical and defensible in court.

At first, only work samples and situational tests were to be numbered under the headings of content-based selection devices, but in recent years other sample type predictors have been developed, for example: biographical questionnaires and related devices (Pannone, 1984; Hough, 1984; Ash and Levine, 1985) and the situational interview (Latham et al., 1980; Latham and Saari, 1984).

The validity of work samples and situational tests has been well documented in the past (according to reviews of Asher and Sciarrino, 1974; Robertson and Kandola, 1982) and nowadays work samples can still be reckoned to be the more predictive instruments. Schmitt et al. (1984) report an average validity coefficient of 0.38 in 18 studies over an eighteen-year period (1964–82). For the situational interview almost all reported validities are impressive and some go as high as 0.40–0.45, values that contrast sharply with an average validity of the selection interview of 0.14 as reported in a review by Hunter and Hunter (1984). Finally, with respect to assessment centers an average level of 0.41 has been reported (Schmitt et al., 1984).

High validities alone do not account for all the popularity of content-based selection devices. An equally important aspect concerns the solid reputation of these methods in courts. Job analysis fulfills a key position in court procedures, according to Thompson and Thompson (1982) who base their opinion on selected federal court cases. Tasks, duties and activities must be identified, suggesting job-oriented job analysis procedures. Terms used by the courts which denote types of information to be described through job analysis are: elements, aspects, characteristics, aptitudes, knowledge skills, abilities and critical incidents. Data should be collected from several up-to-date sources; interviews with job incumbents, supervisors and administrators, training manuals, observations, questionnaires etc. All in all, courts procedures are suggestive of job analyses methods which result in detailed, minute description of jobs.

The job relatedness of content-based selection devices can be demonstrated by adhering to job analysis alone. It is not necessary to demonstrate predictive or concurrent validity. At the outset there was some dispute about the acceptability of content validation but in the case *Kirkland* vs *New York Department of Correctional Service* (1974), content validation was recognized as an adequate validation strategy and necessary qualifications for this research paradigm were laid down. In *Kirkland* vs *New York* evidence was judged to be insufficient but later court cases show an advantageous record in favor of content validation (cf. Arvey, 1979). Kleiman and Faley (1985) have reviewed twelve recent Title VII cases. They stated that judges often demanded stronger evidence for substantiating the predictive validity of the predictor, if it was not developed on rational grounds, i.e. on an extensive job analysis. In this respect Hogan and Quigley (1986) noted that at least three questions regarding job analysis arise in court cases. The first is whether a job analysis has been completed at all. The second concerns the material adequacy of the job analysis. The third asks whether the method selected is appropriate for the validation strategy subsequently used.

Naturally not having conducted a job analysis (first question) is an obvious disadvantage. The accuracy of job information (second question) has received differential attention by the courts. Sometimes, job analysis is given a general and superficial review, but it can also be scrutinized and technical matters can be inspected too. For example, in *Berkman* vs *City of New York* (1982, cited by Hogan and Quigley, 1986, p. 1201) the court recognized interrater correlation coefficients as an expression of the degree of agreement among raters. Also, agreement between different job analysis methods, illustrating convergent validity, has been considered: Five job analysis methods were presented to support the use of a physical test battery. The results were contradictory and conflicting. The court criticized the job information by stating that some of the comparisons made between the two most important job analysis methods, 'smack of an effort at rationalization of apparent conflicts in the results' (Hogan and Quigley, 1986, p. 1201).

The third issue relates to the adequacy of the job analysis method with respect to validation strategy. Hogan and Quigley (1986) discuss the case of *United States* vs *New York*, a case in which job analysis identified knowledge, skills, abilities and other worker characteristics necessary for succesful perform-ance as a trooper. However, this kind of analysis was judged to be inappropriate for conducting a content validity study as was originally planned. In *Berkman* vs *City of New York*, already briefly mentioned above, the appropriateness of the job analysis had also been attended to by the court. The court recognized that a criterion-referenced validation study was the correct strategy to use given an ability-oriented job analysis.

Although the above mentioned examples illustrate an increasingly more pervasive and detailed inspection of job analysis methods and predictor devel-opment by the court (especially for content-oriented selection strategies) there is not much literature illuminating systematic procedures for identifying job content and transforming job content into content-based selection devices. A noticeable exception is a recent article by Schmitt and Ostroff (1986). These authors propose a series of steps in developing content-oriented selection devices. The first step consists of conducting a rather elaborate job analysis procedure in which different job analysis methods are taken together (this procedure, called C-JAM, is adapted from Levine, 1983). Task statements are generated in two meetings with job incumbents. After several revisions a final version is proposed. By then, task statements have been grouped in major performance dimensions. Next, meetings are held to generate KSAs (*K*nowledge, *S*kills, *A*bilities) and questionnaires are developed to rate the importance of task dimensions and KSAs. Finally, content-based tests are constructed. In the example provided by Schmitt and Ostroff, a selection procedure for an emergency telephone operator, several work samples (spelling test, telephone call recording task, typing test, monitoring task), a situational interview and a telephone call simulation were constructed. All these instruments were evaluated in terms of content validity using a procedure outlined by Lawshe (1975; so-called Content validity Ratio). Except for one dimension, all major task dimensions were sufficiently represented in the test materials. Estimates of interrater reliability were usually in the area of 0.60. Unfortunately, no evidence of predictive validity was presented. However, the Schmitt and Ostroff procedure can be credited for the systematic and rational way in which predictors are derived from job content. By also generating KSA-schemes it bridges the gap between the signs and sample approach. Altogether the procedure seems to be a considerable improvement upon the hazarduous nature of developing content-oriented devices until now. Content-based selection devices seem to mature.

3.2 Validity generalization

In the area of personnel selection one of the most important issues discussed in the last ten years is the question of validity generalization. Contrary to former 'beliefs', Schmidt, Hunter and others (e.g. Schmidt and Hunter, 1981; Pearlman *et al.*, 1980; Schmidt *et al.*, 1981) claimed that observed differences in validity coefficients can be explained by sampling error and other methodological artifacts, such as differences between studies in criterion reliability and degree of range restriction.

These findings would imply that test validities are much less situationally specific than thought before, and that a validity study is not necessary in the case where validity information on similar job-test combinations is available. What has to be shown then is that the job at hand can be considered as belonging to the same class of jobs as the original validity generalization study. Hence, the crucial question is what job classification techniques are most appropriate within the framework of validity generalization. This question has been addressed by several researchers.

Level of grouping jobs and type of job descriptor

Pearlman (1980) discusses the concept of job families and the implication for personnel selection. Grouping of jobs can be established at different levels of analysis, for example on the level of occupations, or on the level of positions within the same organization by grouping persons who carry out the same or very similar tasks.

Colbert and Taylor (1978) empirically derived homogeneous job families of insurance company jobs in one firm on the basis of data from the Position Analysis Questionnaire (PAQ). Three job families, which contained jobs into which a substantial number of entry-level clerical personnel were hired, were used to study validity generalization.

From the viewpoint of personnel selection the issue of job family construction has traditionally been under discussion in the question how to combine samples for validation and how to apply validity results to similar situations. Probably the most important issue in job classification, besides the level of grouping, is the question of the content basis of job families. This concerns the type of job data on which the system is built or according to McCormick (1976) the type of 'job descriptor'.

In the literature (McCormick, 1976; Pearlman, 1980) four categories of job descriptors are often distinguished. The first category contains job descriptors that refer to the *job-oriented content* of jobs. This type of descriptors refer to the work that is performed, mostly in terms referring to the specific technology and context of jobs. Examples of this category are the OAI (Cunningham *et al.*, 1983) and task inventories which usually contain many task element items. The second category comprises job descriptors that refer to the *worker-oriented content* of jobs. In this case the emphasis is on the human behaviors involved in the work. This type of descriptors is less tied to specific technological processes than the job-oriented descriptors. The most well-known examples of this category are McCormick's Position Analysis Questionnaire (PAQ), Flanagan's (1954) 'critical incidents' technique of job analysis and Fine's (1955) Functional Job Analysis (FJA).

In terms of the conceptual bases for task analysis as mentioned in paragraph 2, both worker-oriented and job-oriented type of descriptors would fall into the category behavior description. The third category consists of job descriptors that refer to the *attribute requirements* of jobs, which means that jobs are described in terms of the human traits or attributes related to job performance. Examples are the Ability Requirement Scales developed by Fleishman and others (Fleishman and Quaintance, 1984). Another example is the Minnesota Job Requirements Questionnaire (Desmond and Weiss, 1973), a questionnaire which consists of 45 items referring to the nine aptitudes of the GATB. Referring to the categories in paragraph 2 this type of job descriptors fall into the category abilities requirements. The fourth category contains job descriptors that reflect the overall nature of the job, mostly in terms of rather *global descriptions* (e.g. job titles), expressed in a qualitative format. Examples of this category are government job classification systems (U. S. Department of Labor, 1977).

It should be stated that the borderline between these four categories is not always sharp. For example the items in the PAQ (McCormick *et al.*, 1972) which are in general of a worker-oriented nature also contain items that could be classified as job-oriented (Scheltens *et al.*, 1979). Moreover, some researchers (e.g. Krzystofiak *et al.*, 1979) deliberately use both job-oriented and worker-oriented items within one instrument. The importance of this issue is illustrated by the study of Cornelius *et al.* (1979). In their study the type of job descriptor was varied, to examine the effect on the resulting job classification. Seven nominally different foreman jobs in a chemical processing plant were analysed by the same hierarchical clustering algorithm, but using three different types of job descriptors. It turned out that not only the number of similar foreman jobs differed according to the type of job descriptor but also there were differences relating to which jobs were most similar.

Grouping method

The third issue in job family construction is the grouping method used. Two broad classes of grouping methods can be distinguished (Pearlman, 1980): grouping on the basis of some rational or judgmental process and grouping on the basis of some quantitative, statistical procedure.

Recently, Harvey (1986) reviewed quantitative approaches to job classification. He made a distinction between descriptive techniques (e.g. cluster analysis, factor analysis) and inferential techniques (e.g. analysis of variance, discriminant analysis). One of the main differences between these two types of techniques is that descriptive job-classification techniques are more explorative, producing a job taxonomy on the basis of the job information, while the inferential techniques require an *a priori* classification scheme.

Thus, the latter techniques seem useful in deciding whether a new job can be regarded as a member of an existing job family. The former techniques would be valuable in establishing job classifications. Harvey (1986) further states that the specificity of job elements will affect the types of differences revealed and therefore the purpose for job classification should be matched with the specificity of job elements. For purposes of validity generalization he advocates the use of a modest number of job dimensions as is used in the PAQ. We agree with Pearlman (1980) that discussions on the 'best' grouping method are far less important than more substantive issues in job family development. Whether differences between jobs on statistical grounds (e.g. on the basis of cluster analysis, or analysis of variance) are also meaningful in a practical sense should be decided on the basis of the purpose in mind. What makes matters complex is that both differences in the type of job descriptor and grouping method can lead to different job family structures, even when the same jobs are involved.

Returning to the subject of validity generalization, the issue is to determine

the transportability of validity results to similar jobs within or across organizations. Pearlman (1980) defines the objective of job family construction for
validity generalization as: 'It is to create groupings of jobs that moderate test
validities, that is, groupings within which specified test validities will generalize
and between which such validities will not generalize.' On the basis of a
number of validity generalization studies Pearlman (1980) concludes that there
is evidence that 'validities are likely to be generalizable within job families'.
He argues that job family groupings based on job-oriented or worker-oriented
content are unnecessarily restrictive for validity generalization purposes. He
further argues that the attribute requirements approach to job family development is most promising. A number of comments seem to be in order here.

First, job analysis comes into question within the framework of validity
generalization in two places: (a) on deciding which jobs are to be grouped for
doing a validity generalization study, and (b) when validity generalization is
established, deciding on whether a similar job belongs to the job family on
which the validity generalization study was based. Most validity generalization
studies to date (e.g. Pearlman *et al.*, 1980) are based on job groupings using
overall nature type job descriptors. In the Pearlman *et al.* (1980) study jobs
were grouped on the basis of DOT occupational groups. The crucial question
now is whether in the validity generalization procedure there exists the possibility to detect moderators in the data set used. A number of recent articles
(e.g. Algera *et al.*, 1984; Sackett *et al.*, 1986; James *et al.*, 1986; Spector and
Levine, 1987; Kemery *et al.*, 1987) questions the power to detect moderator
variables under some conditions.

For example, Sackett *et al.* (1986) conclude: 'with sample sizes, numbers of
studies and reliabilities typical of those found in much current meta-analysis
research, the power to detect true differences in the magnitude of relations
across studies may be very low.' With these warnings in mind, the earlier
conclusions of Schmidt *et al.* (1981) that large task differences between jobs do
not moderate the validities and that molecular job analyses are unnecessary
in practice look premature. What seem to be needed here are more studies
such as Colbert and Taylor (1978), using job-oriented and/or worker-oriented
molecular job analyses to test the objective of job family construction as formulated by Pearlman (1980).

Second, the kind of criteria used seem to be another important issue. Validity
generalization studies to date nearly always use overall job performance or
overall training success as a criteron measure. When only overall criteria are
used it is sensible also to use molar job analysis methods without reference for
specific tasks, duties or behaviors. However, when specific dimensions of job
performance are used in validity generalization studies, molecular job analysis
methods would probably be called for. There seems to be enough empirical
evidence (see, e.g. Smith, 1976) to conclude that job performance is
multidimensional.

Third, validity generalization and situational specificity are not mutually exclusive. That is to say that it is possible that validities are generalizable across a variety of jobs but at the same time the possibility exists of situational effects on the size of the validity coefficient (see also Tenopyr and Oeltjen, 1982). Tenopyr and Oeltjen suggest that overall criteron measures as supervisory ratings may give rise to extensive generalizability because of the general factor underlying those kind of ratings but that more specific criteria may be associated with more situational specificity of validity.

James *et al.* (1986), in reviewing validity generalization procedures, present alternative models to the existing validity generalization approach to explain variation in validity coefficients. They advocate studies that include situational variables, and further state that: 'Measures representing membership in gross categories such as job families (cf. Pearlmen, 1980) are helpful but lack the explanatory power furnished by measurement and explicit analysis of specific aspects of situations (e.g. stress, leadership) that presumably influence correlations between person variables and job performance.' Fleishman and Quaintance (1984) state that better control over the measurement of criterion performance will make it possible to show that different task requirements can moderate test validities. They conclude that: 'As long as improved predictions of performance can be obtained through an understanding of task requirements, it seems reasonable to proceed with efforts to develop taxonomic systems to categorize tasks in terms of those moderating requirements.' Taking these opinions together, there seems to be enough reason not to restrict the attention to attribute requirements alone as job descriptors in personnel selection research and practice within the framework of validity generalization.

Fourth, Cornelius *et al.* (1979) make a very important distinction between selection systems to be developed for selecting applicants who are expected to demonstrate task performance almost immediately (e.g. typists) and selection systems to be developed for selecting applicants in settings that require training (e.g. managerial trainees). Cornelius *et al.* (1979) propose a task-oriented job classification approach in the former situation while in the latter situation an abilities-oriented or aptitudes-oriented approach to job classification would be appropriate. This indeed seems very logical. In the former situation the selection system would be more oriented to the specific task performance using simulations, work samples and probably situational interviews. In the latter situation, the selection system would be more oriented to abilities or aptitudes of a far more general nature which underly performance in a wide variety of situations as encountered in training.

Fifth, Schmidt and his co-workers (e.g. Schmidt, Hunter and Pearlman, 1981) have used their validity generalization procedure for different groups of jobs, e.g. a wide range of clerical occupations, a great number (35) of army jobs, computer programmers. On the basis of this research they come to the conclusion that the hypothesis of situational specificity is false where *cognitive* abilities are concerned. One could imagine other groups of jobs (e.g. managerial jobs) where cognitive abilities as measured by general mental abilities are relatively less important. In that case one probably would also need job data based on molecular job analysis methods of a job- or worker-oriented nature, referring to noncognitive predictors.

3.3 Synthetic validity

The concept of synthetic validity has traditionally been defined as: 'the inferring of validity in a specific situation from a logical analysis of jobs into their elements, a determination of test validity for these elements, and a combination of elemental validities into a whole' (Balma, 1959, p. 395). The main difference between validity generalization and synthetic validity is that the former refers to the possibility of transportability of validity for a job as a whole, while the latter refers to the possibility of transportability of validity for specific job elements (or components). It is evident from this definition that job analysis plays a major role, namely in the determination of the relevant job components. The word *synthetic* in fact refers to the process of inferring the validity of a test battery from predetermined validities of the tests for work components.

Synthetic validity has been recommended in situations where sample sizes are too small to conduct a validity study or in situations where jobs change rapidly in their content. Although the synthetic validity concept has existed for quite some time now it has not been applied in practice very often. However, recently a revival of interest in the synthetic validity concept (Mossholder and Arvey, 1984; Algera and Groenendijk, 1985; Trattner, 1982; Hamilton, 1981; Hamilton and Dickinson, 1987) has become apparent.

Mossholder and Arvey (1984) note that initial test-work component validities may occur within content-, construct-, or criterion-related validity strategies. The appropriate validation strategy would be partly dependent on the type of predictor used, e.g. work sample vs aptitude. Within the framework of synthetic validity two approaches have become well known in the literature (Mossholder and Arvey, 1984).

(1) The *J-coefficient* is intended to give an estimate of the validity coefficient to be used when an adequate coefficient of the (predictive) type is not available and cannot be obtained because of practical considerations, such as new jobs for which there are not workers or the absence of an adequate sample of workers (Hamilton, 1981). The J-coefficient is based on the idea that the relationship between predictors and job performance is composed of relationships between predictors and job elements, the interrelationships between job elements, and the importance of these job elements to performance. Various J-coefficient formulas are available in the literature. Although empirical methods can be used, mostly judgmental methods are used to determine the three types of relationships involved in the calculation of the J-coefficient.

Hamilton (1981) illustrates that the J-coefficient approach can be considered for different validation options, e.g. content validity, validity generalization and cooperative validation. The differences between validation options determine the manner in which job elements are defined.

A major advantage of the J-coefficient approach probably is the usefulness of information that results from the examination of job element relationships. For example, Hamilton (1981) illustrates this point in his discussion of cooperative validation where more than one organization cooperates in validation studies. One condition for such validation studies is the necessity to demonstrate the similarity of jobs across organizations.

According to Hamilton (1981) in that situation it is likely that similar types of jobs would share many of the same job elements, but it is less likely that these elements would combine in the same manner to determine job success. The J-coefficient approach can accommodate this situation by accounting for such differences through differential weighting of elemental validities according to the situation.

For our discussion, the most interesting point is what kind of job descriptor data are most relevant within this framework. Trattner (1982) in discussing the use of the J-coefficient within the same class, e.g. lower level clerical occupations, elaborates on this point. He states that work behaviors are preferable to knowledge, skills and abilities as modules for analyzing test validity. There are two main reasons for his preference, the first being that less inference is involved in using ratings of time spent in work behavior (as a measure of importance) than in rating the importance of knowledge, skills and abilities for success. The second reason is that better measures of employee performance are expected when they refer to work behavior rather than to traits.

(2) Probably the best known research effort under the label of synthetic validity is the work of McCormick and his co-workers (McCormick *et al.*, 1972, 1979). He developed the *Position Analysis Questionnaire* (PAQ) which consists of about 190 worker-oriented 'job elements' divided into six chapters. Besides these job elements, also 68 'human attributes' were defined by McCormick *et al.* (1972), referring to human traits. Expert judgments were obtained concerning the relevance of the 68 human attributes for each job element. Several principal component analyses were performed, both on the basis of job analysis data and on the basis of attribute profile data. The resulting dimensions were used by McCormick and his associates to illustrate their ideas on synthetic validity. In McCormick *et al.*'s (1972) view jobs can be broken down into a number of dimensions. The underlying assumption for their Job Component Model is that jobs which have certain behaviors (components, dimensions) in common should also require the same human attribute(s) to carry out those behaviors. If the relationships between PAQ work descriptors (e.g. dimension scores) and the human attribute required for performance were

known and tests measuring such human attributes were identified, test batteries could be synthesized on the basis of work descriptor data.

McCormick *et al.* (1972) conclude that: 'In general, the results lend support to the basic notion that aptitude requirements for jobs can be established synthetically on the basis of a structured job analysis questionnaire such as the Position Analysis Questionnaire' (p. 363). However, there are a number of remarks to be made from the viewpoint of synthetic validity. In the first place, the studies are based on the assumption of 'natural selection' or 'gravitation', by using mean scores of job incumbents as criteria supposing that only people with relevant attributes gravitate toward and survive in the job.

It is evident that job membership is not the same as job success, i.e. performance differences between job incumbents in the same job are not taken into account. Second, no empirical validity coefficients are computed and there is no direct link between the tests and job behavior (see also Mossholder and Arvey, 1984; Algera and Groenendijk, 1985).

Nevertheless, the job component approach can provide information that is possibly useful for choosing selection tests (Sparrow *et al.*, 1982). The choice and weights of predictors on the basis of such an indirect approach as in the job component model could probably be legitimated by establishing a prediction model that is tested subsequently.

4 DISCUSSION

This chapter has presented an overview of job analysis methods in relation to personnel selection. Throughout the chapter it has been emphasized that job analysis is an important cornerstone in building prediction models. This 'modelbuilding capacity' cannot be fulfilled otherwise in most instances. Also, some recent developments with regard to validity generalization, synthetic validity and content-oriented selection devices were discussed. Together, these three topics seem to exhaust the domain of practical and scientific endeavors at this moment. Although it can be stated that research in these areas has enhanced the availability and quality of job analysis tools, it is also counterproductive in the sense that some relevant questions have not been given much attention.

We wish to pinpoint a number of these questions. The first one touches upon the already briefly mentioned role of situational moderators of the relations between job content and job requirements. Most job analysis methods are strictly job-oriented. They focus on job content and aspects of the organizational context are not systematically analyzed, except for some characteristics of the physical environment.

The problem is that there is not much literature or research focusing on (potentially) relevant situational variables to be selected for prediction models.

Possible candidates are various organizational climate variables (Schneider, 1978) and 'situational constraints': factors in the work setting that have a negative impact on job holder behavior (Peters and O'Connor, 1980; Peters *et al.*, 1980, 1982; O'Connor *et al.*, 1984).

A second problem to be solved is related to the increasing (technological) complexity of work nowadays. Cognitive operations come into play in a rapid and pervasive way in a variety of jobs (e.g. operators). This makes it productive to look at task performance as a sequence of information-processing operations. On the basis of information-processing theories one might try to construct a theoretical account of what happens between the presentation of the task stimulus and the observed response. A classical example is the Task Strategies Approach of Miller (1973; see also Fleishman and Quaintance, 1984). In this model the human performer is pictured as an information-processing system with a minimum of four system functions: input reception, memory, processing and output effectors. The human information processor must scan the environment to detect task-relevant cues, eventually filter these cues and identify message entities or other patterns. In the next stage, short-term and long-term memory are activated to make comparisons, to store information on a temporary or long-term base, etc. Situational and task cues are interpreted and decided upon, including activities of counting, computing, planning, problem solving. Finally an appropriate response is chosen.

Although the potential utility of the information-processing model in task and job analysis is generally recognized (e.g. McCormick *et al.*, 1972; Cunningham *et al.*, 1983), it is elaborated in a rudimentary fashion most of the time. For example the paradigms of the PAQ and the OAI are both based on simple SOR-models that do not give much attention to the *process* of performing. In Germany, some promising departures of this black box paradigm have been worked out in job analysis methods such as *Verfahren zur Ermittlung von Regulationserfordernissen in der Arbeitstätigkeit* (VERA; Volpert *et al.*, 1983), *Tätigkeitsbewertungssystem* (TBS, Hacker *et al.*, 1983). A characteristic feature of these methods is that they are theory-based, i.e. they are related to *Handlungs und Tätigkeitstheorien* ('theories of performance acts') of Hacker (1978) and others. The specific content of this theory does not have to concern us here: what matters is the observation that more theoretically and cognitively oriented job analysis methods enhance our understanding of performance behaviors.

A third point of discussion has to do with the source of the information. Studies on the type of rater and/or data source include the attempt by Cornelius *et al.* (1984) to replicate Smith and Hakel's (1979) findings on the convergent validity between expert and naïve raters. They found lower values between these two types of raters and criticized the earlier conclusions on methodological grounds. Arvey *et al.* (1982) manipulated the amount of job information and the degree of job interest exhibited by incumbents. Both types of manipulations had only very minor effects on the PAQ and no effects on the JDS (Job

Diagnostic Survey). That job analysts were not biased by incumbents' positive or negative statements about the job is probably reassuring. However, the fact that no effects resulted from giving more job information is more problematic. It becomes unclear how much job information is needed for accurate description of jobs. If high agreement between raters rests on stereotypes of jobs, independent of the amount of information, then the accurateness of these stereotypes becomes a central question.

Although agreement between and within different types of raters tends to be rather satisfactory in a number of studies (e.g. Crowley, 1981; Sackett et al., 1981; Jones et al., 1982: Schmitt and Fine, 1983), some questions still are unanswered. Probably the most interesting issue is the role of job stereotypes in raters' responses. Especially in an era where jobs are changing rather fast because of technological developments, job stereotypes can be inaccurate and could lead to invalid results if they played a major role in the responses of raters who provide job-related information.

REFERENCES

Algera, J. A. (ed.) (in press) Analyse van arbeid vanuit verschillende perspectieven.

Algera, J. A. and Groenendijk, B. (1985). Synthetische validiteit: een vergelijking van benaderingen. *Nederlands Tijdschrift voor de Psychologie*, **40**, 255–269.

Algera, J. A., Jansen, P. G. W., Roe, R. A. and Vijn, P. (1984). Validity generalization. Some critical remarks on the Schmidt–Hunter procedure. *Journal of Occupational Psychology*, **57**, 197–210.

Arvey, R. D. (1979). *Fairness in Selecting Employees*. London: Addison-Wesley.

Arvey, R. D., Davis, G. A., McGowen, S. L. and Dipboye, R. L. (1982). Potential sources of bias in job analytic processes. *Academy of Management Journal*, **25**, 618–629.

Ash, R. A. and Levine, E. L. (1985). Job applicant training and work experience evaluation: an empirical comparison of a few methods. *Journal of Applied Psychology*, **70**, 3, 572–576.

Asher, J. J. and Sciarrino, J. A. (1974). Realistic work sample tests: a review. *Personnel Psychology*, **27**, 519–533.

Balma, M. J. (1959). The development of processes for indirect or synthetic validity (a symposium). 1. The concept of synthetic validity. *Personnel Psychology*, **12**, 395–396.

Bosman, A. (1977). *Een metatheorie over gedrag van organisaties*. Leiden, Stenfert Kroese.

Brinkman, J. A. (1983). *Een klassifikatiesysteem voor arbeidsanalyse-methoden*. Technische Hogeschool Eindhoven, Vakgroep Organisatiepsychologie.

Carroll, S. J. and Schneier, C. E. (1982). *Performance Appraisal and Review Systems. The Identification, Measurement and Development of Performance in Organizations*. Glenview, Illinois: Scott, Foresman and Company.

Colbert, G. A. and Taylor, L. R. (1978). Empirically derived job families as a foundation for the study of validity generalization. Study 3: Generalization of selection test validity. *Personnel Psychology*, **31**, 355–364.

Cornelius, E. T., De-Nisi, A. S. and Blencoe, A. G. (1984). Expert and naïve raters using the PAQ: Does it matter? *Personnel Psychology*, **37**, 453–464.

Cornelius, E. T. III, Carron, Th. J. and Collius, M. N. (1979). Job analysis models and job classification. *Personnel Psychology*, **32**, 693–708.

Crowley, A. D. (1981). The content of interest inventories: Job titles or job activities? *Journal of Occupational Psychology*, **54**, 135–140.

Cunningham, J. W., Boese, R. R., Neeb, R. W. and Pass, J. J. (1983). Systematically derived work dimensions: Factor analysis of the Occupation Analysis Inventory. *Journal of Applied Psychology*, **68**, 232–252.

Darlington, R. B. (1978). Reduced-variance regression. *Psychological Bulletin*, **85**, 1238–1255.

Dunnette, M. D. (ed.) (1976). *Handbook of Industrial and Organizational Psychology*. Chicago: Rand McNally.

Fine, S. A. (1955). A structure of worker functions. *Personnel and Guidance Journal*, **34**, 66–73.

Flanagan, J. C. (1954) The critical incidents technique. *Psychological Bulletin*, **51**, 327–358.

Fleishman, E. A. and Quaintance, M. K. (1984). *Taxonomies of Human Performance. The description of human tasks*. New York: Academic Press.

Frederiksen, N., Jensen, O. and Beates, A. E. (1972). *Prediction of Organizational Behavior*. New York: Pergamon.

Guion, R. M. (1976). Recruiting, selection and job placement. In: Dunnette, M. D. (ed.), *Handbook of Industrial and Organizational Psychology*. Chicago: Rand McNally, pp. 777–828.

Hacker, W. (1978). *Algemeine Arbeits- und Ingenieurspsychology*. Berlin (DDR): Dt Verlag der Wissenschaft.

Hacker, W., Iwanowa, A. and Richter, P. (1983). *Tätigkeitsbewerkungssystem (TBS)*. Berlin (DDR): Psychodiagnostisches Zentrum der Humboldt Universität.

Hamilton, J. W. (1981). Options for small sample sizes in validation: a case for the J-coefficient. *Personnel Psychology*, **34**, 805–816.

Hamilton, J. W. and Dickinson, T. L. (1987). Comparison of several procedures for generating J-coefficients. *Journal of Applied Psychology*, **72**, 49–54.

Harvey, R. J. (1986). Quantitative approaches to job classification: A review and critique. *Personnel Psychology*, **39**, 267–289.

Hirsch, H. R., Schmidt, F. L. and Hunter, J. E. (1986). Estimation of employment validities by less experienced judges. *Personnel Psychology*, **39**, 2, 337–345.

Hogan, J. and Quigley, A. M. (1986). Physical standards for employment and the courts. *American Psychologist*, **41**, 11, 1193–1217.

Hough, L. M. (1984). Development and evaluation of the 'Accomplishment record' method of selecting and promoting professionals. *Journal of Applied Psychology*, **69**, 135–146.

Hunter, J. E. and Hunter, R. F. (1984). Validity and utility of alternative predictors of job performance. *Psychological Bulletin*, **96**, 1, 72–98.

In 't Veld, J. (1981). *Analyse van organisatieproblemen*. Amsterdam: Elsevier Nederland BV.

James, L. R., Demaree, R. G. and Mulaik, S. A. (1986). A note on validity generalization procedures. *Journal of Applied Psychology*, **71**, 440–450.

Jones, A. P., Main, D. S., Butler, M. C. and Johnson, L. A. (1982). Narrative job descriptions as potential sources of job analysis ratings. *Personnel Psychology*, **35**, 813–828.

Kemery, E. R., Mossholder, K. W. and Roth, L. (1987). The power of the Schmidt and Hunter additive model of validity generalization. *Journal of Applied Psychology*, **72**, 1, 30–37.

Kleiman, L. S. and Faley, R. H. (1985). The implications of professional and legal guidelines for court decisions involving criterion related validity: a review and analysis. *Personnel Psychology*, **38**, 803–833.

Krzystofiak, F., Newman, J. M. and Anderson, G. (1979). A quantified approach to measurement of job content procedures and pay offs. *Personnel Psychology*, **32**, 341–357.

Landy, F. J. and Farr, J. L. (1983). *The Measurement of Work Performance*. New York: Academic Press.

Latham, G. P. and Saari, L. M. (1984). Do people do what they say? Further studies in the situational interview. *Journal of Applied Psychology*, **69**, 4, 569–573.

Latham, G. P., Saari, L. M., Pursell, E. D. and Campion, M. A. (1980). The situational interview. *Journal of Applied Psychology*, **65**, 4, 422–427.

Latham, G. P. and Wexley, K. M. (1981). *Increasing Productivity through Performance Appraisal*. Massachusetts: Addison Wesley.

Lawshe, C. H. (1975). A quantitative approach to content validity. *Personnel Psychology*, **28**, 563–575.

Levine, E. L. (1983). *Everything You Always Wanted to Know about Job Analysis and More . . . A Job Analysis Primer*. Tampa, FL: Marines Publishing Co.

McCormick, E. J. (1976). Job and task analysis. In: M. D. Dunnette (ed.), *Handbook of Industrial and Organizational Psychology*. Chicago: Rand McNally, pp. 651–696.

McCormick, E. J., De Nisi, A. S. and Shaw, J. B. (1979). Use of the Position Analysis Questionnaire for analysing the job component validity of tests. *Journal of Applied Psychology*, **64**, 1, 51–56.

McCormick, E. J., Jeanneret, R. R. and Mecham, R. C. (1972). A study of job characteristics and job dimensions as based on the Position Analysis Questionnaire. *Journal of Applied Psychology*, Monograph, **56**, 4, 347–368.

Miller, R. B. (1973). Development of a taxonomy of human performance: Design of a systems task vocabulary. *JSAS Catalog of Selected Documents in Psychology*, **3**, 29–30 (Ms no. 327).

Monaham, C. J. and Muchinsky, P. M. (1983). Three decades of personnel selection research: A state-of-the-art analysis and evaluation. *Journal of Occupational Psychology*, **56**, 215–225.

Mossholder, K. W. and Arvey, R. D. (1984). Sythetic validity: A conceptual and comparative review. *Journal of Applied Psychology*, **69**, 322–333.

O'Connor, E. J., Peters, L. H., Weekley, A. P. J., Frank, B. and Erenkrantz, B. (1984). Situational constraints effects on performance, affective reactions and turnover. A field replication and extension. *Journal of Applied Psychology*, **69**, 4, 663–672.

Pannone, R. D. (1984). Predicting test performance: A content valid approach to screening applicants. *Personnel Psychology*, **37**, 507–514.

Pearlman, K. (1980). Job families: A review and discussion of their implications for personnel selection. *Psychological Bulletin*, **87**, 1–28.

Pearlman, K., Schmidt, F. L. and Hunter, J. E. (1980). Validity generalization results for tests used to predict job proficiency and training success in clerical occupations. *Journal of Applied Psychology*, **65**, 373–406.

Peters, L. H., Fisher, C. D. and O'Connor, E. J. (1982). The moderating effect of situational control of performance variance on the relationship between individual differences and performance. *Personnel Psychology*, **35**, 609–623.

Peters, L. H. and O'Connor, E. J. (1980). Situational constraints and work outcomes: The influence of a frequently overlooked construct. *Academy of Management Review*, **5**, 391–397.

Peters, L. H., O'Connor, E. J. and Rudolf, C. J. (1980). The behavioral and effective consequences of performance-relevant situational variables. *Organizational Behavior and Human Performance*, **25**, 79–96.

Primoff, E. S. (1955). *Test Selection by Job Analysis: The J-coefficient*. Washington D. C.: U. S. Civil Service Commission, Assembled Test Technical Edition, May.

Robertson, I. T. and Kandola, R. S. (1982). Work sample tests: validity, adverse impact and applicant reaction. *Journal of Occupational Psychology*, **55**, 171–183.

Roe, R. A. (1983). *Grondslagen der Personeelsselektie*. Assen: Van Gorcum.

Roe, R. A. (1984). Advances in performance modeling: the case of validity generalization. Paper presented at the Symposium 'Advances in Testing'. Internal Test commission. Acapulco, Mexico.

Roe, R. A. (1986). *A Technological View on Personnel Selection*. Delft, University of Technology.

Sackett, P. R., Cornelius, E. T. III and Carron, Th. J. (1981). A comparison of global judgment vs task oriented approaches to job classification. *Personnel Psychology*, **34**, 791–804.

Sackett, P. R., Harris, M. M. and Orr, J. M. (1986). On seeking moderator variables in the meta-analysis of correlation data: A Monte Carlo investigation of statistical power and resistance to Type I error. *Journal of Applied Psychology*, **71**, 302–310.

Scheltens, R., Meyman, T. and Simmelink, J. (1979). Werkgedragdimensies: Werkelijkheid of artefact. *Psychologie en Maatschappij*, **8**, 64–79.

Schmidt, F. L. and Hunter, J. E. (1980). The future of criterion-related validity. *Personnel Psychology*, **33**, 141–160.

Schmidt, F. L. and Hunter, J. E. (1981). Employment testing: old theories and new research findings. *American Psychologist*, **36**, 1128–1137.

Schmidt, F. L., Hunter, J. E. and Pearlman, K. (1981). Task differences of aptitude test validity in selection: A red herring. *Journal of Applied Psychology*, **66**, 166–185.

Schmidt, F. L., Hunter, J. E., Croll, P. R. and McKenzie, R. C. (1983). Estimation of employment test validities by expert judgment. *Journal of Applied Psychology*, **68**, 550–601.

Schmitt,,N. and Fine, S. A. (1983). Inter-rater reliability of judgements of functional levels and skill requirements of jobs based on written task statements. *Journal of Occupational Psychology*, **56**, 121–127.

Schmitt, N., Gooding, R. Z., Noe, R. A. and Kirsch, M. (1984). Meta-analysis of validity studies published between 1964 and 1982 and the investigation of study characteristics. *Personnel Psychology*, **37**, 407–422.

Schmitt, H. and Ostroff, C. (1986). Operationalizing the 'Bahavioral Consistency' approach: Selection Test Development based on a content-oriented strategy. *Personnel Psychology*, **39**, 91–108.

Schneider, B. (1978) Person–situation selection: a review of some ability–situation interaction research. *Personnel Psychology*, **31**, 281–297

Smith, J. E. and Hakel, M. D. (1979). Convergence among data sources, response bias, and reliability and validity of a structured job analysis questionnaire. *Personnel Psychology*, **32**, 677–692.

Smith, P. C. (1976). Behaviors, results and organizational effectiveness: The problem of criteria. In: Dunnette, M. D. (ed.), *Handbook of Industrial and Organizational Psychology*. Chicago: Rand McNally, pp. 745–775.

Sparrow, J., Patrick, J., Spurgeon, P. and Barwell, F. (1982). The use of job component analysis and related aptitudes in personnel selection. *Journal of Occupational Psychology*, **55**, 157–164.

Spector, P. E. and Levine, E. L. (1987). Meta-analysis for integrating study outcomes: A Monte Carlo study of its susceptibility to Type I and Type II errors. *Journal of Applied Psychology*, **72**, 3–9.

Taylor, L. R. and Colbert, G. A. (1978). Empirically derived job families as a foundation for the study of validity generalization. Study 2. The construction of job families based on company-specific PAQ job dimensions. *Personnel Psychology*, **31**, 341–353.

Tenopyr, M. L. and Oeltjen, P. D. (1982). Personnel selection and classification. In: Rosenzweig, M. R. and Porter, L. W. (eds), *Annual Review of Psychology*, **33**, 581–618.

Thompson, D. E. and Thompson, T. A. (1982). Court standards for job analysis on test validation. *Personnel Psychology*, **35**, 865–874.

Trattner, M. H. (1982). Synthetic validity and its application to the uniform guidelines validation requirements. *Personnel Psychology*, **35**, 383–397.

Tucker, L. R. (1966). Some mathematical notes on three-mode factor analysis. *Psychometrika*, **31**, 3, 279–311.

U.S. Department of Labor (1977) *Employment and Training Administration, Dictionary of occupational titles* (4th edn). Washington D.C.: U.S. Government Printing Office.

Volpert, W., Oestereich, R., Gablenz-Kelakovic, S., Kregell, T. and Resch, M. (1983). *Verfahren zur Ermittlung von Regulations-erfordernissen in der Arbeitstätigkeit (VERA)*. Köln: TÜV Rheinland.

Wernimont, P. F. and Campbell, J. P. (1968). Signs, samples and criteria. *Journal of Applied Psychology*, **52**, 372–376.

3

Some Advantages and Problems of Job Analysis

HEINZ SCHULER
University of Stuttgart-Hohenheim

Jen Algera and Martin Greuter's chapter on 'Job Analysis for Personnel Selection' competently summarizes and updates the state of the art in job and task analysis research. In particular the different types of methods are thoroughly presented and linked to their respective conceptual bases and the 'model-building capacity' of task analysis in general for personnel selection is stringently presented.

What becomes less clear after reading and discussing this article is a problem that is obvious when comparing theory and practice—the question of how it is that job analysis is almost unequivocally demanded and actually seldom practically performed in an adequate manner. For this reason some of the problems still to be resolved will be discussed here in addition to those already mentioned by Algera and Greuter. Before this, however, some arguments will be considered concerning the usefulness or even necessity of job analysis in personnel selection. These considerations should help us in determining the amount of effort we should be willing to make in order to overcome the obstacles. Finally, some expectations and, eventually, perspectives will be noted, based on both benefits and difficulties.

Just as various as the problems in task analysis are the contributors to this comment: members of the discussion group at the Buxton Conference were Jen Algera, Martin Greuter, Michael Gregg, Steve Glowinkowski, and the present author. Besides that, a number of arguments are taken from a research report

Advances in Selection and Assessment. Edited by M. Smith and I. T. Robertson
© 1989 John Wiley & Sons Ltd

the author has prepared together with his co-workers (Schuler, Donat, Funke and Moser, 1987).

SOME ADVANTAGES OF JOB ANALYSIS-BASED SELECTION

According to Algera and Greuter the dominant function of job analysis is performance modeling. This is true in a very general sense and without differentiating job or task analysis from other forms of identifying predictors of job success. On a more detailed level, more directed towards differential advantages of job analysis—especially in comparison to the most common 'competing' method, namely explorative validation studies—the utility of a job analytical approach can be considered with respect to the following aspects:

(1) Detection of new and relevant dimensions at different levels of abstraction as a basis of differentiation between employees and applicants.

(2) Determination of relevant dimensions even if not differentiating between actual performers. Gains in validity are to be expected when base-rates change.

(3) Validity of selection based on job analysis should hold longer—i.e. as long as job demands remain constant—and can be held under control when demands are changing. In contrast to the 'blind empirical approach' using a given distribution of employees or extreme groups as prominent parts of this population a job-oriented selection battery can—ideally—be used like a unit construction, exchanging just the elements or dimensions that have varied. (It should be added, however, that we still do not know enough about the interrelationship of different requirements, which could render this ideal an inapt expression of elementarism.)

(4) Transparency of the diagnostic process and the personnel decision for the applicant as well as for the people in organizations, thus improving acceptability.

In the list above the differences between job analysis and explorative validation are overaccentuated. Explorative validation is almost never completely blind but implies at least intuitive job analysis to determine the selection of assessment instruments. On the other hand, job analysis does not usually lead to unequivocal information about all psychological constructs relevant for performance. But if we, for the sake of differentiation, continue to consider ideal types, we can contrast the two methods by stating that explorative validation aims at the selection of *discriminating* items while the objective of job analysis is to supply a pool of *relevant* items. Only when taken together will both approaches provide what we need for selection of persons for jobs—relevant as well as differentiating items. In terms of methodology, norm-referenced and criterion-referenced diagnosis can be referred to in this way. Job analysis represents the criterion-referenced approach while explorative validation has affinity to the norm-referenced way of testing and selecting applicants (Hambleton, 1985).

SOME PROBLEMS OF JOB ANALYSIS

Given that doing job analysis is a useful or even indispensable basis for personnel selection, why is it actually so seldom performed, at least seldom in a way which would satisfy scientific standards? Indolence is not likely to be the essential reason for this discrepancy because the human tendency to do no more than necessary should be more than outweighed by the rewards any organization provides for those of their members who demonstrate rare competencies and are able to convince important others that their skills are useful for the organization. Concerning this last factor, the banality of results obtained may well be an important factor hindering further dissemination of job analysis.

But there are other reasons. One of the reasons may be the following: scientists in personnel selection seem to pretend that the usual case is the selection of a person for a certain job that is well known in its nature and requirements and can be expected to remain stable in this regard. Actually quite the contrary is the case. A large number, if not most, personnel decisions are decisions whether to hire a person or not for an organization where he or she is expected to perform a variety of tasks and roles, only a part of which is known at the time of the decision and even a smaller part of which can be unequivocally identified in reference to the relevant skills and abilities. Instead, this person is expected to develop within and together with the organization towards a largely unknown future. Little wonder then that employers act like meta-analysts and prefer the idea of hiring people with regard to abilities which are likely to be useful for a wide variety of jobs and organizational roles. What remains is something like intelligence, achievement motivation, emotional stability and extraversion or social competence.

But even if we believe in the situation-specificity hypothesis there is a number of unsolved problems and unanswered questions concerning job analysis. Only some of them can be listed and briefly discussed here. The first and probably most central deficiency is what we could call the *missing-link problem*. When Dunnette ten years ago spoke of the two worlds that have to be brought together he well knew that there was no logical way of deducing one from the other. There are a lot of approaches to transforming task characteristics into abilities or behavior, but there seems to be no logical-deductive way to do it.

The four 'basic approaches' Algera and Greuter depicted—behavior description, behavior requirements, ability requirements and task description—should be thoroughly investigated with reference to their helpfulness in overcoming this gap. Although there are some transformational devices at hand (e.g. McCormick, DeNisi and Shaw, 1979; Banks, Jackson, Stafford and Warr, 1983) so called 'experts' do not seem to be replaceable whatever approach we choose. J-coefficients and repertory grids (Smith, 1986) have been suggested for translating work into people, but both of them are based on judgements concerning the similarity or equivalence of objects belonging to different levels of cognizance—semantically as well as epistemologically.

Taxonomies of human behavior or performance like those of Fleishman (Fleishman and Quaintance, 1984) or Peterson and Bownas (1982) are likely to be helpful as general categorial systems not dissimilar to those that were of inestimable value in the natural sciences, especially in biology and chemistry. Interrelating them to job characteristics within the programmatic concept of a 'job-requirement matrix' (Fleishman, 1975) may be the best general tool we have at hand to date for matching jobs with personal qualities and synthetic validation. Its main shortcomings may lie in the assumptions of objective job characteristics that can be described totally independently of the incumbent and of unequivocal noncompensatory assignment of task and ability elements. For most jobs we have to assume that tasks and task elements are not completely independent of the incumbent. There is a certain amount of freedom of choice for all and a large amount for some jobs, going so far as to include the responsibility of creating new tasks for the incumbent. Additionally, systematic changes over time have to be taken into account (Brousseau, 1984). Concerning the relationship between tasks and abilities we have to assume that only for very simple jobs may it be true that a defined set of abilities is necessary and sufficient for performance. More often it may be true that abilities can compensate each other, and especially in combination with the individual redefinition of jobs the individual performance may have a partly idiosyncratic character. Finally, for the use of ability-labels we may find the same problems as we recognized in performance assessment where it has been shown, quite convincingly, that we are not able to use trait-like terms in a reliable manner (e.g. Ilgen and Feldman, 1983). Taking all of these limitations together we actually cannot expect more than a relatively vague assignment of work and person by means of job analysis.

A further bundle of problems greatly unsolved and often not even discussed (as in Algera and Greuter's chapter) is connected with the psychometric properties of job analysis methods. Information about reliability and validity would carry users' decisions about which of the various techniques to apply beyond the criteria of feasibility and practicality—or even beyond that of face validity, which may be a special problem with sample-type methods. The Critical Incidents Technique (CIT), for example, seems to provide no more than a framework or even only an idea which is varied in different ways by its users leaving everybody satisfied although there is a lack of standardization and presumably of psychometric sufficiency. Most psychometric criteria of the kind conducted routinely in test construction are usually not calculated in job analysis, and no advances have been made, as far as I can see, concerning the comparability of results gained by different methods, especially those belonging to the different categories of 'sample' and 'sign'.

As there seems to be little clarity about how to define even the most central psychometric concepts, reliability and validity, we concentrate here on some clarifying remarks on their definition and measurement. Different operational aspects of reliability, test-retest-reliability, internal consistency, parallel-test-reliability and objectivity (interrater-reliability) can be distinguished. If reliability is estimated by repeated measurement of the same job, components of unreliability can not only consist of instability of rating behavior but also of instability of the job in question. Seldom, if ever, are both components differentiated. For estimation of reliability by calculation of mean item-correlations, that is, by testing internal consistency, we have limited possibilities as most instruments usually consist of heterogenous items that are intended to measure distinct single aspects of tasks or jobs. So we have to keep in mind that internal consistency is a measure of homogeneity of the job or job requirements. If reliability is estimated by using parallel forms of job analysis instruments equivalence of these instruments has to be assured. As was mentioned earlier, comparability of results from different instruments is questionable in most cases. Raters can be thought of as being different methods, then interrater reliability (objectivity) is a special case of equivalence. This last form of estimation (i.e. interrater reliability) is the most common, gaining usually satisfactory results for standardized instruments (e.g. Banks and Miller, 1984). Of interest, in this context, is the correlation between supervisors' and subordinates' ratings of the latters' jobs, as a common question is, who should be taken as the more relevant source of information. Several studies demonstrated that task-perception may be dependent on personal characteristics like job satisfaction (e.g. Schnake and Dumler, 1985). The common expectation that subordinates' job descriptions reflect more social desirability than do supervisors' descriptions was called into question by Smith and Hakel (1979). Other components of differences between subordinates' and job incumbents' views, however, may well contribute to the validity of each of these perspectives.

A special problem in job analysis reliability is the number of 'does-not-apply' responses. As shown by Harvey and Hayes (1986) using the PAQ, as much as 21 percent of items of this kind can account for a correlation of 0.50 between two raters, 56 percent for 0.78. So reliability calculations have to be corrected in order to produce a reasonable estimation. On the other hand, the same 'does-not-apply' responses have to be considered as bearing valid information, so their scores should not be totally ignored for reliability calculation. DeNisi,

Cornelius and Blencoe (1987) investigated 'does-not-apply' responses as an index of appropriateness of the method for analyzing certain types of jobs.

The amount of evidence that job analysis represents veridical information about jobs, tasks and requirements, i.e. validity, can be estimated using the trichotomy of strategies usual for validation of person-related measures: criterion-referenced, content-referenced and construct-referenced. However, as is argued in Schuler et al. (1987), several restrictions and specialities have to be taken into account, characterizing the peculiarities of job-diagnostic data. One of them is the difficulty of separating measures of validity from those of reliability in certain cases, e.g. when assessments stemming from job incumbents and from their supervisors are compared. In predictive strategies, variance between jobs is the basis of validation, whereas differences between persons are part of the error variance (the opposite is true for the validity of person-related measures: calculation is based on variance between persons while situations have to be held constant).

For empirical validation basically two types of criteria are at issue: (a) other methods of job analysis, and (b) criteria of job success (performance, job satisfaction, health etc.). In case (a), for a certain job, the same elements should be nominated, or scaled as being relevant. As discussed above in the context of reliability, comparability between the results of different methods is actually very restricted due to the divergent quality of the responses. While assessments of unimportant job elements are easier (leading to overestimated correlations) the essence of validation would probably be better met by assigning higher weights to important or central elements of the jobs. Considering the 'autonomy' of a job (Breaugh, 1985) as a moderator variable, parts of the variance could probably be explained that otherwise would be attributed to error variance and thus lowered validity/reliability.

In case (b), validating a selection device against criteria of job success can not only be interpreted as a validation of the test but also of the underlying job analysis procedure. Out of several competing procedures, the one delivering the more successful line of prediction can be taken as the more valid. An example for this type of comparison is meta-analytic studies comparing job analysis procedures of different types (e.g. Cornelius, Schmidt and Carron, 1984) showing that rather simple procedures are not necessarily inferior to elaborate ones. Methodological difficulties lie in probable contaminations of the two levels of predictors among each other and with the criteria as well. Although there are no systematic comparisons known to the author, we can assume that in job analysis measures of predictive validity covary poorly with measures of content validity, as shown for selection instruments by Ostroff and Schmitt (1987). None the less content validation—and this means inclusion of 'subject matter experts' in the process—is not dispensable if the analysis is not to be restricted to differentiating elements but is to be extended to 'all' job elements.

Content validity is usually operationalized by having expert judges rate the representativeness of items for the jobs in question or for job dimensions, respectively. As a quantified index Lawshe (1975) proposed a coefficient of content validity for each item, relating the number of experts who named this item as relevant to the total number of experts.

As Schuler *et al.*, (1987) have argued, there is a special methodological problem with content validity: as criterion-related validity always is based on correlations and thus on variances, reliable differences between elements (persons or jobs) are crucial for calculations of validity. In contrast, for content-related evidence discrimination cannot be the crucial aspect, as the same elements can very well have equal importance for different jobs—thus lacking variance as a basis for computing any validity coefficient. In this case estimations of validity will not do without expert ratings of, e.g. importance or extent of the task or behavior for the job.

The most common scoring key of an item's job relevance is 'importance'; besides that 'difficulty', 'frequency', 'applicability' and some other scoring keys are in use. Not all of these scoring keys are likely to be adequate for rating all job elements (with the exception, probably, of 'importance'); but rules of adequacy are not established nor is there enough information concerning the interrelationship of keys among each other.

As far as a tool for job assessment not only delivers a pure description of movements or results, but also aggregates movements into more abstract concepts of tasks or even deals with job demands, we can conceive the appropriateness of these, as descriptions of the job, as a question of construct validity. The sources of these constructs may not only be formal or implicit theories of tasks and of jobs, but also theories of human performance and its basic situational conditions, of abilities, skills, motivation, and even of distributions and interactions among all these possible determinants of job success. There seems to be no way from 'pure' description of task or behavior elements to human attributes without building this bridge in the form of hypotheses from the other side. Or, to restate the picture in a metaphor somewhat more common in scientific reasoning, to synthesize the induction-deduction-cycle at a higher level of the spiral. Ideally, this process results in testable hypotheses concerning three modeling or transformation relations: (a) categorization (dimensionalization) of job characteristics, (b) measurability of dimensions by a given instrument, (c) relationships between job constructs (dimensions) and ability constructs.

As with the diagnosis of persons, so it is in analyzing jobs. We may not find any single procedure to test construct validity and seldom a result unequivocally indicating any precise amount of construct validity. One procedure to quantitatively assess at least components of construct validity is the multitrait-multimethod matrix (MTMM) (Fiske, 1987). In research on personnel testing as well as on performance assessment useful analyses have been done with this procedure wherever multimodal types of diagnosis have been involved (Schuler and Schmitt, 1987). In job analysis, however, experience with this type of comparison is rare as, in general, thinking in terms of construct validity of job analysis procedures has not been common. In the Hohenheim research group we have recently conducted an MTMM analysis including job analysis data with engineers in industrial research and development units collected by two different methods from two sources (job incumbents and supervisors). First results show low convergent and discriminant validity, correlations between raters being somewhat higher than those between methods. But, as was discussed before, comparison of different methods is one of the basically unsolved problems in job analysis, especially when they belong to different types (sign vs sample approach).

   Dimensionality is the central focus of most of the other studies of construct validity in job analysis. The usual procedure is to use factor analysis of importance ratings (and/or ratings of other keys) to form behavior categories. As demonstrated by Cranny and Doherty (1988), the resulting factors are not interpretable as important dimensions of the job while those dimensions raters agree to be important are not likely to emerge as factors. Irrelevant dimensions have to be excluded according to their low means in the expert ratings. It is more difficult, however, to be sure that all relevant dimensions are included. For this reason it can be recommended that item-generating procedures be integrated not only in the development of a job analysis instrument but also in the first stages of its application to new job families. More appropriate methods of grouping than factor and cluster analysis may be multidimensional scaling or other methods based on conceptual similarity of item content.

EXPECTATIONS

This discussion of some problems in job analysis began by considering why job analysis is so seldom practiced in a satisfying manner although generally being requested. I think we found a number of reasons for this discrepancy, the central one being that there is no satisfactory method of job analysis, at least when the intention is to use it for personnel selection purposes.

   If we consider job analysis indispensable for personnel selection we are well advised to intensify our research efforts to improve our knowledge, especially concerning the links between job analysis and predictors as well as between job analysis and criteria. Maybe validity generalization research will soon be able to supply us with stronger indications where detailed analyses really are necessary, where broad content types and procedures—e.g. classification by experts—are sufficient or where we can even rely on generalization of existing knowledge and totally skip job analysis. Validity generalization may be especially helpful in view of its capacity for the development of performance theories (e.g. Hunter, 1983) that could be a basis for improved job analysis instruments.

It is not only about job analysis in general that our knowledge is highly deficient, but also in regard to the usefulness of different types (e.g. sign vs sample approach) or single methods for special purposes. The work of Levine and his associates (Levine, Bennett and Ash, 1980; Levine, Ash, Hall and Sistrunk, 1983) was a meritorious start in this respect. They had expert users rate seven different methods of job analysis concerning their relative strengths and weaknesses for different purposes. By and large, ratings were mostly on an average with a rather small range. But, nevertheless, some useful information is given especially with regard to practicality of methods. The most important question for our context, however, cannot be answered by these studies, that is which method is the best one to allow the assembly or construction of valid selection procedures.

In many cases we may be well advised to choose a multimodal procedure. By using several methods simultaneously we not only have better chances to have the 'right' method included, but we open possibilities for construct validity research—e.g. for improving knowledge on specific analysis-predictor-criterion-relationships. One plausible hypothesis to test would be the expectation of closer relationships between levels of analysis and performance criteria of the same types—e.g. tasks/results, behaviors/work samples, abilities/tests—compared to relationships between different kinds of observations.

While it is obviously useful for research purposes to make simultaneous use of different (types of) analyses, utility in practical contexts has still to be demonstrated. Again, extensions on both sides of the procedure should be more fruitful than restricting multiplicity to one of their ends: analysis may be more adequate if it includes not only job elements but also specific requirements and constraints in a given organization. Utility calculations, on the other hand, may be more realistic when calculations of validity and economic gains are completed by an evaluation of parameters relevant to those specific requirements and constraints and thereby to decisions within the given context. Otherwise psychologists may further miss the point of actual decisions and their calculations may further be ignored even if their impressive numbers seem to demonstrate obvious gains for the organization.

Lately approaches to job analysis have been demonstrated by cognitive psychologists; in Germany especially action theorists claim that the investigation of processes of cognitive regulation is a basic tool of understanding tasks and human work. One of the principles thought to be essential is to neglect distinctions between thought and behavior, both being integrated in the concept of action (Hacker, 1978). Another 'strain' of cognitive psychology, presumably of somewhat more relevance for personnel selection, is the simulation of complex decision-making, usually performed by using computer programs that interconnect large numbers of variables (e.g. Dörner, Kreuzig, Reither and

Stäudel, 1983). Although several research teams are currently trying to make systems of this kind operational for ability testing, no especially remarkable success has been demonstrated so far. Perhaps the new branch of a 'psychology of knowledge' (Wissenspsychologie; Spada and Opwis, 1987) including, among other activities, computerized modeling of knowledge acquisition and trying to formulate a psychological basis of artificial intelligence, could support, in the longer run, the development of superior theories of human work and performance.

A last aspect I want to mention that could be of importance in future is the inclusion of social processes. In a twofold way social processes could be taken into account: the first one is to consider determinants of peoples' responses to task analysis apart from a factual description of what they do and what their job demands. Presumably descriptions are biased by considerations about the consequences of the answers. As results of job analysis are often connected with job evaluation and can be relevant for payment and for organizational changes, we should include these aspects of 'micropolicy' in our understanding of task-related data as is tentatively done in other stages of the selection process (Herriot, in this volume). Possibly some methods of job analysis are less prone to this type of reactivity than are others. CIT, for example, may provoke less impression management than most standardized rating methods, but we are completely in the realm of speculation regarding this first aspect of social processes.

The second aspect is the inclusion of social psychological characteristics of the work environment in the analysis and in the information communicated to the applicants. Concerning this aspect, there are already some data at hand. Wanous' realistic job previews, for example (Premack and Wanous, 1985), produce positive effects from the use of such information. In the Hohenheim research group we collected applicants' responses which indicated that they were especially interested in this kind of information, as it is almost completely missing in traditional presentations of organizations to prospective job incumbents. In general, selection devices based on job analysis—especially, of course, if both are of the 'sample' kind—may be better accepted by applicants than instruments that include less task-relevant information. Recent work demonstrated that climate information on organisations enhanced validity of self-selection. Griffin, Bateman, Wayne and Head (1987) experimentally demonstrated support for their hypothesis that objective facts of workplaces and social information jointly determine perceptions and affect.

It might be worthwhile to consider using standard instruments for this type of information, for example measures of organizational climate, of leadership and interaction style; in this way, personnel selection could be developed somewhat more in a direction of an equitable or even joint decision process or at least towards the view that personnel decisions involve the participants more than hitherto taken into account. In an intuitive manner this kind of consideration may have been included for a long time, especially if the whole selection and decision process is in one person's hand. This is one of the many gateways where the art comes into the science of selection.

Taken altogether, we have to confess that our claim that job analysis is an indispensable basis of personnel selection may be more a rhetoric script than one of action. In many cases—out of the few where it is actually practiced—job analysis seems to be a kind of garnishing to justify the selling of selection procedures like 'organization-specific assessment centers'. The impossibility of reconstructing the, allegedly, job analysis-based assessment dimensions (Robertson, Gratton and Sharpley, 1987), should be a warning sign (although there is not much information justifying Robertson *et al.*'s expectation that validity would be improved by making exercises instead of dimensions the basis of predictions).

Even those of us who share a less pessimistic view and believe in principle in the advantages—or even necessity—of job analysis will concede that competitive tests of different methods are urgently needed. Methodological progress will only be made by critical comparative evaluations. Applying test-theoretical strictness to job analysis should be a good start.

REFERENCES

Banks, M. H., Jackson, P. R., Stafford, E. M., and Warr, P. B. (1983). The job components inventory and the analysis of jobs requiring limited skill. *Personnel Psychology*, **36**, 57–66.

Banks, M. H. and Miller, R. L. (1984). Reliability and convergent validity of the Job Components Inventory. *Journal of Occupational Psychology*, **57**, 181–184.

Breaugh, J. A. (1985). The measurement of work autonomy. *Human Relations*, **38**, 559–570.

Brousseau, K. R. (1984). Job-person dynamics and career development, *Research in Personnel and Human Resources Management*, vol. 2, JAI Press, Greenwich, pp. 125–154.

Cornelius, E. T. III, Schmidt, F. L. and Carron, T. J. (1984). Job classification approaches and the implementation of validity generalization results. *Personnel Psychology*, **37**, 247–260.

Cranny, C. J. and Doherty, M. E. (1988). Importance rating in job analysis: Note on the misinterpretation of factor analysis. *Journal of Applied Psychology*, **73**, 320–322.

De Nisi, A. S., Cornelius, E. T. III and Blencoe, A. G. (1987). Further investigation of common knowledge effects on job analysis rankings. *Journal of Applied Psychology*, **72**, 262–268.

Dörner, D., Kreuzig, H. W., Reither, F. and Stäudel, T. (1983). *Lohhausen: Vom Umgang mit Unbestimmtheit und Komplexität*, Huber, Bern.

Fiske, D. W. (1987). On understanding our methods and their effects. *Diagnostica*, **33**, 188–194.

Fleishman, E. A. (1975). Toward a taxonomy of human performance. *American Psychologist*, **30**, 1127–1149.

Fleishman, E. A. and Quaintance, M. K. (1984). *Taxonomies of human performance*, Academic Press, Orlando.

Griffin, R. W., Bateman, T. S., Wayne, S. J. and Head, T. C. (1987). Objective and social factors as determinants of task perceptions and responses: An integrated perspective and empirical investigation. *Academy of Management Journal*, **30**, 501–523.

Hacker, W. (1978). *Allgemeine Arbeits- und Ingenieurpsychologie.* Deutscher Verlag der Wissenschaften, Berlin.

Hambleton, R. K. (1985). Criterion-referenced assessment of individual differences. In: C. R. Reynolds and V. L. Wilson (eds), *Methodological and Statistical Advances in the Study of Individual Differences,* Plenum Press, New York, pp. 393–424.

Harvey, R. J. and Hayes, T. L. (1986). Monte Carlo baselines for interrater reliability correlations using the position analysis questionnaire. *Personnel Psychology,* **39**, 345–357.

Hunter, J. E. (1983). A causal analysis of cognitive ability, job knowledge, job performance, and supervisory ratings. In: F. Landy, S. Zedeck and J. Cleveland (eds), *Performance Measurement and Theory,* Erlbaum, Hillsdale, NJ, pp. 257–266.

Ilgen, D. R., and Feldman, J. M. (1983). Performance appraisal: A process focus. *Research in Organizational Behavior,* vol. 5, JAI Press, Greenwich, pp. 141–197.

Lawsche, C. H. (1975). A quantitative approach to content validity. *Personnel Psychology,* **28**, 563–575.

Levine, E. L., Ash, R. A., Hall, H. and Sistrunk, F. (1983). Evaluation of job analysis methods by experienced job analysts. *Academy of Management Journal,* **26**, 339–348.

Levine, E. L., Bennett, L. J. and Ash, R. A. (1980). Exploratory comparative study of four job analysis methods. *Journal of Applied Psychology,* **65**, 524–535.

McCormick, E. J., DeNisi, A. S. and Shaw, J. B. (1979). Use of the Position Analysis Questionnaire for establishing the job component validity of tests. *Journal of Applied Psychology,* **64**, 51–56.

Ostroff, C. and Schmitt, N. (1987). *The relationship between content and criterion-related validity indices: An empirical investigation,* Michigan State University; unpublished manuscript.

Peterson, N. G. and Bownas, D. A. (1982). Skill, task structure, and performance acquisition. In: M. D. Dunnette and E. A. Fleishman (eds), *Human Performance and Productivity. Vol 1: Capability Assessment,* Erlbaum, Hillsdale, NJ, pp. 49–105.

Premack, S. L. and Wanous, J. P. (1985). A meta-analysis of realistic job preview experiments. *Journal of Applied Psychology,* **70**, 706–719.

Robertson, I., Gratton, L. and Sharpley, D. (1987). The psychometric properties and design of managerial assessment centres: Dimensions into exercises won't go. *Journal of Occupational Psychology,* **60**, 187–195.

Schnake, M. E. and Dumler, M. P. (1985). Affective response bias in the measurement of perceived task characteristics. *Journal of Occupational Psychology,* **58**, 159–166.

Schuler, H., Donat, M., Funke, U. and Moser, K. (1987). *Entwicklung eines eignungsdiagnostischen Personalauswahlsystems für Wissenschaftler und Ingenieure im Bereich industrieller Forschung und Entwicklung. 1. Zwischenbericht,* Universität Hohenheim, Stuttgart.

Schuler, H. and Schmitt, N. (1987). Multimodale Messung in der Personalpsychologie. *Diagnostica,* **33**, 259–271.

Smith, J. E. and Hakel, M. D. (1979). Convergence among data sources, response bias, and reliability and validity of a structured job analysis questionnaire. *Personnel Psychology,* **32**, 677–692.

Smith, M. (1986). A repertory grid analysis of supervisory jobs. *International Review of Applied Psychology,* **35**, 501–512.

Spada, H. and Opwis, K. (1987). Wissenspsychologie: Erwerb, Repräsentation und Nutzung von Wissen. In: M. Amelang (ed.), *Bericht über den 35. Kongress der Deutschen Gesellschaft für Psychologie in Heidelberg 1986,* Hogrefe, Göttingen, pp. 253–264.

4

Using Job Analysis as a Basis for Selection

R. S. KANDOLA
Pearn Kandola Downs, Oxford

A large brewery wished to recruit new employees into a bulk packaging plant which was undergoing construction and was nearing completion. High-speed filling lines of an advanced nature were being introduced which required fifteen people to work on each line in a shift. Although the technology was not a great advance on that used elsewhere in the brewery the lines were considerably faster.

The objectives of the study were to analyse the new jobs: identify relevant job-related criteria: and to draft employee specifications for each job or group of jobs for use in the selection process. The grouping of jobs into broad bands was considered important as the brewery wanted to recruit people into a group rather than into a specific job. Accordingly, each employee once recruited should be capable of doing all the jobs within the group. The new plant was being constructed in an inner-city with a high ethnic minority population and so another important consideration was the fairness of any selection procedure which was to be introduced.

A variety of data-gathering methods were used (see Table 4.1). First of all observations and questioning of experienced workers in another packaging plant of the brewery where similar, though not identical, lines had already been introduced. The Job Components Inventory (Banks *et al.*, 1979) was used because it was ideal for identifying in great detail the kinds of tools used, the levels of arithmetic reasoning, etc. involved in a job. In addition, the Position Analysis Questionnaire (McCormick *et al.*, 1972) was used because it was the only technique currently available which could scale a particular job against all jobs by reference to its norm base. In this way, a direct comparison was

Advances in Selection and Assessment. Edited by M. Smith and I. T. Robertson

possible between jobs in terms of the skill, effort and other demands made on the individual. The cluster analysis option of the PAQ on computer processing facilities would determine whether the jobs could be meaningfully grouped.

Table 4.1   Summary description of techniques used.

Technique	Description	Purpose
Observation	Visits to different areas of plant. Watching job holder carrying out tasks and asking questions.	To obtain an overview of task being carried out. To become familiar with the plant and environment.
Job Components Inventory (JCI)	A structured questionnaire split into 7 sections: A Tools and equipment. B Physical and conceptual skills. C Mathematical skills. D Communication skills. E Decision-making and responsibility. F Job conditions. G Perceived job characteristics. Most suitable for skilled, semi-skilled and unskilled work.	To provide detailed descriptions of each area of work. Information to be used in drawing up person specifications.
Position Analysis and Questionnaire (PAQ)	A structured questionnaire containing 187 items, split into 6 categories: A Information input. B Mental processes. C Work output. D Relationships with others. E Job context. F Other job characteristics. Data are computerised, analysed and jobs are normed against 2200 jobs contained in computer data back	To enable direct, quantifiable and normative comparisons to be made between jobs in terms of skills required. To cluster into groups those jobs which were most similar
Critical Incidents Technique	Interviews with supervisors of jobs being analysed. Asked for actual occasions when job holders did something extremely well or badly. Interview follows a laid down procedure.	To provide information on the most critical aspects of some of the jobs. To provide more information on the skills to be measured in the assessment procedure.

In addition, the more complex jobs were subjected to critical incident interviews with supervisors. The interviewer asked the supervisor for descriptions of real job behaviour which they had witnessed which they felt was particularly good, and also descriptions of actual job behaviour which they felt was less effective or where avoidable mistakes were made. Altogether, twelve PAQ interviews and twelve critical incident interviews were conducted; together with the eight JCI interviews.

Five distinct groups of jobs were identified. These were:

(1) quality controller;
(2) pasteuriser, cleaning in place, and cleaner;
(3) forklift truck driver, stock control;
(4) palatiser, depalitiser, labeller, capsuler, decant operator;
(5) decoder.

For each group of jobs a person specification was developed and the critical features of each group were identified; altogether 22 specific skills and abilities were identified from all the jobs though the number relevant for a group of jobs ranged from 5 up to a maximum of 13.

For each of the 22 skills identified, an interview checklist was developed. This provided interviewers with guidelines on the types of questions to ask candidates and how to interpret their responses. In addition, recommendations were made on appropriate aptitude tests to be used for each group of jobs.

The study showed that a common set of job behaviours can be developed from which the requirements for specific jobs can be selected, thus greatly reducing repetition and demands on the interviewers. The study also demonstrated the usefulness of the JCI in helping to prepare job descriptions, which compensated for the lack of detailed information of that kind from the PAQ.

In terms of fairness, approximately 30 per cent of staff taken on were from ethnic minorities, which was in proportion to the numbers who had applied. In addition it was found that the quality of people appointed was higher than that in other comparable plants. The most powerful indication of this was that the new staff were learning the jobs more quickly. As a result, average training was 3 weeks compared with 12 weeks in the company's other bulk packaging plant.

REFERENCES

Banks, M. H., Jackson, P. R., Stafford, E. M. and Warr P. B. (1979). *Job components Inventory Mark II.* Sheffield, Manpower Service Commission.

McCormick, E. J., Jeanneret, R. R. and Meacham, R. C. (1972) A study of job characteristics and job dimensions as based on the Position Analysis Questionnnaire. *Journal of Applied Psychology, Monograph,* **56**, 347–368.

5

Criteria for Selection

FRANK J. LANDY and HALEH RASTEGARY
Pennsylvania State University

This chapter is the product of three processes. The first of these processes was the preparation of an outline for a presentation at a conference held in Buxton, England, in May of 1987 on the topic of personnel selection and assessment. The second process involved actually presenting and discussing the topic of criteria at that conference in the context of the other presentations and reactions of the participants to our presentation. The third process was the formal response of a colleague who was given the responsibility of considering the presentation, the resulting paper and the implications of these two products. This third process has resulted in a discussion section at the end of the chapter prepared by our colleague Tom Akermann.

Some assumptions

In preparing for the conference, we made some assumptions about what was expected of us. First, we assumed that our colleagues wanted someone to identify relevant literature that they might access at some other time. They simply wanted to be able to scan the activity of those doing research in the area called criterion measurement. In addition, we assumed that they would count on us to alert them to any changes or radical alterations in ways of measuring or thinking about criteria. Finally, we assumed that they would like us to express an opinion on an optimistic-pessimistic continuum with respect to various classes of performance measures. It was with these assumptions in mind that we prepared the outline, the presentation and this chapter.

Advances in Selection and Assessment. Edited by M. Smith and I. T. Robertson
© 1989 John Wiley & Sons Ltd

THE REVIEW

Boundaries

It is important for the reader to know how we conducted our search and what limits, if any, were placed on our review. In the first place, we assumed that there was not much reason to go back beyond 1980. We chose that line of demarcation for several reasons. In the first place, Landy and Farr (1980) published a review of rating scales as criteria that covered the literature from the mid 1940's through 1979. In addition, Landy and Farr also published a book (1983) that covered other types of performance measures that had been used through 1980. Thus, the interested reader has available detailed reviews in order to assess trends prior to 1980. Since there have been no exhaustive general reviews since that time, in combination with these earlier reviews, the period from 1980 through 1986 is most useful for the individual interested in criterion measurement.

The title of the book (and the conference) as well as the other chapters in the book imply that the critical issue for concern is selection. Thus, it might have been appropriate to consider only the issue of selection (and promotion) in reviewing the literature. We felt that this, although useful and responsive as far as the conference was concerned, was wasteful. Since we had to review all of the literature to find the selection studies, we thought that we might just as well cast a wider net and report on trends on all areas of criterion measurement. Thus, we developed many different subcategories for the research we reviewed. As an example, in the rating area, we did not simply consider those papers that used ratings as criteria in a selection study, we also considered the papers in which the influence of demographic characteristics of raters (e.g. race, gender) might influence ratings.

In determining which journals would be sampled, we tried to be as inclusive as possible. Thus, we reviewed the following journals for the years in question: *Journal of Applied Psychology, Personnel Psychology, Journal of Occupational Psychology, Journal of Occupational Behaviour, Organizational Behavior and Human Decision Processes* (formerly *Organizational Behavior and Human Performance*), *Academy of Management Journal, Journal of Educational Psychology, Psychological Bulletin, Applied Psychological Measurement, Academy of Management Review,* and *Human Factors.* Undoubtedly, we missed some articles in other journals but we felt that these journals would fairly represent what was being done currently in the area of criterion measurement.

Criterion categories

Ratings

When considering criterion variables, it is clear that there are several distinct classes that must be considered. The most ubiquitous measure is the supervisory rating. But rating studies can take many different forms. They can be 'real' ratings in field settings or they can be 'paper' or 'video' people ratings of simulated workers. They might even involve the rating of actors in role-playing situations. As you will see in the tables to follow, we have noted these distinctions for the reader.

Objective measures of productivity

The term *objective*, as it is used here, is meant to imply that the behavior under consideration lends itself to unambiguous counting (though not necessarily unambiguous interpretation). In a normal production setting, this would include measures like the number of units produced, the amount of time necessary to produce a unit, the number of errors that occur in producing each unit, etc. As was the case with ratings, however, the studies that address objective measures of performance do not always occur in the field. Sometimes these studies occur in simulation and role-playing designs and in other instances, they occur in laboratories with no attempt to simulate a work setting in any important manner. We will note these distinctions in presenting the results of the review.

Ancillary measures of performance

Traditionally, in addition to ratings and objective indices, several other measures have been considered reasonable criteria in selection studies. It has been assumed that it is valuable to an organization to be able to predict, understand and control absenteeism, turnover, and accidents. Although these are not 'performance' in any real sense, they certainly do affect organizational effectiveness. Further, it seems fairly clear that psychological variables are implicated in the variation of these measures in a given population of workers. For these reasons, we consider these ancillary measures separately in the review.

Hands-on measures

Recently, there has been a great deal of interest in a new class of measures that we will refer to as hands-on measures. Hands-on measures are samples of work performance chosen on some *a priori* basis (e.g. importance or frequency) to represent a particular job. The data are not gathered in the context of more general job performance. The subject is usually asked to perform a very specific set of tasks extracted from the job and performed at a work station that has been developed specifically for purposes of collecting the criterion data. This has the advantage of providing behavioral data on aspects of the job that might not otherwise occur with sufficient frequency or in suitable contexts or environments to allow for high-quality measurement. Frequently, these measures resemble work sample predictors. The point to keep in mind for purposes of this chapter is that these measures are gathered as *criterion* data not predictor data.

Knowledge tests

An additional category of criterion data that might be considered is a knowledge or task mastery measure. Although this type of measure is used most frequently as a criterion in training studies, it might also be considered a reasonable criterion for a selection or promotion study.

Multiple indicators

In many of the studies that we reviewed, more than one type of criterion measure was under consideration. Thus, some studies might consider both ratings of performance and ancillary data (e.g. absence rates) or performance ratings and objective performance measures. Rather than enter these articles in several independent categories, we have simply created a category to deal with multiple-measure studies.

Coverage by journal

Major trends

Table 5.1 presents data that permit one to determine where criterion-related articles are being published. On an absolute basis, it is clear that the *Journal of Applied Psychology* has produced the greatest number of performance-related articles in the past seven years. The 139 articles in *JAP* represent 34 percent of all articles appearing on performance-related topics during that time period. *The Academy of Management Journal* and *Personnel Psychology* represent a distant second—each accounting for approximately 15 percent of the performance-related articles. The numbers and percentages look somewhat different, however, when you consider the total number of articles published by each source during the years reviewed. Table 5.2 shows that based on total articles published, *Personnel Psychology* and the *Journal of Applied Psychology* seem more 'performance intensive' in terms of subject matter. Three other journals (*Journal of Occupational Psychology*, *OBHDP* and the *Academy of Management Journal*) all have similar percentages represented in their ratios of performance articles to total articles. At this level, there is nothing startling. The good news is that most of the journals that purport to deal with the prediction of work-related performance do publish that type of research. The bad news is that the reader interested in criterion research cannot limit his or her reading to one or two journals. It was, however, somewhat surprising to see the small percentage of total pages devoted to research that actually gathered criterion measures by journals such as *Human Factors, Applied Psychological Measurement* and the *Journal of Occupational Behaviour*. A literature review cannot determine whether this is the result of choices made by editors or choices made by authors, but it is interesting to note.

Table 5.1 Performance measurement[a]

| | Absolute # Articles | | | | | | | | | | | |
	J. Appl. Psych.	Pers. Psych.	J. Occup. Psych.	OBHDP	Acad. Man. Jour.	Ed. Psych.[b]	Psych. Bull.	Appl. Meas.	Acad. Man. Rev.	Hum. Fac.	Occup. Beh.	TOT
Real rat.	47	24	9	9	19	20	3	1	5	1	2	140
Other rat.	13	8	1	13	4	7	–	–	–	–	–	46
Real prod.	17	5	4	4	3	–	1	–	1	9	1	45
Other prod.	19	4	–	8	3	–	–	–	–	10	–	44
Abs.	11	2	2	2	5	–	–	–	2	–	–	24
Turn	17	4	4	1	17	1	–	–	7	–	2	53
Acc.	2	–	1	–	1	–	–	–	–	–	–	4
Hand-on	1	3	1	1	1	–	–	–	–	2	–	9
Knl.	–	2	1	–	–	–	–	–	–	–	–	3
Mult.	12	5	4	5	10	–	–	–	3	–	1	40
Tot	139	57	27	43	63	28	4	1	18	22	6	408

[a] Literature reviews were not included unless a new theoretical position was presented in the body of the review.
[b] Teacher performance was considered but not student performance.

Table 5.2 Performance measurement

| | Percentage of total articles devoted to performance (in each journal) | | | | | | | | | | |
	J. Appl. Psych.	Pers. Psych.	J. Occup. Psych.	OBHDP	Acad. Man. Jour.	Ed. Psych.	Psych. Bull.	Appl. Meas.	Acad. Man. Rev.	Hum. Fac.	Occup. Beh.
Tot # Art.	662	260	210	332	428	560	552	238	447	428	87
% Perf in journal	20	21	12	12	14	5	0.7	0.4	4	5	6

Journal/performance measure interactions

Table 5.1 presents data that relate to absolute numbers of articles. Table 5.2 deals with criterion-related articles compared to total articles. Table 5.3 presents data that provide a clearer picture of which journals tend to 'specialize' in which types of criterion-related articles. In this table, we are considering the breakdown of criterion-related papers by type *within* each journal. Thus, the columns will sum to 100 percent. As an example, Table 5.1 tells us that 139 criterion-related articles appeared in the *Journal of Applied Psychology* between 1980 and 1986. Of this total, 47 included rating data in which the ratings were of real (as opposed to 'paper' or video) performers in field settings. Thus, in Table 5.3 we see that 43 percent (i.e. 34 + 9 percent) of the articles that appeared in *JAP* dealt with ratings of one form or another. In *Personnel Psychology*, this percentage is even higher—56 percent. In the *Journal of Educational Psychology*, 27 of 28 performance-related articles considered ratings as criterion measures. If we look at the far right-hand column in Table 5.1, we see some general trends. Across all journals reviewed, rating studies account for 46 percent (140 + 46) of the publications, objective measures (i.e. productivity) account for 22 percent, and absence and turnover account for 19 percent of the published research. Studies that deal with multiple performance indicators account for 10 percent of the published research, hands-on measures account for 2 percent and knowledge measures, and accidents account for 'trace' amounts of the published research.

Table 5.3   Performance measurement

	J. Appl. Psych.	Pers. Psych.	J. Occup. Psych.	OBHDP	Acad. Man. Jour.	Ed. Psych.	Psych. Bull.	Appl. Meas.	Acad. Man. Rev.	Hum. Fac.	Occup. Beh.
	\multicolumn{11}{l}{Percentage in each journal (columns sum to 100)}										
Real rat.	34	42	35	21	30	67	60	100	29	4	33
Other rat.	9	14	4	31	6	23					
Real prod.	12	9	12	10	5	7	20		6	39	17
Other prod.	14	7		19	5				44		
Abs.	8	4	7	5	8				12		
Turn.	12	7	15		26	3	20		35		33
Acc.	1		4		2						
Hand-on	1	5	4	2	2					13	
Knl.		3	4								
Mult.	9	9	15	12	16				18		17

There is one final way to cut the data that might be of interest to the reader. Many researchers are interested in one or a few types of performance measures. The researcher may be interested in ratings as measures of performance or turnover or accidents. If we consider the total number of articles appearing on a particular type of performance measure and then look at where they appear, on a proportional basis, we get a somewhat different view of who is publishing what. Consider Table 5.4. In this table, we discover that the *Journal of Applied Psychology* and *Human Factors* take the lead in publishing articles in which productivity measures gathered in field settings are represented. Similarly, the *Journal of Applied Psychology* and the *Academy of Management Journal* seem to be publishing most of the research that uses absenteeism as a criterion variable. Other percentages may be intriguing but misleading because of the small number of total articles published on the topic.

Table 5.4 Performance measurement

	Percentage by each journal (rows sum to 100)										
	J. Appl. Psych.	Pers. Psych.	J. Occup. Psych.	OBHDP	Acad. Man. Jour.	Ed. Psych.	Psych. Bull.	Appl. Meas.	Acad. Man. Rev.	Hum. Fac.	Occup. Beh.
Real rat.	34	17	6	6	14	14	2	1	4	1	1
Other rat.	28	18	2	28	9	15					
Real prod.	37	11	7	9	7	4	2		2	19	2
Other prod.	43	9		18	7					23	
Abs.	46	9	8	8	21				8		
Turn.	32	7	8	2	32	2	2		11		4
Acc.	50		25		25						
Hand-on	11	33	11		12					33	
Knl.		67	33								
Mult.	30	13	10	13	25				7		2

Annotated reference list

As a service to the reader, we have identified all of the articles that make up the tables presented to this point in a separate publication. Since space limitations did not permit the inclusion of the specific references or the identity of the studies in the various matrices that appear in Tables 5.1 through 5.4, we will make this information available to anyone who requests it. Simply send the request to the authors of this chapter. In that publication, we have indicated which cells in the tables each of these references occupies. We hope that this will help the reader interested in a particular criterion measure to identify the most recent research on that measure.

The ubiquitous caveat

In our literature review, we have attempted to identify most of the current important work in the area of criteria for selection and assessment. Unless something miraculous has happened to change the vagaries of human performance (i.e. ours!), we have probably missed a few articles. The object of our review was not to be obsessively complete but to identify trends and draw attention to some areas. Thus, we pre-congratulate the reader who finds the study or paper that we missed. It will serve to confirm the fact that our feelings of modesty for this chapter are deserved.

THE STATE OF THE ART

Having reviewed much of the recent work on various measures of performance and having considered the logic and theory that support these various measures, we will now venture some opinions regarding their usefulness and integrity for purposes of selection and assessment research and practice.

Ratings

Supervisory ratings have been variously lionized and maligned over the last several decades. They were introduced and promoted with great enthusiasm in the 1930s, integrated with judgment theory and practice in the 1940s (particularly by Wherry), used extensively in the 1950s and 1960s for the validation of various selection devices and vigorously bashed in the 1970s for proneness to errors of judgment. In the midst of this roller coaster profile, work continued on developing rating scales that resisted some of the more common forms of errors. The results of these efforts were the Behaviorally Anchored Rating Scale (BARS) (Smith and Kendall, 1963; Schwab, Heneman and De-Cotiis, 1975) and the Behavioral Observation Scale (BOS) technique (Latham and Wexley, 1977; Latham, Fay and Saari, 1979). The BARS technique is the older and more thoroughly studied of the two procedures but both seem to result in decent estimates of important aspects of behavior in a wide range of settings.

Landy and Farr (1980) published an extensive review of the rating literature and concluded that rating formats did not make a substantial difference in the variance in actual ratings *if the rating scales were well constructed and had certain critical characteristics*. We add emphasis because it is common to hear the first part of that conclusion quoted but not the second part. The characteristics that seem to be crucial include a well-defined domain of behavior, behavioral anchors for the scales and an effective range of scale points between 3 and 9. Within those limits, it does not seem to matter if the scale is developed as a traditional graphic rating scale with arbitrary scale values or a BARS scale with empirically placed anchors. Further, the earlier review concluded that a good deal of the observed variation in rated behavior was the result of variation in true scores rather than the result of systematic error or bias.

Landy and Farr (1980) and Feldman (1981) both called for more extensive research into the cognitive mechanisms that were involved in the rating process. This call may have led to some inappropriate emphasis and inference. It became obvious to these reviewers that the ratings were the result of some fascinating and complex cognitive operations, just as job performance is the result of complex combinations of interdependent systems. It did *not* follow from this observation that rated performance was an epiphenomenon that was the result of combinations of judgment errors. Unfortunately, many colleagues in the user community were left with this impression. The fact that cognitive approaches to rating research have dominated the research landscape for the past seven years has helped to institutionalize that negative impression of the integrity of ratings as criteria in selection and assessment research. This negative impression is unwarranted. To be sure, ratings are not without unwanted variance. There are problems of reliability and domain validity. Nevertheless, it is fair to say that in most instances, true score variance easily overwhelms error variance (both random and systematic). Further, when the issue is *unreliability* of the criterion measure, there are methods of estimating relationships that can correct for this attenuation.

We see no data to encourage disaffection from supervisory rating scales. When they are well developed and administered, they retain the capacity to show substantial relationships to appropriate selection devices in the form of significant validity coefficients. It is likely that meta-analyses of various rating studies conducted in the past decade will demonstrate that various artifacts can account for the observed variation of rating 'errors' illustrated in rating studies published in the past 30 years. The issue of true score variation is somewhat more difficult to deal with directly since the only studies that are capable of estimating such values are those employing various simulated (e.g. videotape) performance scenarios.

Objective measures of performance

Traditionally, objective measures have been unattractive for several reasons. First, there are relatively few jobs where incumbent performance can be characterized using an objective measure of performance that is not trivial. What is it that managers or police officers or firefighters or college professors or research scientists 'produce'—that can be counted? What they do produce, they produce in such small quantities that it would take years or decades to gather sufficient 'observations' to be at all useful. In addition, most jobs require interaction among workers—or at least a certain interdependence or sequencing of operations. As a result, workers in these jobs are not individually or uniquely responsible for the 'production'. There is really no unique criterion variable to match with a predictor score. Although we might consider using group measures of output, the problem is that we do not hire work *groups*—we hire individuals.

There have been, however, some interesting developments in certain work settings. It is no secret that computerized operations are sweeping the clerical and administrative environments. Most offices have switched or are in the processing of switching to VDT technology. Such technology provides an interesting opportunity for criterion measurement. It is now possible to monitor quite closely the operations of clerical, administrative and professional staff who make extensive use of VDT technology (Landy, Rastegary and Motowidlo, 1987; Frese, Ulich and Dzida, 1987). As an example, the speed and accuracy of the insurance claims agent is easily determined. The efficiency of dispatchers, telephone operators, and even retail clerks is easy to monitor through the same computer equipment that helps incumbents to carry out their duties and responsibilities. This can be seen as either good news or bad news. The good news is that it is no longer necessary for someone to sit and count certain behaviors in order to assign an 'objective' performance score. The bad news is that this type of technology can be easily (and possibly *correctly*) perceived as an attempt to impose performance 'standards' by the employees. Nevertheless, if we consider only the good news, there is some hope for the development of new objective performance measures of high psychometric integrity in jobs that can be monitored using computer technology. Since computer technology is rapidly expanding in work settings, it is safe to say that the future for objective measures is more promising than its past. For many jobs, however, the possibility of identifying objective measures of performance will never be realized.

Ancillary measures

Absences

The prediction of worker absence remains an attractive goal for personnel research. At one level, the impact of absence is clear and quantifiable. Its costs can be estimated and its reduction 'sold' to managers dubious of the contributions of the behavioral sciences to the world of commerce and industry. Unfortunately, there are more than a few problems associated with absence research and the use of absence measures as criterion variables. First, there is a problem of frequency. Absence is an infrequent event. On the average, 4 percent of the workers have 100 percent of the absence. Further, only a small portion of those workers have more than one absence. These problems have been well described in a recent book by Goodman and his colleagues (1984). The fact is that there are rather formidable analytic problems related to absence measures. In addition, there is the problem of what an absence *means*. Chadwick-Jones, Nicholson and Brown (1982) make a compelling argument for considering absences as part of a larger social contract between employer and employee. As such, they cannot be rightly understood in the context of individual characteristics of workers. In other words, from the social contract perspective, it is rather silly to even *contemplate* predicting absences from ability, motivational or dispositional characteristics of the worker.

Most research has centered on trying to understand the social-psychological foundation for absence behavior. There are few studies that place absence in the role of a criterion variable in a selection program. It should be obvious why this is the case. At this stage, we can generate little optimism that this circumstance is likely to change.

Turnover

Although there are considerably more published research articles dealing with turnover than absence, virtually all of these articles address the social-psychological characteristics of decisions to quit. Moreover, most of the studies measure the *desire* or *intention* to quit rather than quitting behavior *per se*. From the psychometric perspective, turnover measures are infinitely more problematic than absence measures and for many of the same reasons. The level of aggregation is critical with these studies and it is seldom possible to isolate an individual measure of turnover. Instead, turnover probability can be assigned to work group, shift, plant or cohort status.

There is little hope for the emergence of turnover as a realistic criterion variable in most public and private sector settings. The one possible exception to this is the military environment. Research on retention is now quite vigorous. In the US, the various armed service branches are anxious to know who will re-enlist and how re-enlistment rates can be increased. Given the number of enlisted personnel involved, the regularity with which this decision must be made (e.g. every several years depending on the branch of the service), and the frequency with which enlisted personnel *do* re-enlist, it may be possible to identify individual predictors of turnover that will have meaning and transportability to private sector employers.

Accidents

The simple fact is that virtually no one is studying accidents from the perspective of individual differences among incumbents. There certainly is a great deal of discussion about safe behavior in environments such as nuclear power plants, air traffic control towers, and airplane cockpits. Nevertheless, the published literature considering these topics from a selection perspective is non-existent. Needless to say, the number of industrial deaths and lost time injuries remains unacceptably high. It is hard to believe that applied psychologists have run out of ways to study or understand safety behavior. It may be that the differential psychologist has simply deferred to the human factors psychologist to solve the problem. This may be a little premature. At best, the answer to safe behavior is likely to come from the joint efforts of the personnel psychologist and the human factors psychologist rather than from the unique contribution of either of them.

Knowledge tests

Knowledge tests are well known and frequently used as predictors of later performance but seldom used as criteria in selection studies. They are, however, often used as criteria for training studies. Most often knowledge tests are thought of as written multiple-choice or essay-type tests but they need not be limited to that format. For example, in the nuclear power industry, it is common to give control room operators what is known as a 'walk-through' interview. Individuals are taken on a tour of a working facility and asked questions about the various displays and controls. They are given hypothetical situations and asked to describe what is occurring and what actions might be taken. They might be asked actually to point to the control that they would use to deal with the situation, describe how they would manipulate that control, and indicate what displays they would then monitor and what information they would look for to determine if the action taken was the correct action.

Other knowledge tests might involve items presented on a VDT that allow for interactive responses. This type of knowledge testing might be attractive as a criterion measure for positions in laboratory, computer-interactive, and continuous-process industries of various types. The problem with knowledge tests as criteria may be, however, that they describe the *necessary* but not *sufficient* condition for effective performance. They represent what the worker *might* or *could* do but not what he or she *will* do or *has* done. An additional drawback of traditional paper and pencil knowledge tests as criterion measures is that they have frequently been associated with adverse impact against members of ethnic minority groups when they have been employed as predictors. The possibility of 'creating' validities from matching method variance in predictor and criterion is legitimate cause for caution.

Hands-on measures

The most promising criterion measure to receive attention in some time is the work sample or hands-on measure. Work samples are well known as predictors.

A typing test for clerical workers, a programming test for computer programmers and a one-game 'try out' for an aspiring athlete are all examples of work samples as predictors. Conceptually, the work sample as a criterion is no different. As a criterion measure, the work sample has some attractive characteristics not possessed by alternative criterion measures. In the first place, the criterion work sample or hands-on performance measure is a carefully developed and clearly delimited *piece* of the entire job. It is selected and developed to represent a central or important part of the job. It is administered in carefully controlled conditions that permit accurate observation of behavior and the standardization of equipment and environment. This accomplishes two things. First, it reduces the common contaminating influences in most attempts to measure performance on the job—factors such as equipment differences, production demands, and day-to-day environmental variation. In addition, it permits one to observe certain behaviors that occur infrequently or could not be easily observed on the actual job.

Currently, the US Department of Defense is supporting a large-scale validation of the Armed Services Vocational Aptitude Test Battery (ASVAB) in each of the branches of the military. Each service has identified one or more job titles for study and is developing multiple criterion measures for a criterion-related validity study of the ASVAB. In each of these service projects, one or more hands-on measure is being developed as a criterion variable.

As an example of hands-on measures, in the armed services study, the army is studying the position of tank crewman. As part of the study, they have developed a hands-on battery that is administered to incumbent crewmen. The battery requires the subject to complete several different exercises for which a tank crewman would be expected to possess proficiency. This battery requires the subject to climb into an actual tank and:

(1) operate the radio system that would be used to communicate with friendly ground forces outside the tank;
(2) operate the internal communication system that would be used to speak with other tank crew personnel in that tank when it is in operation;
(3) position the tank cannon for firing;
(4) disassemble and re-assemble an automatic hand-held weapon.

Each subject is asked to complete these tasks one at a time. The subject is carefully observed and scored on a checklist for the various operations necessary to successfully complete the action in question. The scoring is done by trained observers. These scores represent criterion measures and they will ultimately be correlated with ASVAB scores as part of the criterion-related validity study of that predictor. Descriptions of this research can be found in several sources. A report edited by Wigdor and Green (1986) and a recent article in TIP (Harris, 1987) both describe this project.

The hands-on measures seem to produce reliable scores and since they are samples of tasks identified as important in a job analysis, their validity seems to be well grounded. Nevertheless, as is the case with work samples as predictors, these measures are complex, expensive to develop and demanding to administer. It may be that their expense and complexity place them out of the reach of the garden-variety validity study. Nevertheless, just as predictor work samples are becoming more popular, inexpensive and feasible, so might criterion work samples. There is little doubt about the potential that they offer for validation research. Manuscripts describing these measures and their value in validation research are just beginning to reach journal editors. In all likelihood, much of this research will be available to the psychological community in published form in the next 12 to 18 months.

A PROBLEM: THE STATUS OF CRITERION-RELATED VALIDITY STUDIES

As we indicated in the beginning of the chapter, although we chose to complete a rather extensive review of criterion measures and research related to them, it was obvious to us that we were expected to say something in particular about the value of various alternative measures in validation research. To a large extent, that is what we have just done. In the course of the review, however, we discovered some surprising and disquieting things about published criterion-related validity research. We discovered that there has very little of it appearing in the journals in the past 7 years.

When we looked back at the 408 studies that comprised our domain of identified articles, we discovered that only 28 of them fell into the category of traditional criterion-related validation. Remember, this is 28 articles over a 7-year period in 11 different journals. As you might expect, the bulk of these articles appeared in the *Journal of Applied Psychology* and *Personnel Psychology*. Of the 11 studies that appeared in *JAP*, 6 used ratings as criteria, 2 used turnover, 1 used absence and 2 used productivity measures. Of the 10 that appeared in *Personnel Psychology*, 7 used ratings as criteria, 1 used turnover, 1 used a hands-on measure and 1 used a knowledge test. Thus, the trend reported by Guion in 1965, and Landy and Trumbo in 1976 and 1980 has not changed—most criterion-related studies depend on supervisory ratings as criteria. What has changed, however, is the number of criterion-related studies being published. An examination of the publication trends in *JAP* is instructive. From 1949 until 1952, *JAP* published approximately 50 criterion-related studies. In 1953, 17 were published. In 1960, 13 were published. From 1970 until 1976, approximately 37 studies (about 5 per year) were published. From 1980 until early 1987, a total of 11 criterion-related studies were published (or slightly more than 1 per year). In 1986, two articles that might be construed as criterion-related studies were published and one of those was a meta-analysis. It seems clear that the number of criterion-related studies being published has been radically reduced in the past decade.

Causes for the reduction in published articles

There are a number of possible reasons that might account for the disappearance of validity studies in the industrial psychology literature. We will describe the most likely reasons, but readers might think of other, equally plausible, factors.

Litigation

Within 5 years of the passage of the Civil Rights Act, mechanisms for initiating litigation under that Act had been set in place and employers were finding themselves in court on a frequent basis. One result of this new-found exposure to what had previously been fairly pedestrian personnel research and application was a desire on the part of defendants to consider all material that might in any way at any time become involved in Title VII litigation as privileged and proprietary. Plaintiffs' experts became expert reviewers of scientific research, eager to point out its ambiguities and shortcomings. As a result, many organizations that had previously encouraged their personnel staff to publish validity studies now actively discouraged this type of publication.

Similarly, many organizations simply chose an 'ostrich' response to the threat of litigation—they stopped using tests and other standard predictors and, as a result, stopped doing validity studies.

Editorial policies

The procedures for validating predictors were institutionalized in the late 1950s and early 1960s. Articles appeared describing how it should be done and variations designed for unusual circumstances (e.g. synthetic validity) began to replace the more standard validation studies that had appeared previously. It is safe to say that most editors (and editorial boards) of the 1970s and 1980s saw traditional validity studies as simple mechanical demonstrations of the obvious and not worth valuable journal pages. It is not uncommon today to have a reviewer comment that a particular paper is 'just another validity study.' Thus, even though studies might have been conducted and submitted, it was unlikely that they would be published.

Tenure and promotion policies

It does not take a Nobel winner to realize that the decisions of editors have a substantial impact on the well being of the members of a research community—

particularly one based in a university setting. The academic form of the basic Darwinian Mechanism is known as the 'publish or perish' decision rule. It is practiced most skillfully by tenure and promotion committees. If editors would not publish validity studies, it was not likely that academic researchers would bother to conduct them or produce manuscripts describing them. Instead, efforts were directed toward studies of organizational climate, expectancy theory and behaviorally anchored rating scales.

The validity generalization juggernaut

In the late 1970s and early 1980s, Schmidt and Hunter began to disassemble the empire of situational specificity (Hunter and Schmidt, 1979; Schmidt, Gast-Rosenberg, and Hunter, 1980; Schmidt and Hunter, 1981). They demonstrated that many of the assumptions that had fueled validity studies of the past were questionable. Specifically, they demonstrated that much of the variance in previously reported validity coefficients could be accounted for by three arti-facts—sample size, restriction of range on the predictor and criterion unre-liability. When these three factors were controlled, validity coefficients covered a rather narrow range. Further, they demonstrated that the mean of this distribution of validity coefficients was commonly significantly greater than 0.00. In other words, they proposed that most tests were valid in most settings. This is a gross oversimplification and it is treated in greater detail (and with greater respect) by Neal Schmitt in another chapter of this book. Nevertheless, this brief description illustrates a temperament that seemed to appear in the mid-1980s. It was a feeling that these tests that had been developed 30 years ago were valid all along and that there had never been any real reason to doubt their value. Since validity studies can be expensive to do well, this was another reason to minimize their value.

It is likely that one or more of these factors is implicated in the drastic reduction in published validity studies. In fact, it is likely that all have played some role in the decline. There is good reason to be concerned about this situation.

The problem

If there were no reason to be concerned with the changing nature of predictors, criteria, jobs or theories of work performance, then the absence of criterion-related validity studies would not be worth mentioning. Unfortunately, change has been endemic in personnel and differential psychology for the past several decades. We need only look at the topic of this chapter—criteria and their measurement. As an example of change, the BARS technology has revolution-ized supervisory ratings. It is likely that both Type I and Type II errors were part of the validation scene when it was at its peak and depending on casually developed graphic rating scales. Similarly, earlier research seldom employed criterion work samples. We should expect to learn a great deal of new and useful things about abilities and performance when criterion work samples are more commonly used.

On the predictor side, the change has been even more substantial. We have greatly refined and developed the interview. We have introduced assessment center technologies. Work samples are widely used in prediction systems today. Knowledge tests are common and well developed in promotional testing. The fact is that there is a wide variety of predictors that was not well developed two decades ago. Many of the cognitive tests have changed as a result of newly emerging theories and taxonomies of cognitive activity such as Sternberg's propositions about componential intelligence (Sternberg, 1984) and Fleishman's taxonomy of human abilities (Fleishman and Quaintance, 1984).

In addition to predictors and criteria, the nature of work has changed substantially. This change is likely to continue for some time to come. The most obvious transformations have been brought about by computer technology. Twenty years ago we had machine operators. We now have machine tenders. Ten years ago, we had stenographers and typists. We now have word processing specialists. Ten years ago, we had draftsmen. We now have CAD/CAM specialists. The fact is that the demands on workers are different than they had been when the original validity studies were carried out.

Finally, the nature of applicant populations has changed substantially. These changes are apparent not only in demographic variables such as gender, age and race, but also in areas such as test-wiseness, capacities to read and write, and general knowledge levels. We are not testing or hiring the same types of applicants described in the validation studies of the 1950s.

For all of these reasons, criterion-related validity studies need to regain the exposure that has been denied them for the past ten years. Personnel researchers have a good deal of basic work to do. This work stretches well beyond the broad goals of validating the GATB or ASVAB for mass testing purposes. We need to rediscover the lost art of predictor development and empirical validity documentation. This type of research is the raw material for inductive theory building.

The solution

Many of us are old enough (much to our distress) to remember the 'Validity Information Exchange' that appeared in *Personnel Psychology* until 1963. This was a useful section of the journal for practitioners. It was discontinued a few years before it would have become a valuable adjunct to Title VII litigation. It was very basic and presented concise descriptions of criterion-related validity studies. The reports included the nature of the job (with DOT number), a description of the organization or location, descriptive data about the predictor(s), descriptive data about the criterion (or criteria) and the validity coefficient. It was nothing fancy. There was no introduction, no discussion, no theory, no extensive speculation. Just plain empiricism. That may have been part of the problem. The field was beginning to recoil from attacks by social critics such as Whyte (in the *Organization Man*) or Gross (in *The Brain Watchers*). Empiricism became 'dust-bowl' empiricism.

It seems to us that times have changed and that we need once again to consider the nature and extent of empirical relationships between predictors and criteria. We are not arguing that we return to mindless correlation calculation. Criterion-related data of the traditional variety need to be integrated with data and theory provided through other validity designs (Landy, 1986). Although it is unlikely that any of our journals would be willing to reintroduce the 'Validity Information Exchange' in its original form, there is no reason why an annual volume of validity information could not be published. It need not be elaborate and the format adopted by the 'Validity Information Exchange' would work just fine. Such a volume would serve several purposes. First, it would provide a new impetus for conducting criterion-related validity studies. It would also provide a forum for the exchange of validity information on an international basis. In addition, after a reasonable period of time, it would provide a wealth of information for meta-analysis. As it stands now, most meta-analytic approaches to validation research may be substantially compromised by study availability. Such a volume would also provide a point of contact between the research and practitioner communities.

The first step

As a result of the review that we conducted for this chapter, we discovered what we consider to be this unreasonable void in the criterion-related validity literature domain. After several initial inquiries, we have identified a publisher who agrees that there is a need that should be filled. Beginning in 1989, a series known as the *Test Validity Yearbook* will appear on a yearly basis. This series will be published by Lawrence Erlbaum and Associates and we feel that it will represent a substantial addition to the current data base available in the area of selection and assessment.

A CONCLUDING COMMENT

We have greatly enjoyed preparing this chapter. We learned some things we did not know before. We think that we discovered a substantial problem. Whether our enjoyment becomes the reader's enjoyment is arguable. We think that the conference that instigated the preparation of the chapters in this book as well as the chapters themselves illustrate the vitality and excitement of personnel research on the topics of selection and assessment. We hope that you will agree.

REFERENCES

Chadwick-Jones, J. K., Nicholson, N. and Brown, C. (1982). *The Social Psychology of Absenteeism*. New York: Praeger.

Feldman, J. M. (1981). Beyond attribution theory: cognitive processes in performance appraisal. *Journal of Applied Psychology*, **66**, 127–148.

Fleishman, E. A. and Quaintance, M. K. (1984). *Taxonomies of Human Performance*. Orlando: Academic Press.

Frese, M., Ulich, E. and Dzida, W. (eds) (1987). *Psychological Issues of Human Computer Interaction in the Workplace*. Amsterdam: North-Holland.

Goodman, P., Atkin, R. and associates (1984). *Absenteeism*. San Francisco: Jossey-Bass.

Guion, R. M. (1965). *Personnel Testing*. New York: McGraw-Hall.

Harris, R. (1987). Joint service job performance measurement/enlistment standards project. *The Industrial-Organizational Psychologist*, **24**(4), 36–42.

Hunter, J. E., Schmidt, F. L. and Hunter, R. (1979) Differential validity of employment tests by race: a comprehensive review and analysis. *Psychological Bulletin*, **86**, 721–735.

Landy, F. J. (1986). Stamp collecting versus science. *American Psychologist*, **41**, 1183–1192.

Landy, F. J. and Farr, J. L. (1980) Performance rating. *Psychological Bulletin*, **87**, 72–107.

Landy, F. J. and Farr, J. L. (1983). *The Measurement of Work Performance: Methods, Theory and Applications*. Orlando: Academic Press.

Landy, F. J., Rastegary, H. and Motowidlo, S. (1987). Human computer interactions in the workplace: psychosocial aspects of VDT use. In M. Frese, E. Ulich and W. Dzida (eds) *Psychological Issues of Human Computer Interaction in the Workplace*. Amsterdam: North Holland.

Landy, F. J. and Trumbo, D. A. (1976). *Psychology of Work Behavior*. Homewood: Dorsey.

Latham, G. P., Fay, C. and Saari, L. M. (1979) Application of social learning theory to training supervisors through behavioral modeling. *Journal of Applied Psychology*, **32**, 299–311.

Latham, G. P. and Wexley, K. N. (1977). Behavioral observation scales for performance appraisal purposes. *Personnel Psychology*, **30**, 225–268.

Schmidt, F. L., Gast-Rosenberg, I. and Hunter, J. E. (1980). Validity generalization results for computer programmers. *Journal of Applied Psychology*, **65**, 643–661.

Schmidt, F. L. and Hunter, J. E. (1981). Employment testing: old theories and new research findings. *American Psychologist*, **36**, 1128–1137.

Schwab, D., Heneman, H. G. III, and DeCotiis, T. (1975). Behaviorally anchored rating scales: a review of the literature. *Personnel Psychology*, **28**, 549–562.

Smith, P. C. and Kendall, L. M. (1963). Retranslation of expectations: an approach to the construction of unambiguous anchors for rating scales. *Journal of Applied Psychology*, **47**, 149–155.

Sternberg, R. (1984). Toward a triarchic theory of human intelligence. *The Behavioral and Brain Sciences*, **7**, 269–315.

Wigdor, A. and Green, B. F., Jr (1986). *Assessing the Performance of Enlisted Personnel*. Washington, DC: National Academy Press.

6

Criteria and Individual Assessment

ANTHONIE E. AKKERMAN
LTP, Amsterdam

INTRODUCTION

The review of Frank Landy and Haleh Rastegary gives a thorough overview of criterion research in relation to personnel selection and as such it gives a good idea of 'the state of the art'. It does not need much comment. That is why instead I want to step back and discuss the role of criterion research for personnel selection for I/O psychologists engaged in psychological assessment for selection. Results of criterion research do not have scientific relevance only; they form the foundation on which responsible personnel selection methods are based.

This point of view was introduced in the discussion following the presentation of the paper by Frank Landy. Though we, that is the participants in the discussion, agreed on most topics and this presentation is certainly coloured by the discussion, I must take responsibility for the opinions stated here. My contribution is written from a double point of view. As a research psychologist I am interested in the role of criterion research for theory building in industrial psychology. At the same time, as the employee of a consultancy firm in the field of industrial psychology I am interested in the practical relevance of (criterion) research: what direct implications do the results of current research have for daily work? As you will see, this leads me to the opinion that what we need most is a sound theoretical basis to give meaning to the relations between predictors and criteria.

Advances in Selection and Assessment. Edited by M. Smith and I. T. Robertson

WHAT IS A CRITERION?

In their review Landy and Rastegary wisely avoided this question, probably because it does not have an easy answer. That this is true may become clear when we think about the amount of attention that has been given to this topic in several handbooks (i.e. Smith, 1976; Roe, 1983). One of the main things that become clear is that most of the time the criterion used is not the same as the criterion meant. What one intends to predict is the 'ultimate' criterion (Thorndike, 1949), but that seems to be an ideal that can only be approximated but never attained. To this we may add the notion of Hofstee (1985) that the criterion is emergent in the sense that it is never completely defined. At any moment the judge as well as the judged may introduce new elements that have their impact on judgment of the criterion. For example, the judge may suddenly arrive at the conclusion that being an enthusiastic golf player is essential for becoming a brain surgeon; a judged person may suddenly become more appreciated because s/he did something no one ever thought of before. In this sense the criterion always carries elements of creativity, it can never be fully specified.

According to Hofstee personnel selection is choosing those persons whose expected contribution to the organisation is greatest. In this sense the criterion is the balance of the material and immaterial gains minus costs for the organisation, integrated over time until the person leaves the job or even longer (Hofstee, 1985). Of course this kind of criterion is useless for practical prediction research. The time horizon would be too far away to be practical and, even if not, the criterion thus defined carries too many subjective elements to be very predictable. Nevertheless we should never forget that in the end it is this kind of target at which prediction is aimed.

A logical consequence is that this ultimate target is one-dimensional. For if job holders are compared on their contribution to the organisation, necessarily we are talking about a one-dimensional scale. One of the objections against using a single criterion is that in fact the criterion is not one-dimensional. There are many aspects to job behaviour and on each and every one of them the judged may be better or worse independently of the performance on other aspects. Therefore, it is argued, it would be meaningless to project judgments on one dimension. But still decisions have to be made and it is impossible to hire someone for only one aspect of a job and not for the others. So the decision-maker ranks the applicants in terms of attractiveness (for the organisation that is) and hires the topmost. This is the normal situation and it implies the final ranking of applicants is on only one dimension. This is quite logical, for either you hire an applicant or you do not.

COVERAGE OF THE CRITERION

Following Hofstee it was argued that the ultimate criterion or, in other words the criterion as meant, is at least partly subjective. Furthermore, the ultimate criterion has creative elements. So, even in principle, it will be rather difficult, if not impossible, to construct objective instruments to predict the ultimate criterion. Yet for pure pragmatic reasons we need a predictable criterion, for without it it would be impossible to choose or construct predictor instruments. This creates the challenge to construct a criterion which is as close as possible to the criterion as meant, but yet is measurable. The criterion measure is an operationalisation of the criterion construct and thus will suffer from the same problems of coverage (de Groot, 1961) as any operationalisation of a theoretical construct. For any operationalisation it will be true that coverage of the meant criterion is not perfect: some aspects are left out while other, unmeant, aspects creep in.

The bias to construct instruments that are reliable and have proven validity produces a new risk because of validation research: criterion drift. To make this idea clear a thought experiment will be done. Suppose one has two criteria. The first one, UC (= ultimate criterion) is the criterion as meant, the other is CC, the constructed predictable criterion. Because of the problem of coverage both criteria will not correlate perfectly. Now suppose we have two predictors X and Y. X is very reliable and correlates highly with the constructed criterion. Y is relatively unreliable and has lower validity towards CC. What is the best predictor, if the correlation of Y with UC would be higher than the correlation of X with UC? (See Figure 6.1; the length of the arrows indicates the size of the correlations.) The visible validity is the correlation of the predictors with the constructed, predictable, criterion. It will be higher for X than for Y. So in this thought experiment empirical validation research would lead to the choice of a predictor that is biased towards the constructed criterion, away

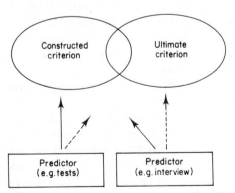

Figure 6.1   Correlations between predictors and constructed and ultimate criterion

from the criterion as meant. New personnel would be hired on arguments derived from the results of the validation study. Because the 'best' predictor is reliably slightly off the mark, there is a considerable risk that in the long run the character of the organisation will change and in the end this implies a change in the criterion as meant as well. This is what we mean with criterion drift and this kind of argument is reason for Hofstee (1985) to suggest that we should be careful in discarding instruments with low proven validity. For, it may be true that more clinical instruments like the interview, although unreliable, may be better aimed on the target (the criterion as meant) than instruments that have a higher proven validity against a measurable criterion.

There is a moral in this thought experiment. As researchers we are biased towards quantitative measures. We must never forget that not everything of what we are trying to measure or to predict is represented by our numbers. A certain measure of modesty in relation to what we are able to predict is appropriate.

DIVISION OF RESPONSIBILITY

The above thought experiment has practical implications as well. A short summary of the experiment is that there are things we can predict and other things we cannot predict. In his relation with the client organisation the I/O psychologist as a consultant must explicitly state what he or she can predict and what not. As noted, a criterion like 'contribution to the organisation' is not really predictable. There are too many subjective facets and too much of it is emergent. As the statements in a psychological report ought to be based on sound scientific reasoning, the psychologist must restrict his/her advice to aspects of job behaviour that are measurable and thus predictable. The other aspects belong to the responsibility of the organisation. They are certainly not irrelevant and may be the reason why a person is hardly ever hired without an interview. For the decision-maker the results of the psychological assessment are only (a relevant) part of the data on which the decision is made to hire or reject an applicant. As an example: a missionary could be psychologically tested in order to assess his qualities for the job. But someone had better ask him about his religious convictions as well.

As a consultant the psychologist concentrates on predicting the predictable aspects of the job. The personnel manager is responsible for hiring people who will make a positive contribution to attaining the goals of the organisation. Because of these different roles for the personnel psychologist and the personnel manager validation research is possible and useful. As the criterion the psychologist uses those aspects of job behaviour that can be predicted (the constructed criterion), while the personnel manager tries to predict the ultimate criterion 'contribution to the organisation' (the validity of the latter is almost never researched). Because of this distinction in roles the organisation remains responsible for possible criterion drift.

DIFFERENT ROLES FOR THE CRITERION

In psychological assessment for personnel selection criteria play several roles (Roe, 1983). For one thing they are the target at which the predictor must be aimed; for another thing they set the standard on which the performance of the job holder will be measured. There are other roles as well. As was brought forward in the discussion during the conference, constructing criterion variables may be an aid in the process of organisation development. For example by the process of constructing criterion variables the contents of the job become clear to job holders and the organisation. For the job holder this may have the positive outcome that finally he or she can explain to others what he or she is doing on the job. For the organisation the result of criterion analysis might be that the job in question ought to be changed. In other words, criterion analysis is never an isolated process in a static environment. It always occurs in the dynamic system formed by the organisation and its employees.

As Roe (1983) points out the function of the criterion as the target for prediction has been neglected for a long time. Emphasis has always been on the predictor side and only in recent times (and probably especially in academic circles) have things changed. Theorising about the criterion (i.e. Thorndike, 1949) made it clear that a haphazard criterion measure as an index of the ultimate criterion would not do. So attention in criterion research shifted away from what *has to* be predicted (the ultimate criterion) to what *can* be predicted. This research has led to the different approaches for criterion measurement as reviewed by Landy and Rastegary (this volume).

INDIVIDUAL ASSESSMENT

As individual psychological assessment plays an important part in personnel selection it is in order here to discuss the role of the criterion therein. Recently Ryan and Sackett (1987) surveyed the field of I/O psychology to gain insight into the activities of I/O psychologists. From their survey it shows that individual selection is not a minor part of the work of an I/O psychologist. In order to gain an idea of the importance of criterion research for I/O psychologists it is useful to reflect on the activities involved in individual assessment.

Individual psychological assessment is a process that starts with gathering information about the applicant and the job. Next this information is aggregated and used to produce a conclusion about the applicant. Information about the applicant is mostly obtained from more or less structured instruments like ability tests, personality questionnaires and personality history forms (Ryan and Sackett, 1987). Even the ubiquitous interview becomes more structured following the views of, for example, Latham *et al.* (1980). While the information about the applicant is obtained in a more or less structured way, the same is not true for information about the job. Ryan and Sackett (1987) describe for example that information about the job was most commonly obtained by interviewing organisational members and by other informal means. This appears to be true especially for I/O psychologists in consultancy firms. It seems that more formally structured devices like the PAQ (McGormick, 1976) are rarely used to derive formal criteria for individual selection. In other words in individual assessment most of the time an informal, *ad hoc* criterion is predicted, not a formally derived criterion measure.

THE CRITERION AND THE PSYCHOLOGICAL REPORT

Most of the time the outcome of the psychological assessment is reported as a narrative description of the individual (Ryan and Sackett, 1987). The situation in Holland will be about the same. Though the narrative report is still mostly used, since World War Two the emphasis in the contents of the report has shifted from the person to the job. Formerly the psychological report contained a more or less clinical description of the applicant (Jansen, 1979; van Strien, 1964). The idea with this kind of report was that with the information provided the organisation could do a better job of selecting employees and introducing them into their organisation. This point of view has been abandoned because nowadays such psychological reports would be thought of as an invasion of the privacy of the candidate as they contain information that is not strictly relevant as concerns the job (Jansen, 1979). At present most assessment reports contain statements about the adequacy of the person in fulfilling distinct job requirements. Most of the time these statements are summarised in a recommendation. This evolution in the contents of the assessment report suggests I/O psychologists do pay more attention to what has to be predicted; they do the predicting themselves instead of furnishing the personnel manager with data to do the predicting. In the extreme form the assessment report contains only standard criterion statements and the psychologist marks the adequacy of the person with respect to each of the criterion aspects. The criterion statements in the assessment report may be derived from formal criterion research, but most of the time they will be based on informal infor-mation and common sense.

The psychological report containing marks on very specific criterion state-ments has several advantages. Especially when the criterion statements in the report have been discussed with the client organisation beforehand the meaning of the report will be clear; there is little room for ambiguity. This is why Roe

(1983) considers this the optimal way to transfer information about the applicant to the client organisation. As the marks on the criterion statements put by the psychologist can be used as numbers, the 'criterion-related report' becomes an excellent tool for validation research. For the criterion would be identical to the assessment report, the only difference being that in validation research the criterion statements would be marked by the employer. It is here criterion and validation research would merge.

The advantages of the 'criterion-related report' can be summarised as: more privacy for the assessed, better aimed psychological assessment, improved transfer of information and ideally suited for validation research. But there are drawbacks as well. Focussing of the assessment report on the criterion implies that the applicant as a person moves out of focus. There will be less room for counselling or development suggestions. Furthermore it will be more difficult to generalise the results of the assessment to different jobs. And this brings us back to the criterion problem. How useful is a very specific criterion? Predicting for a very specific job has paradoxical elements. In this time of rapid technological development most jobs exist only a few years. New machines will be introduced into the organisation and/or the organisation is reshuffled. The original job at which the psychological assessment was aimed will no longer exist. The new machines have to be operated as well, so we need not be afraid that the person hired will be fired. But as far as the original prediction was better aimed at the old job the person may fit worse in the new job and this cannot be the intention of good individual assessment for selection.

CLINICAL PREDICTION

Criterion research as well as validation research can only be carried out when enough observations are possible. So most of the published research is biased to situations where there are relatively large numbers of vacancies for one type of job for which a large number of applicants is available. A typical example of where this kind of research can be done is the army. In any army there is a large pressure to standardise jobs so that someone selected for a job can do it anywhere in the world. In this the armed forces are special. Most organisations are not as large and certainly not as standardised. In the same vein, in common validation research large numbers of cases are needed to construct prediction formulae, especially if these formulae will be cross-validated. Real life situations in which this is feasible are rare. The low Ns in published validation studies bear witness to this while cross-validation studies are even more rare. In contrast, most I/O psychologists are engaged in individual assessment (Ryan and Sackett, 1987). That is, when there is a vacancy in the organisation the employer calls upon the psychologist to assess one or more applicants for the job. Most of the time the feedback to the employer is in absolute terms: candidates are not compared. So instead of many applicants for many vacancies of a particular job, the most common situation is a vacancy in a more or less unique job for which there are only a few applicants. In this situation construction of prediction formulae is virtually impossible. It would be like constructing a prediction formula for the selection of the President of the United States. Even if in cases like this construction of a criterion measure might be technically feasible, the cost would be prohibitive while the time needed to produce a prediction formula would be too long to be practical.

When doing individual assessment psychologists use their heads instead of the formula. This does not make them better predictors; almost any formula would improve on them (Meehl, 1954; Dawes, 1979; Dawes and Corrigan, 1974; Carroll, 1987). But the formula approach has several inherent short-comings that make it unpopular. For one thing, the use of a formula implies comparison of applicants: the candidate with the highest score will be hired. Often neither the employer nor the applicant wants to know if the other guy is the better. Especially in the case of only a single candidate for the job the real question is whether he or she can do the job. Results of criterion or validation research hardly ever supply objective information to support this kind of judgment. Still those judgments are asked and given and, as it seems, in an acceptable way, seeing that I/O psychologists are still in business.

Formulae are quite rigid in terms of information that can be used and criteria that can be predicted. Formulae have fixed slots in which only well-defined information fits. If only one piece of information is missing the formula cannot be applied or one would need to use some default value. Relevant extra information cannot be put into a formula: there are no free slots. Furthermore, the research needed to construct a prediction formula results in a prediction formula for a well-defined criterion. Without further research it cannot be used to predict different criteria. The psychologist on the other hand is very flexible in the kinds of information he can utilise and with it he can predict any criterion. And though the relevant literature concludes that prediction by formula is always better, this does not mean clinical prediction is random! Of course prediction formulae can be and are generalised to different situations. But in doing so (clinical) judgment is involved and not formal, scientific knowledge.

UNDERSTANDING

In my opinion the most important reason for the existence of the narrative report and the clinical use of information to predict future success in a function is that people want to understand judgments. The outcome of a formula is something like 'your score is OK' or 'you have four points below the cutting score'. This is very unsatisfactory as it gives no insight in the cause of this score and other conclusions that may be drawn. The employer as well as the applicant wants an explanation in terms of demands of function and aptitudes, abilities and traits of the assessed in concepts understandable by both. And, if relevant, they want additional advice/comments on future training or career development. In a way this alludes to the difference between psychological testing and psychological assessment (Matarazzo, 1986).

In my opinion there is an enormous gap between the procedures and outcomes of academic criterion and validation research and the needs of the practitioner in I/O psychology. The information derived from formal academic research is restricted in terms of explaining the causes of results. It is more supportive of psychological testing than of psychological assessment. Furthermore, I/O psychologists involved in individual psychological assessment are, at least to my experience, not inclined to think in terms of standard errors, validity coefficients or regression formulae. What they do may be conceived as an example of diagnosis and from the research on diagnostic processes may be inferred that the diagnostic process is guided by an internal, qualitative model (Bouman, 1978). (To some conceptions all thinking is guided by mental models, e.g. Johnson-Laird, 1983.) It is in the context of such mental models that the results of (validation) research are used. And not in quantitative terms but in semantic terms like 'to be a good programmer you must be able to reason about . . . and that implies a high level of verbal ability'. With this kind of idea, for example, literature is consulted when choosing new tests. My assumption is that conclusions from the research literature are utilised as far as they fit into the mental model the psychologist uses in assessment. This model will be the product of formal knowledge, informal, common sense knowledge and experience. As far as knowledge is automated (that is, closed for conscious reflection) one might even call it intuition. The quality of the assessment will be dependent on the quality of the mental model. So in order to improve individual assessment the quality of the mental model of the I/O psychologist has to be improved. The question is how this can be attained and how criterion research has a role in this.

SOME GENERAL CONCLUSIONS ABOUT CRITERION RESEARCH

There are two classes of criterion measures. There are those criterion measures that reflect parameters of the organisation and those that reflect individual differences in job performance. The former criteria, like turnover and absenteeism, have a large conceptual distance from psychological characteristics and there are too many factors not related to individual differences that influence these so-called ancillary criterion measures. These criteria may be most useful for organisational development; as criterion measures for validation studies they seem less effective.

From the review of Landy and Rastegary it seems criterion research is biased to concreteness. One way to arrive at concreteness is using some kind of objective measure like number of units produced. The problem with objective criteria is that they do not refer to job behaviour and there are often several ways of reaching a certain criterion. (For example do productive persons work harder, or do they work smarter?) Therefore objective criteria do little to increase understanding of the causes of differences in productivity. Furthermore, as noted by Landy and Rastegary, there are not many jobs where performance can be objectively measured in a non-trivial way. So it is better to derive criterion measures from job behaviour directly. The most typical example of this is the work sample or as Landy calls it the 'hands-on' approach. The advantage of these kind of criterion measures is that they are very close to the actual job. This is, of course, at the same time a disadvantage. By staying close with actual job behaviour one has a very relevant criterion measure, but only for that job. As the description will be in concrete 'job' terms there is little room for generalising to other jobs or for understanding the job behaviour in terms of traits and abilities measured by common psychological tests.

There are many jobs for which criterion measures in the form of actual behaviour would be rather nonsensical. Such as describing the work of a conductor in terms of arm movements. Abstraction of concrete job behaviour is often inevitable in order to obtain sensible criterion measures and in those cases rating scales are popular measures. One of the common objections against rating scales is that when they are not properly structured and formulated raters tend to give trait ratings instead of performance ratings. In order to work well they, amongst other things, ought to refer to a defined domain of behaviour (Landy and Rastegary, this volume). So ratings also are biased to dimensions of job behaviour. By the way, it is interesting in itself why people should much more easily give trait ratings than behaviour ratings. Research as to why people do so seems to be missing.

The problem with remaining as close as possible to actual job behaviour is that because of this there is a lack of generally acceptable concepts for describing job behaviour that can easily be applied to different jobs. This being the case it is extremely difficult to develop acceptable theories that can explain why certain job behaviour is shown and how it relates to individual differences. I/O psychologists need such theories to produce valid arguments with regard to why a person would qualify in a job.

To make the idea clear Figure 6.2 is presented. In regular validation research results are expressed in the direction of the thick arrow between predictor behaviour and criterion behaviour in the form of correlations or whatever quantitative indices are relevant. The explanation of the empirical relation can

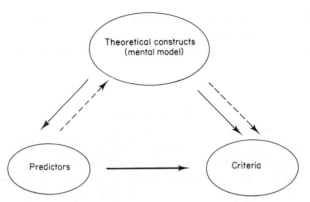

Figure 6.2 Relations between predictors, criteria and theoretical constructs

be found in theories about human behaviour. From theoretical constructs both the scores on predictor measures and criterion measures can be explained. In the figure this is indicated by the thin arrows coming from the top oval. (The arrows point in this direction, because it would be nonsense to understand behaviour on predictor instruments as causes of criterion behaviour.) In daily practice I/O psychologists do not have exact information about the relation between predictor and criterion because it is not available. Therefore they use theory to infer future criterion behaviour from assessment data. In figure 6.2 this line of reasoning is indicated by the dotted arrows. Accordingly in this model the top oval in Figure 6.2 may be interpreted as the mental model of the I/O psychologist. It highlights a central problem for I/O psychologists: the lack of a common theoretical framework to describe behaviour on predictor and criterion measures.

To make criteria more predictable one might use predictor instruments that resemble criterion measures as close as possible: the work sample. It is intuitively clear that validity coefficients will rise. But it will also be clear that understanding will decrease. For when, with two measures that are much alike, one is used as a predictor for the other, the explanation for validity is that the person performs well because he or she performs well on this kind of task. This kind of problem shows up with assessment centres. Assessment centres are predictive but it is not clear why (Klimoski and Brickner, 1987).

Of course things are not as black as has just been painted. Though still most work is done on the bottom part of Figure 6.2, the validity generalisation movement was at least partly driven by the idea of filling in the top half (see Hunter, this volume). To round things up it is good to quote Dubin (1976): 'If accurate prediction is the practical outcome of utilizing scientific models, then the intellectual outcome is the understanding they provide of the characteristics of the empirical domain they model.' Current criterion research seems to emphasise prediction and measurement, but in the words of Dubin (1976) understanding is knowledge of process, while prediction is knowledge of outcome. In my opinion we ought to be more theoretical in order to be more practical.

SUMMARY

In my comment on the contribution of Landy and Rastegary I discussed several aspects of criterion research, the common theme being their practical relevance for I/O psychologists involved in individual assessment. For one thing the point was made that in the end a criterion is always one-dimensional: a person is either hired or not. Additionally, the ultimate criterion is not completely tangible. It is emergent and contains creative elements. The overlap of the constructed criterion as used by the psychologist and the ultimate criterion as relevant for the employer is not perfect. This was reason to acknowledge and emphasise the different responsibilities of the psychologist and employer in the selection process.

Many I/O psychologists are engaged in individual assessment and necessarily produce narrative, clinical predictions of a job criterion. Besides reasons of understanding the rationale of the judgment, clinical prediction is used because generally the empirical knowledge to apply to specific selection problems is not available. Theoretical support is insufficient or lacking as well so I/O psychologists tend to make up their own minds. That is, they make their own theories. This gives two reasons to put more emphasis on building a common theoretical framework for predictors and criteria: to increase understanding and to improve quality of assessment. The observation of Guion (1987) that a single correlation is viewed with less sanctity may be an indication that a change in research direction as advocated may be in progress.

Finally, Landy noted that validation research is an endangered species in the journals and he thought of it as a bad sign. Though it may seem that I propagate a more clinically oriented approach to selection, I very much agree with Landy. We can only arrive at good useful theories when enough data are available to build those theories and subsequently they are thoroughly put to the test and the results thereof published.

REFERENCES

Bouman, M. J. (1978). *Financial Diagnosis, a Cognitive Model of the Processes Involved.* Unpublished dissertation, Carnegie-Mellon University, Graduate School of Industrial Administration.
Carroll, B. (1987). Artificial intelligence. Expert systems for clinical diagnosis: are they worth the effort? *Behavioral Science*, **32**, 274–292.

Dawes, R. (1979). The robust beauty of improper linear models in decision making. *American Psychologist*, **34**(7), 571–582.

Dawes R. and Corrigan, B. (1974). Linear models in decision making. *Psychological Bulletin*, **81**(2), 95–106.

Dubin, R. (1976). Theory building in applied areas. In: Dunnette, M. D. (ed.), *Handbook of Industrial and Organizational Psychology*. Chicago: Rand McNally.

Groot, A. D. de (1961). *Methodologie. Grondslagen van onderzoek en denken in de gedragswetenschappen*. Den Haag: Mouton.

Guion, R. M. (1987). Changing views for personnel selection research. *Personnel Psychology*, **40**, 199–213.

Hofstee, W. K. B. (1985). Liever klinisch? Grenzen aan het objectiviteitsbeginsel bij beoordeling en selectie. *Nederlands Tijdschrift voor de Psychologie*, **40**, 459–473.

Jansen, A. (1979). *Ethiek en praktijk van personeelselectie*. Assen: Van Gorcum.

Johnson-Laird, P. N. (1983). *Mental Models. Towards a Cognitive Science of Language, Inference, and Consciousness*. Cambridge: Cambridge University Press.

Klimoski, R. and Brickner, M. (1987). Why do assessment centers work? The puzzle of assessment center validity. *Personnel Psychology*, **40**, 243–260.

Latham, G. P., Saari, L. M., Purcell, E. D. and Campion, M. A. (1980). The situational interview. *Journal of Applied Psychology*, **65**, 422–427.

Matarazzo, J. D. (1986). Computerized clinical psychological test interpretations. *American Psychologist*, **41**(1), 14–24.

McGormick, E. J. (1976). Job and task analysis. In: Dunnette, M. D. (ed.), *Handbook of Industrial and Organizational Psychology*. Chicago: Rand McNally.

Meehl, P. E. (1954). *Clinical versus Statistical Prediction*. Minneapolis: University of Minnesota Press.

Meehl, P. E. (1957). When shall we use our heads instead of the formula? *Journal of Counseling Psychology*, **4**, 268–273.

Roe, R. A. (1983). *Grondslagen der personeelselektie*. Assen: Van Gorcum.

Ryan, A. M. and Sackett, P. R. (1987). A survey of individual assessment practices by I/O psychologists. *Personnel Psychology*, **40**, 455–488.

Smith, P. D. (1976). Behaviors, results, and organizational effectiveness: the problem of criteria. In: Dunnette, M. D. (ed.), *Handbook of Industrial and Organizational Psychology*. Chicago: Rand McNally.

Strien, P. J. van (1964). *Problemen van de bedrijfspsychologische rapportering*. Assen: Van Gorcum.

Thorndike, R. L. (1949). *Personnel Selection*. New York: Wiley.

7

Criterion Measures in Selection Research

RODGER D. BALLENTINE
United States Air Force Human Resources Laboratory

The United States Air Force (USAF), along with the other military services, is participating in a large-scale project (a) to develop methodologies for measuring on-the-job performance and (b) to link enlistment standards to such measures of performance (Harris, 1987; OASD, 1987; Wigdor and Green, 1986). This paper focuses on the USAF approach to on-the-job performance criterion development, with emphasis on an innovative work sample measure called Walk-Through Performance Testing. More specific information about the USAF component of this study can be obtained from the author.

BACKGROUND

The test used by the United States Department of Defense (DoD) to determine aptitude levels of military service enlisted applicants is the Armed Services Vocational Aptitude Battery (ASVAB). Applicants are screened for entry based on their Armed Forces Qualification Test (AFQT) scores; the combined score from four (i.e., word knowledge, paragraph comprehension, arithmetic reasoning, and numerical operations) of the ten ASVAB subtests. Service-specific composites of abilities measured by these ten subtests are used to assign recruits to skill training courses and subsequent jobs.

Given the importance of the ASVAB for accessing military manpower, the DoD initiated a joint-service research program in the early 1980s to validate enlistment standards against job performance, instead of training success. Linking enlistment standards to job performance would improve the military

Advances in Selection and Assessment. Edited by M. Smith and I. T. Robertson
© 1989 John Wiley & Sons Ltd

services' ability to determine more accurately accession quality requirements
(OASD, 1987).

UNITED STATES AIR FORCE PROJECT

The overall program of research calls for the development of measurement
techniques that allow for the collection of valid, accurate, and reliable performance data (Hedge and Teachout, 1986). High-fidelity hands-on measures are
used as benchmarks against which surrogate indices of performance (less
expensive, easier-to-administer interview tests and performance ratings) are
evaluated as substitutes for the more expensive labor-intensive hands-on measures. The conceptual performance measurement model underlying this
approach is described in a report by Kavanagh, Borman, Hedge, and Gould
(1987).

The following eight job specialities were selected to cover the range of jobs
in four Air Force ASVAB aptitude composite areas (mechanical, electronics,
general, and administrative): Jet Engine Mechanic, Air Traffic Control Operator, Avionic Communications Specialist, Ground Radio Operator, Aircrew
Life Support Specialist, Precision Measuring Equipment Laboratory Specialist,
Aerospace Ground Equipment Specialist, and Personnel Specialist. Based on
the findings from these specialities, the measurement system will be finalized
and tested in a small sample of specialties representing these aptitude areas.

Types of measures developed

Walk-through performance testing (WTPT)

The cornerstone of this criterion development effort is a work sample testing
approach (Hedge and Lipscomb, 1987). This task-level job performance
measurement system expands the range of job tasks on which an individual is
measured by combining hands-on and interview testing procedures to provide
a high-fidelity measure of technical job competence. The interview testing
component has been added as a means of assessing those tasks that would
have been eliminated because of these constraints, thereby providing a more
thorough coverage of the work domain.

The hands-on component resembles traditional work sample tests designed
to measure performance on a sample of tasks that have survived the imposition
of measurement constraints such as testing time/cost or risk of personal injury/
equipment damage. These measures provide direct observation of proficiency
on 10 to 15 critical tasks (e.g., installing a starter on a jet engine). The
examiner's booklet provides the information needed for setting up test items

and a yes/no checklist with standards to record whether required steps were performed correctly.

Interview testing takes place in the work setting and requires the job incumbent to demonstrate his/her capability by 'showing and telling' the evaluator how the task is accomplished. The procedure is designed to uncover procedural strengths, weaknesses, and knowledge related to the performance of that task. The format of the examiner's booklet parallels comparable hands-on test materials to the greatest extent possible.

Rating forms

A wide range of rating forms have been developed as alternate job performance measures. These include peer, supervisor, and self-ratings at four different levels of measurement specificity. The most detailed rating forms include all the tasks in the WTPT plus additional critical tasks that examinees are likely to perform. Rating forms were also developed to reflect groupings of tasks, or dimensions, of technical proficiency; and a global rating form provides overall ratings of technical and interpersonal competencies. Finally, an Air Force-wide scale allows evaluation of general competencies required across specialties.

Job knowledge tests and additional questionnaires

In order that all service surrogates and hands-on measures may be collected from the same job incumbents, job knowledge tests have been developed for the last four specialties. Also, data collection instruments are included in the measurement system to assess factors related to performance (e.g. task/job experience, situational constraints, level of motivation) and its measurement (e.g. perceived acceptability of measures, understandability of instructions) so these effects on job performance can be measured and considered while studying the accuracy of the performance measures.

Construction strategy

Items developed for WTPT and task and dimension rating forms are selected based on job analytic information available in the USAF Occupational Research Data Base. Subject-matter experts (SMEs) aid test developers in dichotomizing these critical tasks into those which can be measured by hands-on procedures and those which must be measured by interview. Next, test developers and SMEs outline procedures for observing task performance, interviewing, and specifying the performance standards for scoring responses. Other SMEs review the instruments and administration/scoring procedures. Using information learned in the WTPT development process, rating forms are developed. Once the candidate measures have been developed, the assessment package is administered to a small sample to evaluate testing time estimates, procedural stability, and reliability.

DATA COLLECTION AND RESULTS

Whenever possible, approximately 300 first-term airmen who have been on the job at least 6 months are assessed. In some specialties, the sample is limited further to airmen working in certain types of jobs because the work domain is broad and heterogeneous, encompassing many jobs. In such cases, measurement development and sample selection are limited to those jobs most representative of the specialty (i.e. those jobs in which the majority of the incumbents work).

To the maximum extent possible, WTPT takes place at the work site where the tasks are actually performed or at installation training facilities where required equipment is available. Such 'real-world' settings enhance confidence in the adequacy of testing procedures and performance evaluations obtained. The WTPT examiners, if possible, are former enlisted personnel with experience in the specialty who have no prior knowledge of the examinee's performance. The training of job-experienced WTPT administrators focuses on specific test content and standards for determining correct performance; logistical testing arrangements; and observation, interviewing, and scoring skills. Videotapes of incumbents performing tasks correctly and incorrectly, as well as role playing, were used extensively in the training (Bierstedt and Hedge, 1987).

Supervisor, peer, and self-ratings are collected by group administration in large centralized locations. All raters receive training to familiarize them with the purpose and use of rating forms just prior to administration of the rating forms.

Preliminary findings

Data collection has been completed on all eight specialties. Preliminary analyses completed on one of these specialties are briefly summarized here. The remaining analyses will be completed this year and results will be available by late 1989. The most recent Joint-Service Project report (OASD, 1987) summarized the findings available across services.

In the first specialty, 255 jet engine mechanics were administered the measurement system. This sample closely matched the larger population on key demographic characteristics. Analyses of these data suggest (a) reliable and valid performance measures can be constructed and administered, (b) supervisor rating forms and interview testing are promising surrogates/substitutes for expensive hands-on criterion data, and (c) the ASVAB selection test score (AFQT) can predict hands-on performance. In the future, the focus of this project will shift to identification of the most cost-effective measurement procedures and the establishment of methodologies for strengthening the relationship between predictor tests and performance, thereby increasing the likelihood that recruits will be capable performers.

LESSONS LEARNED

Throughout this effort a number of issues surfaced that had to be addressed for the work to continue. These lessons learned have been categorized for convenience, but this organization is not meant to imply that issues in one category are independent of issues in another.

Research design

A real strength of the research design was the way in which each service could focus resources on development of a single measurement technique. While the use of hands-on measures as a benchmark for determining the equivalence of less expensive measures of technical proficiency is justifiable, there are limits to the types of behavior that can be adequately assessed by this technique. For example, standardized hands-on test items for tasks with multiple acceptable approaches to a product are a challenge to develop and score. The hands-on method seems most appropriate for observable procedural tasks. Equivalence of hands-on and surrogate data for procedural tasks represents measurement comparability; however, non-equivalence for other types of work may represent performance variance accounted for by a surrogate (e.g., interpersonal behavior) but not captured by hands-on items. Therefore, one must be careful when developing a measurement strategy and analyzing the equivalence of measures to determine what portion of the performance criterion space each method covers.

Test item development

Multiple objectives of project designers may create conflicts when one attempts to carry out the research. For example, selecting job content most suitable for hands-on test items could unintentionally exclude other key performance (non-procedural) aspects of the job. Even a comprehensive task selection plan that uses current job analysis data provides only a starting point for the extensive task analysis input required from job experts to develop work sample test items.

A drawback to using a task-based item selection approach is the risk of reducing the job into minute parts when the work is normally performed in modules made up of several individual tasks.

Multiple measures

Developing multiple measurement techniques, although demanding, provides valuable time, information, and manpower efficiencies. For example, procedures for identifying potential work sample tasks were used to select the additional tasks included in task-level rating forms, and costly job expert input to WTPT construction was used to develop behavioral anchors for several rating forms. In addition, multiple measures of performance also increase the likelihood that the performance criterion space will be adequately covered and that true and error variance can be identified.

Training data collectors

The thorough program of training was instrumental to the success of this project (Bierstedt and Hedge, 1987). Repeated use of videotapes, with known correct and incorrect performance, and role-playing exercises where WTPT administrators had the role of examinee and examiner helped ensure high interrater agreement (Hedge, Dickinson and Bierstedt, 1987).

Support

Obviously, a study of this magnitude requires a tremendous amount of support from all levels. In the USAF alone, approximately 4000 personnel at more than 45 different base locations participated in the study. Their involvement lasted anywhere from 1–1/2 days for job incumbents to 2–4 hours for supervisors and peers.

A key to successful test development and acceptance of data collection was the extensive involvement of field personnel, people who learned how carefully the performance measurement system was developed and administered and its potential value for improving the quality of their airmen. These noncommissioned officers became avid spokesmen for the project, thereby enhancing field cooperation.

AUTHOR NOTES

The views expressed herein represent those of the author and do not necessarily reflect the views of the United States Air Force, other Services, or the United States Department of Defense.

REFERENCES

Bierstedt, S. A. and Hedge, J. W. (1987). *Job Performance Measurement System Trainer's Manual* (AHRL-TP-86-34, AD-A115 294). Brooks AFB, TX: Training Systems Division, Air Force Human Resources Laboratory.

Harris, R. (1987). Joint-Service job performance measurement/enlistment standards project. *The Industrial-Organizational Psychologist*, **24**, 36–42.

Hedge, J. W., Dickinson, J. L. and Bierstedt, S. A. (1987). *Walk-through Performance Testing: The Use of Videotape Technology to Train Test Administrators* (AFHRL-TP-87-71, AD–A195, 944). Brooks AFB, TX: Training Systems Division, Air Force Human Resources Laboratory.

Hedge, J. W. and Lipscomb, M. S. (1987). *Walk-Through Performance Testing: An Innovative Approach to Work Sample Testing* (AFHRL-TP-87-8, AD-A185 479). Brooks AFB, TX: Training Systems Division, Air Force Human Resources Laboratory.

Hedge, J. W. and Teachout, M. S. (1986). *Job Performance Measurement: A Systematic Program of Research and Development* (AFHRL-TP-86-37, AD-A174 175). Brooks AFB, TX: Training Systems Division, Air Force Human Resources Laboratory.

Kavanagh, M. J., Borman, W. C., Hedge, J. W. and Gould, R. B. (1987). *Job Performance Measurement in the Military: A Classification Scheme, Literature Review, and Directions for Research* (AFHRL-TR-87-15 AD-A185 752). Brooks AFB, TX: Training Systems Division, Air Force Human Resources Laboratory.

Office of the Assistant Secretary of Defense (OASD, Force Management and Personnel) (1987). *A Report to the House Committee on Appropriations: Sixth Annual Report to Congress on Joint-Service Efforts to Link Enlistment Standards to Job Performance*. Washington, DC.

Wigdor, A. and Green, B. F., Jr (eds). (1986). *Assessing the Performance of Enlisted Personnel: Evaluation of a Joint-Service Research Project*. Washington, DC: National Academy Press.

8

Personnel Selection Methods

Ivan T. Robertson and Mike Smith
The University of Manchester Institute of Science and Technology

INTRODUCTION

Selection and assessment is fundamently concerned with the prediction of job performance and prediction necessarily implies the existence of predictors. However, in recent years the centre stage of the selection and assessment scene has been given over to other issues such as fairness, criteria and utility. Yet more work *is* needed on the predictors we use.

It is inconceivable that we have discovered all the major possible predictors and we hardly know the features of the predictors which produce the characteristics we desire such as validity and reliability. The main purpose of this paper is to provide a *tour d'horizon* which will bring predictors back into the centre stage of our research. We hope to achieve this in three phases. First we briefly list the main methods of prediction which are used in the selection and assessment of people at work. Then, equally briefly we will outline the ways that these methods can be categorized. At the end of this stage a large schema will have emerged and it will be impossible to deal with all parts of it in detail. Consequently, we will select some aspects which to us seem particularly worthy of attention.

PREDICTORS OF TODAY

Perhaps one of the reasons why there has been little progress in this area is its complexity and diversity. First and perhaps of central interest are the

Advances in Selection and Assessment. Edited by M. Smith and I. T. Robertson

predictors which we currently use. Figure 8.1 gives a list of some of those available.

Of course other types of predictors could be included and the classification system is to some extent subjective. The situation is further complicated by the fact that some predictors can be mixed, as in assessment centres, to produce a combination which becomes a method in its own right. A quick examination of the list suggests that little has changed over the last 20 years. Measures have been refined and improved but there has been nothing really novel except, perhaps, situational interviews and the work on accomplishment records (Latham, Saari, Purcell and Campion, 1980; Latham and Saari, 1984). Work on the situational interview is both interesting and promising but the research base for this method is still very slim. The accomplishment record is in a similar position. Hough's work (Hough, 1984; Hough, Keyes and Dunnette, 1983) on codifying people's accomplishments is very promising but it needs independent verification in a wider range of settings and occupations. There are also some interesting possibilities in the use of computer-assisted testing. Repertory Grid techniques, and the future biography method (Tuller and Barrett, 1976) are in their infancy as selection methods.

A picture of predictors which stopped here would be very incomplete. At the very least we would need to consider the predictors in relation to the job

1 Interviews
— unstructured
— structured
— situational
— behaviour description
2 Tests (analytical or signs)
— cognitive ability (general or specific)
— perceptual-motor
— personality
— interests
3 Tests (analagous or samples)
— work sample
— situational (intrays, role plays, simulations)
— trainability tests
4 Computer Assisted Tests
5 Repertory Grids
6 Biodata and Accomplishment Record
7 Future Autobiography
8 References
9 Graphology
10 Astrology
11 Self-assessment
12 Supervisors/Peer assessment

Figure 8.1   List of some predictors in use

on which performance is being forecast. Here, many classifications could be justified but a classification into managerial, professional, sales, personal service, clerical, operative and technical is in use fairly widely. So at the very least, we need to conceptualize predictors in two dimensions. Already our scheme is taking on some complexity: we have a model with over 50 cells.

Characteristics of predictors

But there is a third dimension, the characteristics of the measure. Muchinsky (1986) calls some of these 'evaluative standards' and Figure 8.2 reflects his views and additional factors. Many of these standards, such as validity, are old friends whose problems and ramifications are well known. Others, such as the time orientation of the data and the concept of impact, are less familiar and require a little further elaboration.

The predictors, occupational categories and characteristics can be combined. Even though this represents a simplification, the final matrix consists of almost 1000 cells. Clearly, it will be impossible here to survey each cell.

EVALUATIVE STANDARDS

— Validity
— Fairness
— Applicability
— Cost
— Availability
— Qualifications of user
— Acceptability
— Other characteristics
— Source of information: self, others, objective
— Driven by theory of empiricism
— Impact on applicants
— Past, present or future oriented

Figure 8.2   Characteristics of predictors

Usage of selection

The literature on various predictors has been accumulating for over half a century. We know quite a lot about many predictors. This information has been thrown into sharp focus by the techniques of meta-analysis which will be considered in greater detail in another section. Although there are many Is to be dotted and Ts to be crossed we have a fair idea of the validity of most of the main classes of predictors in most occupational categories. Furthermore, we are beginning to collect systematic information on the use of these predictors by employers. For example Sneath, Thakur and Medjuck (1976) surveyed the use of tests in British industry and Robertson and Makin (1986) surveyed the way that British industry selects its managers. Figure 8.3 presents a slight oversimplification of some results.

	ALWAYS USE (%)
Interviews	81
References	67
Cognitive tests	5
Personality tests	4
Assessment centre (sometimes 22%)	—
Biodata	2

Figure 8.3   Use of predictors for managerial selection in the UK

The results show that the bedrock of selection in industry is the methods which are among the least valid (interviews and references). Evidence suggests that the same conclusion would be true in other countries. The question then arises 'why do employers persist in using poor methods?' This question suggests that one fruitful avenue of research on predictors is the perceptions that employers and others have of the various predictors and the way that these perceptions guide the choice of methods in practical selection situations.

The state of the art

The development of improved methods of personnel slection has been a crucial issue within occupational psychology since the earliest days of the discipline. A large and varied collection of predictors continue to be studied involving a variety of different occupational groups. Research interest in different predictors and occupational groups has fluctuated over the last 25–30 years. Monahan and Muchinsky (1983) reviewed personnel selection studies reported in the journal *Personnel Psychology* for the period 1950–1979. They noted, for example, that studies focusing on professional and managerial jobs peaked during the 1960s where the number of published studies swelled to four times the rate in the 1950s. In the 1970s however, trades, crafts, sales and professional jobs were studied with more or less equal frequencies. Schmitt *et al.* (1984) surveyed studies published in two journals, *Personnel Psychology* and *Journal of Applied Psychology*; 366 conceptually independent validity coefficients relating to specific predictor-criterion pairs were identified from an original sample of 840 non-independent coefficients. The distribution of these coefficients across different occupational groups is shown in Figure 8.4 in percentage form.

OCCUPATIONAL GROUP	PERCENTAGE OF COEFFICIENTS
Professional	22
Managerial	25
Clerical	10
Sales	14
Skilled labour	13
Unskilled labour	16

Figure 8.4   Percentages of validity coefficients as a function of occupational groups (derived from Schmitt et al., 1984)

In recent years several reviewers have attempted to summarize the large amount of information available and produce general conclusions about the validity of specific predictors for specific criteria. Some of these reviews have taken the form of narrative reviews with some quantification (e.g. Reilly and Chao, 1982; Tenopyr and Oeltjen, 1982; Muchinsky, 1986). Others have used meta-analysis techniques (e.g. Hunter and Hunter, 1984, Schmitt et al, 1984). In general terms, regardless of the approach used, the reviews produce similar conclusions. Of the criteria, suggested earlier in this paper, that may be used to evaluate predictors overriding importance is usually attached to validity (normally predictive validity). Decades of research into selection methods has provided a data base that, in the case of some predictors, can be used to provide a clear, quantifiable estimate of validity coefficients based on large numbers of studies. Drawing on the research mentioned above (particularly Hunter and Hunter, 1984; Schmitt et al, 1984; Ghiselli, 1973; Reilly and Chao 1982) Figure 8.5

SELECTION METHOD	APPROXIMATE TOTAL SAMPLE SIZE	RANGE OF MEAN VALIDITY COEFFICIENTS
Work sample	3,000 +	0.38–0.54
Ability composite	30,000 +	0.53
Assessment centre	15,000 +	0.41–0.43
Supervisor/Peer evaluation	8,000 +	0.43
General mental ability	30,000 +	0.25–0.45
Biodata	5,000 +	0.24–0.38
References	5,000 +	0.17–0.26
Interviews	2,500 +	0.14–0.23
Personality assessment	20,000 +	0.15
Interest	1,500 +	0.10
Self-assessment	500 +	0.15
Handwriting	small	0.00

Figure 8.5   Approximate-total sample sizes and mean validity coefficients for selection methods

shows estimates of validity coefficients for various selection methods. This global view is necessarily an oversimplification since it is appropriate to make such comparisons between methods only when the same criteria are being predicted.

Despite this caveat, as Figure 8.5 shows it is possible to categorize selection methods on the basis of their predictive accuracy. Work sample tests and what Hunter and Hunter (1984) describe as an 'ability composite' (general mental ability and psychomotor ability) produce the best validity coefficients. Supervisor/peer assessments, assessment centres, biodata and general mental ability are the best of the remaining methods. References, interviews, personality, assessment and interest inventories provide very low, but positive validity coefficients. More recent evidence from meta-analytic studies, on the validity of interviews, suggests that different types of interview may have different validities (see Hunter and Hirsch, 1987). For self-assessments and handwriting, the evidence does not provide any support for their use as a predictors of work performance.

For most of the selection methods mentioned above the range of validities reported in different studies is relatively narrow. It is worth noting that for cognitive tests there is a somewhat larger variation in the range of coefficients reported. Ghiselli (1973) reported average validity coefficients of between 0.25–0.30 for intelligence and aptitude tests. Schmitt *et al.* (1984) produce similar results whereas Hunter and Hunter (1984) report a mean validity coefficient of 0.45 with job proficiency as the criterion being predicted. The source of this variation seems to be based on whether or not investigators using meta-analysis techniques have corrected for error of measurement and restriction of range.

Validity is a crucial factor when considering the value of personnel selection methods. As noted above, however, other facets of selection methods are important. Fairness is the topic of another section in this book and will not be discussed in detail further here. It is worth noting, however, that for several methods (e.g. references) only very limited information is available.

RECENT PREDICTORS

The main recent innovations in predictors have been the development of situational and behaviour description interviews and the accomplishment record.

Situational and behaviour description interviews

Successive studies of the validity of interviews have suggested that they have very little predictive power (see Mayfield, 1964; Ulrich and Trumbo, 1965;

Wright, 1969; Arvey and Campion, 1982). Recent work with situational interviews (Latham *et al.*, 1980, Latham and Saari, 1984) has revealed validity coefficients of up to 0.35. Situational interviews use the results of systematic job analyses to produce job-related incidents. The incidents are then turned into interview questions in which job applicants are asked to indicate how they *would behave* in a given situation. Janz (1982) has revealed validity coefficients for behaviourally-patterned, structured interviews of 0.54. Another recent interview study (Arvey *et al.* 1987) has produced even higher validity coefficients (up to 0.61 after correction). It may be, however, that in this particular situation the interviews were functioning as surrogate work-sample tests. Arvey *et al.* (1987) note that 'the behaviours and interpersonal skills observed during the interview were not unlike those exhibited on the job' (p. 10). It is also hypothesized that situational interviews could operate as an impure form of verbal intelligence test.

Accomplishment Record

A recently developed variant of the biodata approach, known as the 'accomplishment record', has been developed by Hough and colleagues (Hough, Keyes and Dunnette, 1983; Hough, 1984). This approach is based on self-reported descriptions of past accomplishments in job-related behavioural dimensions. Validity coefficients with job performance as criterion of 0.23 have been reported, furthermore Hough (1984) reports that accomplishment record scores are unrelated to traditional measures of aptitude and thus may contribute unique information.

CLASSIFICATION OF METHODS

The personnel selection methods mentioned above are all attempting to provide accurate predictions of future behaviour. Robertson (1986) has suggested classifying personnel selection methods on the principle that future work behaviour is potentially predictable from three factors: past behaviour of the person, current behaviour and personal attributes and expectancies concerning future behavious.

It is informative to classify the methods reviewed above on this basis.

Predictors based on the past:

    Biodata
    References
    Supervisor/peer ratings

Predictors based on the present:

Cognitive, personality and interest tests
Interviews
Self-assessments
Work samples
Handwriting
Repertory Grids

Future-orientated predictors:

Future biography
Situational interview

It is clear from recent research in personality and motivation that work behaviour is to some extent predictable from intentions and expectancies that people hold (e.g. Locke *et al.*, 1986).

With the exception of situational interviews, and possibly the Future Auto-biography (Tuller and Barrett, 1976) current methods do not explicitly focus on intentions, goals, expectancies and other similar future-orientated variables. Situational interviews concentrate, in a highly structured way, on how people say that they would behave in realistic work situations. Interviews or other information collection procedures might be devised to collect information on future goals, expectancies, self-efficacy (defined by Bandura, 1986, as 'people's judgements of their capabilities to organize and execute courses of action required to attain designated types of performances', p. 391). Barling and Beattie (1983), for example, demonstrated links between self-efficacy and future sales performance on a sample of 97 insurance sales representatives.

The results concerning the validity of different selection methods, reviewed above, are now increasingly familiar to occupational psychologists and some clear conclusions may be drawn.

(1) There is a set of techniques that provide the best predictions of future work performance:

Ability tests; Work samples; Biodata; Supervisor/Peer ratings; Assessment centres.

(2) Certain approaches have received relatively little research attention. In general these are approaches that appear to have low validity—but perhaps this is a function of lack of research interest.

(3) The ceiling for validity coefficients for a single predictor is approximately 0.5.

(4) Hunter and Hunter (1984) have shown that by combining two specific, closely related predictors, viz. mental ability and psychomotor ability, mean validity coefficients are increased by comparison with the results available for single predictors. Little material is available on the relationships between

various predictors and therefore the gain in validity that might be achieved by using several predictors is unclear. More research on the interrelationships between predictors would be useful.

(5) Within limits, specific predictors are better at predicting some criteria than others. For example, biodata predicts performance ratings better than turnover (see Schmitt *et al.*, 1984; Hunter and Hunter, 1984)

Although it does not follow as a direct conclusion, it is also quite clear that the process of psychological testing may be revolutionized by the use of computer technology.

COMPUTER-ASSISTED TESTING

Brief review of computer-assisted testing 1967–1987

Computer-assisted testing (CAT) is an area of such promise that it deserves a section of its own. The beginning of CAT is best typified by the early modification during the 1960s of teaching machines by, mainly, clinical psychologists (e.g. Gedye, 1967, 1968). Soon, traditional tests such as the Wechsler Adult Intelligence Scale (WAIS), the 16PF, Eysenck Personality Inventory, Raven's Matrices and the Elithorn maze (Elwood and Griffin, 1972; Knights *et al.*, 1973; Karson and Odell, 1975; Katz and Dalby, 1981; Elithorn and Telford, 1969, respectively) had been computerized.

From the early days, developments in computer-assisted testing have been technology driven. The most important of these technological factors is the availability of fairly cheap portable computers (Fletcher, 1978) which have computing power that only ten years ago would have required a mainframe computing department. Other important technological developments have been the vast improvement in graphical output: high-resolution graphics, with colour, has meant that computer-assisted testing has been applied to spatial and diagrammatic items. More recent developments include the touch-sensitive screen, and computer-controlled video discs. All these will enormously expand the range and volume of material which can be used while at the same time simplifying the methods of response and producing a user friendly system. The rate of development in the computer industry is so fast that it is hard to forecast the developments of tomorrow but computer recognition of natural speech and free handwriting cannot be far away.

These developments were fairly slow to percolate through to occupational psychology. Even today the use of computerized tests in selection and assessment is restricted largely to military uses such as the MICROPAT battery for the UK Army Air Corps (Bartram and Dale, 1983), the Graphic Information Processing Tests for the US Navy (Cory, Rimland and Bryson, 1977), Pilot

Selection for the USAF (Stettgen, Gray and Wasmundt, 1979) and the Armed Services Vocational Aptitude Battery (McBride and Martin, 1983; Sands, 1985). Wildgrube (1985) and Steege (1986) describe similar developments in the German Federal armed forces.

The reasons for this slow transfer of CAT to industrial and commercial organizations are a matter of speculation but there are two clear possibilities. First, there are the high set-up costs which inhibit the adoption of CAT except where the throughput of candidates is very high. However, some software houses have now undertaken this function and some computerized tests are available 'off the shelf'. Second, publications on CAT tend to occur in journals such as the *Journal of Educational Measurement*, the *Journal of Computer Based Instruction* and the *International Journal of Man Machine Studies*, which are not routinely scanned by personnel psychologists. Fortunately, there have been a number of useful reviews of computer-assisted testing which have helped bring the information into the mainstream of selection and assessment. They are Kilcross (1976), Denner (1977), McBride (1979), Bartram and Bayliss (1984), Hackel (1986) and Murphy (1988). In essence, these reviews tended to confirm the following points:

(1) Computerized tests tended to correlate highly with the paper and pencil versions.
(2) In many cases (where adaptive testing is used) costs could be reduced by up to 50 per cent.
(3) Computerized tests were generally as valid as the pencil and paper versions.
(4) Subjects were not averse to CAT if it was well presented.
(5) Standardization and control of administration were vastly increased.

The components of CAT systems

McBride (1979) analysed the essential components of the computer system into 8 parts.

A device for displaying the stimulus

This is usually a television-like screen but liquid crystal displays and light-emitting didodes are also used. To produce some uniformity it has been suggested (Bartram, Beaumont, Cornford, Dann and Wilson, undated) that:

(i) the use of the top and bottom lines of the display should be avoided;
(ii) pages should not be overfilled;
(iii) excessive use of highlighting and colouring should be avoided;

(iv) graphical items should use at least 512 × 512 pixels but preferably 1024 × 1024 pixels should be used.

They also provide suggestions for screen layout and the presentation of information and instructions. Generally, sound should be used with discretion—especially, at the present state of the art, when synthetic speech is involved.

A response device

Again Bartram et al. (undated) provide some guidelines concerning the use of keys on a standard QWERTY keyboard together with touch screens, light pens, tracker ball, etc., etc. Generally, auto repeat facilities on keys should be disabled to avoid unintentional duplication of responses.

Item storage medium

Clearly limited storage implies the use of fewer and simpler items. Bartram et al. suggest the use of computers with a minimum of 256K RAM, 10 Mbyte hard disk and single 360K drives.

Internal processing

Often this is not a limiting factor because it is not opaque to the subject and in all but the most minimal systems, processing speed is beyond the limen of most subjects.

Ability to process the responses made by the subject

This may involve more than the simple recording of the reply. Computers offer the possibility of measuring the speed of response, the likelihood of faking, difficulties in reading, conservatism, alignment errors, and guessing (Bartram and Bayliss, 1984). All these are measures which are over and above those provided by pencil and paper tests.

Item selection

Computers have the ability to present to subjects only the items which are relevant or items which provide the maximum information. This lies at the heart of adaptive testing.

Test scoring

This can be undertaken both in the traditional normative way offering the user a choice between the methods of presentation (quotients, stens, T scores etc.) and in a way which aims to track the process of the subject's response.

Data recording

This is either to a magnetic medium or to a hard copy. Recent technological developments suggest that data transmission to other parts of a larger network should also be included under this heading. To facilitate standardization of recording and transmission Bartram *et al.* (undated) give some guidelines and similar standards suggested by Geen, Brock, Humphrey, Linn and Reckase (1984).

Ultimately, standardization of data recording plus the development of computer networks could lead to an international pool of items which are used by personnel psychologists in several countries.

Additional advantages of CAT

The reviews cited earlier outlined some of the major advantages of computer-aided testing: speed, economy, etc. However, one major advantage that has not been discussed is the potential offered for new kinds of test which measure new abilities. The most obvious of these is the capability to make tests *dynamic*. Modern computer graphics mean that elements of a test item can be made to move, rotate, change colour, fade or embolden. Situations can be made to happen in real time (Cory, Rimland and Bryson, 1977; Hunt and Pellegrino, 1985; Greitzer, Hershman and Keeley, 1981). McBride also pointed out in 1979 that the capabilities of computers allow us to break away from the simple yes/no, *dichotomous scoring* of most pencil and paper tests to use polycotomous scoring where each response can contribute to several dimensions (Samejima, 1969; Bock, 1972). As computers grope towards the analysis of natural speech and handwriting, new kinds of tests with *open ended questions* could be produced. Brooks, Dann and Irvine (1984) describe some principles for the use and construction of computer-controlled tasks (CCTs). The greater flexibility of display and response also means that *ways of testing people with handicaps can* be developed. Indeed, the use of computers could revolutionize the very basis of personnel tests. Murphy (1988) points out that the traditional conceptualization of true score plus error score has dominated ability measurement since Binet's time. Yet this approach has been subject to increasing criticism by, for example, Lumsden (1976). The alternatives to traditional test theory include item response theory (*IRT*) sometimes known as latent trait theory. Item response theory will take account of a large number of parameters which usually include item difficulty, discriminating power, and the probability of guessing the correct answer. Probably the most well known exponent of IRT is Rasch (1960)—although there is some recent empirical work suggesting that many items do not behave in the way that Rasch would predict. A good introduction to IRT is provided by Hulin, Drasgow and Parsons (1983). The computer's ability to utilize statistical processes such as IRT underpins the development of adaptive and tailored testing.

The use of computer-assisted testing will influence the type of tests we use in other ways. Tests could be developed which allow us to identify the *processes* which subjects use rather than simply the end result. In some situations the process used may be more predictive than the quantification of the end result because the process chosen may underlie a great deal of performance variability. Hakel (1986) notes that these developments may lead us to a sharper conceptualization of the measures we use. When we are clear on the parameters involved, it may be a simple step to ask the computer to create items within those parameters. For example, it is already very easy for a computer to generate a new series of random numbers for a digit span test and Colberg (1985) suggests rules for the composition of logic-based questions.

Some disadvantages of CAT

Unfortunately the benefits of computer-assisted testing are accompanied by disadvantages. At the most superficial level there are problems associated with set up and hardware costs and, perhaps, problems of person–machine rapport. At a deeper level, there are problems of equivalence and the maintenance of standards. The *problems of equivalence* start with the initial change from pencil and paper to computer. Reviews suggest that the two versions will correlate highly and that the computer version will be valid; however, the scores may not be equivalent in terms of the interpretation to be made from them. The computer version may need to be renormed before it can be used for assessment purposes. Renorming, of course, will require considerable effort and resources. The problem does not stop here. The problem of equivalence will arise each time the test is moved to a different computer configuration with different displays and response method. Renorming at each change will be tedious and wasteful. Perhaps with some empirical work we will be able to identify those changes which destroy equivalence and perhaps we will be able to derive satisfactory statistical corrections. Another solution to this problem would be the adoption of a set of agreed rules for computer tests.

Bartram and Bayliss (1984) draw attention to the need to *maintain standards for computer tests*. They quote the example of Smith (1982) who developed a computer-administered Programme Aptitude Test (PATSY) on the basis of his long personal experience. But he did not conduct proper validation or reliability studies. The fact that the computer administered the test provided an aura of veracity which would have been absent if traditional media had been employed. Bartram and Bayliss arrive at the firm conclusion that 'test development must be carried out by psychologists with both the appropriate skills in test development, standardisation and validation, and the ability to produce a system capable of attaining the necessary level of rapport and test security. The programming skills necessary to produce the required software are relatively easy to acquire or obtain; the psychological expertise and experience is not! The view that automating a test is simply a matter of writing the software is a very common and misleading one.' To a large extent, these are developments for the future. Most computer-assisted testing today consists of 'the translation' of existing tests. In addition there is some use of computers in interpreting the test results (Smith, 1978; Vale, Keller and Bentz, 1986). The use of computers in adaptive testing is less common and largely restricted to the armed services.

THE CURRENT APPROACH

The material presented in the first part of this chapter reviews the knowledge base concerning personnel selection methods. This knowledge base has been derived within the context of a specific perspective on the development of selection methods. One purpose of this chapter is to review the current situation and point the way towards future research and development needs. In this spirit we wish to examine the viability of the current perspective and raise some issues that seem to warrant attention. First a clear statement of the main features of the current perspective is appropriate.

(1) Strategies for designing selection methods follow one of two basic procedures. The difference between the approaches is exemplified in Wernimont and Campbell's (1968) discussion of the use of *signs* or *samples* of behaviour to predict future performance. In this chapter we have also used the term analagous and analytical testing to refer to a similar concept.

Both approaches, in theory, begin with job analysis. When the sample approach is being used, the product of the job analysis is then used to build assessment exercises that simulate the job. The clearest use of this approach is in the development of work-sample tests (Robertson and Kandola, 1982). The sample approach is also often involved in the development of assessment centres and is similar though not identical to the use of content validity. Schmitt and Ostroff (1986) provide an example of a procedure specifically designed to operationalize the behavioural consistency approach advocated by Wernimont and Campbell (1968). It has been argued that the sampling approach can only be used in situations where candidates are competent in the tasks sampled and cannot be used for entry level posts. The use of trainability testing (Robertson and Downs, 1979) where a period of learning is included in the assessment demonstrates that this view is incorrect. The alternative to the sample method involves using the job analysis to identify signs of behaviour including personal characteristics, for example decision-making skills, and then developing assessment exercises to look for these characteristics. The use of psychometric tests, particularly personality, provides clear illustrations of the use of this approach. In practice, not all selection methods are based entirely on one approach or another, for example assessment centres (see Sackett, 1987). A possible third approach is the raw empiricism exemplified in the development of some biodata questionnaires.

(2) Methods are developed which identify the *most suitable candidate* for the job. Despite some attention to other criteria, for example content validity, for evaluating selection methods the most widely accepted criterion of a good selection method is that it provides *an accurate prediction of future work performance*; plus a fairly narrowly defined set of other criteria (e.g. tenure, training success).

Our view is that two increasingly important issues are ignored by this perspective on selection methods. There are:

(1) The dynamic, interactive nature of people and the (work) situations they are in.
(2) The impact of selection processes on candidates.

PEOPLE, JOBS AND SITUATIONS

The current range of selection methods predicts a relatively narrow range of criterion variables. The chief endeavour of our current orthodox selection methodology is to derive methods that predict job performance. Is it appropriate to restrict our range of interest to predictions of job *performance*? There are arguments against this.

The first point concerns the links (or lack of them) between work performance, satisfaction and motivation. The evidence of a direct link between satisfaction and productivity is mixed and there is no certainty about whether satisfaction causes performance or vice versa. A recent meta-analysis (Petty *et al.*, 1984) offers support for a positive relationship between satisfaction and performance and suggests in particular that *dissatisfaction* may result in lower performance. In general the links between satisfaction and other productivity-related variables such as turnover and absenteeism appear to be fairly weak, though results vary (see Mobley, 1982; Hackett and Guion, 1985). Whilst the direct links between satisfaction and performance may not be particularly strong there may be important indirect links. Motowidlo (1983), for example, found that satisfaction was associated with greater consideration and personal sensitivity in the job. Bateman and Organ (1983) and Smith *et al.* (1983)

have found similar results. Thus individual job satisfaction may influence the *performance of others*.

Motivation (i.e. the strength and direction of behaviour) and performance are clearly much more directly associated, to the extent that high ability to perform can be completely negated by low or misdirected motivation. Consideration of motivation requires consideration of psychological factors such ‹as needs, values, goals and cognitions. These are often expressed and/or attained through factors indirectly related to job tasks and are linked to personal and group relationships, organization, climate and culture, etc. Direct consideration of these factors is not normally involved in the job analysis conducted prior to the design of selection methods. The sample approach could, however, be extended to include consideration of these factors.

A further point is that for an individual job holder the factors discussed above (and others) are not fixed and static but are in a state of flux. People, the jobs they do and the situations in which both are embedded are dynamic phenomena. They influence and are influenced by each other. In terms of contemporary personality theory the idea being presented here is represented by Bandura's (1977, 1986) notion of 'reciprocal determinism' (see Figure 8.6).

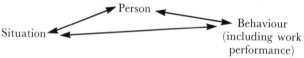

Figure 8.6   Reciprocal determinism (after Bandura, 1977)

Behaviour (job performance included) is a function of person and situational variables and in turn helps to determine these variables. Anecdotal evidence and personal experience support the view that both people and jobs change over time. In many situations poor selection decisions are turned into acceptable ones by adjusting jobs and people until an acceptable degree of fit is found. In other situations managers and supervisors struggle to cope with the job holders who misdirect their undoubted skill.

As well as personal experience, there is clear scientific evidence to show that people change, as a function of the jobs they do (e.g. Kohn and Schooler, 1982; Brousseau, 1984). In our day-to-day working lives we may all recognize this but current selection methodology does not appear to. Work sample exercises and assessment centres may attempt to simulate the *immediate* task situation but even that is debatable. Maybe these factors are partly responsible for the fact that many organizations appear unimpressed by the progress in personnel psychology and do not use contemporary selection methods to the full.

The psychological costs or benefits of a selection decision are not limited to a consideration of the job holder's productivity. This is important for the organization and presumably the job holder's career but, as noted earlier, high productivity does not, for example, necessarily mean high job satisfaction. Psychologists could be expected to be concerned about other aspects of the job—person fit such as psychological well-being, mental health, and general quality of work life. The criterion measures used in personnel selection studies show little concern with such issues. The ubiquitous supervisors' ratings are both limited (to what extent are they linked with true performance?) and limiting.

One challenge to the current orthodoxy in selection is to recognize the reality of the links between people and situations and take into account a broader range of factors both when designing selection methods and when selecting relevant criterion measures. These arguments for a consideration of a broader range of variables could lead to more efficient selection in overall terms, viz. better prediction of work performance and improvements in the quality of work life for individuals concerned. This would attain useful goals for both organizations and individuals.

At the individual level there is another important aspect of selection methodology not yet explored: the impact that selection processes and decisions have on individual applicants.

THE IMPACT OF SELECTION METHODS ON CANDIDATES

By definition in any true selection (rather than assessment) situation some of the candidates will be rejected. The psychological impact of rejection on a candidate may vary according to the context in which the decision is taken, the method used and the personal characteristics of the candidate. Important contextual factors could include the career/life stage that the candidate has reached, whether the candidate was being assessed for internal promotion/tiering, or entry to an organization from outside, etc.

In essence when selection and assessment methods are utilized there are three broad kinds of outcomes: accept, reject, feedback on strengths and weakness. Sometimes (e.g. as in the case of internal assessment centres used to identify candidates for a management development programme) feedback is coupled with accept or reject decisions; other times it is not. In a discussion of utility models in personnel selection Dreher and Sackett (1983) focus on the consequences of a negative decision for the individual job seeker, the organization and society as a whole. To illustrate the potential importance of impact consider a hypothetical but perfectly realistic organization with seven levels of manager grades. The lowest grade (1) contains 50 per cent of the managerial workforce, only 5 per cent of managers reach grade 7. Promotion decisions are taken on the basis of tests, assessment centres and supervisor/peer ratings—all highly valid methods. In due course only 5 per cent of the companies' managers progress through the organization without receiving a negative decision, and having to cope with its consequences. These consequences *could* include reduced work commitment, lowered self-esteem, ill-health, reduced efficiency. Thus, the worst scenario suggests that whilst the top 5 per cent of managers may be very happy with the organization most of the remainder may be alienated from the organization, performing below their optimum level or actively seeking another job. For more traditional selection situations where candidates originate from outside the organization the impact at organization level is more difficult to clarify, but impact at the individual level could be equally damaging. This view of alienated or psychologically damaged individuals represents only one side of the impact coin. It is presumably equally possible that when a candidate is given a negative decision (with or without feedback) this may enable him or her to build a more accurate and realistic self-image and develop realistic, attainable, but still satisfying career goals.

Is there any evidence that selection methods have any impact on candidates? Though the amount of available evidence is quite small the answer seems to be yes. Selection methods might have affective, cognitive or behavioural impacts. One clear example of behavioural impact is given in a study reported by Downs, Farr and Colbeck (1978). In this study candidates were given a trainability test and graded A (high performance) to E (low performance). Candidates were not informed of their grades. Of those graded A, 90 per cent took up a job offer; of those graded E, only 23 per cent did so. Research into the impact of all methods is limited. For several methods information on various types of applicant reactions have been collected, such as self-reports on how anxious interviewees felt when being questioned on certain topics (Keenan and Wedderburn, 1980). Other research has focused on links between reactions to interviews and intentions to accept job offers (Schmitt and Coyle, 1976; Liden and Parsons, 1986).

The reactions of participants in assessment centres, perhaps because of their often explicit development *and* assessment function, seem to have received most attention. Though even here there is little research designed to measure and assess psychological impact on participants.

Early studies (e.g. Kraut, 1972; Bourgeois *et al.*, 1975; Nirtaut, 1977) suggest that, overall, participants' reactions to assessment centres are favourable. For example, participants report that they received a realistic view of their strengths and weaknesses, that participation would have a *positive* effect on morale, and that the assessment centre measured important job-related qualities. More recent studies, often basing their data collection on a standardized question-naire (Dodd, 1977) have produced further data (e.g. Dodd, 1977; Dulewicz, Fletcher and Wood, 1983). One small-scale study, Teel and Dubois (1983) divided participants into high and low scorers and showed some differences in reactions when these groups were compared.

None of the above studies goes beyond exploring applicant reactions. One recent study (Schmitt, Ford and Stults, 1986) has, however, shown that changes in self-perceived ability were related to performance in particular assessment centre exercises. Research recently completed (Robertson *et al.*, in preparation) has examined links between exposure to three mainstream selection methods— situational interview, Biodata and Assessment Centres—on three main groups of person-variables: work commitment (e.g. work involvement, job involvement, job withdrawal cognitions); psychological well-being (e.g. self-esteem, general health); and personal agency (career planning, self-efficacy). Preliminary results are strongly supportive of an impact effect for all of the methods studied. The variables most affected seem to be those grouped under work commitment. In terms of applicant reactions biodata seems to be the least favoured of the three methods and is seen as both inaccurate and unfair. For situational interviews and assessment centres differences on work commitment variables were revealed between high and low performers. As the study was cross-sectional rather than longitudinal it is difficult to be certain of cause and effect.

The implicit notion underlying much personnel selection research is that measuring individual differences and making a selection decision is a psychologically neutral process with no life or career implications. This notion needs to be replaced with a more comprehensive model of methods as interventions into people's careers. At this stage of research only a very tentative model of the key causal and moderator variables can be drawn. Figure 8.7 provides a tentative representation of the variables involved when the impact of personnel selection methods on individual candidates is considered.

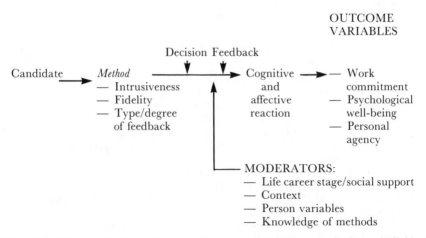

Figure 8.7 The psychological impact of personnel selection methods on individual candidates

Figure 8.7 suggests that the outcome variables are influenced in certain ways depending on the selection method used. Important method factors may include intrusiveness and fidelity (as perceived by candidates), type and degree of feedback. After exposure to one or more methods candidates receive a decision and/or feedback. This information then produces a cognitive and affective reaction. This reaction may be moderated on an individual basis by factors such as the applicant's life/career stage, the context in which the assessment was made (e.g. a one-off speculative job application or a calculated bid to break through into an organization's senior management 'fast track'). Person variables and applicant knowledge of the methods used and perceptions of their validity may also moderate impact. Attempting to conceptualize impact in terms of validity could produce a definition of impact validity as: 'The extent to which a measuring instrument has an effect on a subject's psychological characteristics'.

It is apposite to end this chapter on another future avenue of research. Looking through much of the literature on predictors it is hard to avoid the impression that the development of predictors is governed by the laws of serendipity—someone has a hunch or an idea which is then subjected to empirical examination. With the aid of meta-analysis we are arriving at the position where we can build up a reasonably authoritative list of the characteristics of the predictors. Using the interrelationships among these characteristics in a deductive way, we could begin to establish a picture of what makes a 'good predictor'. This picture could then be used in a hypothetical way to suggest new and better predictors. We may need to give this type of analysis a new name. In view of the impact it could have, an appropriate name would be Mega-Analysis.

REFERENCES

Arvey, R. D. and Campion, J. E. (1982). The employment interview: A summary and review of recent literature. *Personnel Psychology*, **35**, 281–322.
Arvey, R. D., Miller, H. E., Gould, R. and Burch, P. (1987). Interview validity for selecting sales clerks. *Personnel Psychology*, **40**, 1–12.
Bandura, A. (1977). *Social Learning Theory*, Englewood Cliffs, New Jersey: Prentice-Hall.
Bandura, A. (1986). *Social Foundations of Thought and Action*, Englewood Cliffs, New Jersey: Prentice-Hall.
Barling, J. and Beattie, R. (1983). Self-efficacy beliefs and sales performance. *Journal of Organizational Behaviour Management*, **5**, 41–51.
Bartram, D. and Bayliss, R. (1984). Automated Testing: Past, present and future. *Journal of Occupational Psychology*, **57**, 221–237.
Bartram, D., Beaumont, J. G., Cornford, T., Dann, P. L. and Wilson, S. L. (undated). *Recommendations for the design of software for computer based assessment*, University of Hull, UK: Ergonomics Research Group.
Bartram, D. and Dale, H. A. C. (1983). *Micropat version 3.0: A description of the fully automated personnel selection testing system being developed for the Army Air Corps*. Ergonomics Research Group, University of Hull, England, Report ERG/Y6536/83/7.
Bateman, T. S. and Organ, D. W. (1983). Job satisfaction and the good soldier: the

relationship between affect and employee 'citizenship'. *Academy of Management Journal*, **26**, 587–595.

Bock, R. D. (1972). Estimating item parameters and latent ability when responses are scored in two or more nominal categories. *Psychometrika*, **37**, 29–52.

Bourgeois, R. P., Leim, M. A., Slivinski, L. W. and Grant, K. W. (1975). Evaluation of an assessment centre in terms of acceptability. *Canadian Personnel and Industrial Relations Journal*, **22**, 17–20.

Brooks, P. G., Dann, P. L. and Irvine, S. H. (1984). Computerized testing: extracting the levy. *Bulletin of the British Psychological Society*, **37**, 372–374.

Brousseau, K. R. (1984). Job-person dynamics and career development. *Research in Personnel and Human Resources Management*, **2**, 125–154.

Colberg, M. (1985). Logic-based measurement of verbal reasoning: a key to increased validity and economy. *Personnel Psychology*, **38**, 347–359.

Cory, C. H., Rimland, B. and Bryson, R. A. (1977). Using computerised tests to measure new dimensions of abilities. An exploratory study. *Applied Psychological Measurement*, **1**, 101–110.

Denner, S. (1977). Automated psychological testing: a review. *British Journal of Social and Clinical Psychology*, **16**, 175–179.

Dodd, W. E. (1977). Attitudes towards assessment center programs. In J. L. Moses and W. C. Byham (eds), *Applying the Assessment Center Method*, New York: Pergamon.

Downs, S., Farr, R. M. and Colbeck, L. (1978). Self-appraisal: A convergence of selection and guidance. *Journal of Occupational Psychology*, **51**, 271–278.

Dreher, G. F. and Sackett, P. R. (1983). *Perspectives on Employee Staffing and Selection: Readings and Commentary*, Irwin.

Dulewicz, V., Fletcher, C. and Wood, P. (1983). A study of the internal validity of an assessment centre and of participants' background characteristics and attitudes: a comparison of British and American findings. *Journal of Assessment Center Technology*, **6**, 15–24.

Elithorn, A. and Telford, A. (1969). Computer analysis of intellectual skills. *International Journal of Man Machine Studies*, **1**, 189–209.

Elwood, D. L. and Griffin, R. H. (1972). Individual intelligence testing without the examiner: reliability of an automated method. *Journal of Consulting and Clinical Psychology*, **38**, 9–14.

Fletcher, B. C. (1978). Automated testing: an alternative to Denner. *Bulletin of the British Psychological Society*, **31**, 223.

Gedye, J. L. (1967). A teaching machine programme for use as a test of learning ability. In Unwin, D. and Leedham, J. (eds), *Aspects of Educational Technology*, London: Methuen.

Gedye, J. L. (1968). The development of a general purpose psychological testing system. *Bulletin of the British Psychological Society*, **21**, 101–102.

Ghiselli, E. E. (1973). The validity of aptitude tests in personnel selection. *Personnel Psychology*, **26**, 461–477.

Green, B. F., Bock, R. D., Humphreys, L. G., Linn, R. L. and Reckase, M. D. (1984). Technical Guidelines for assessing computer adaptive tests. *Journal of Educational Measurement*, **21**(4), 347–360.

Greitzer, F. L., Hershman, R. L. and Keeley, R. T. (1981). The air defense game: a microcomputer program for research in human performance. *Behaviour Research Methods and Instrumentation*, **13**, 57–59.

Hackett, R. D. and Guion, R. M. (1985). A re-evaluation of the absenteeism-job satisfaction relationship. *Organizational Behavior and Human Decision Processes*, **35**, 340–381.

Hakel, M. D. (1986). Personnel selection and placement. *Annual Review of Psychology*, **37**, 361–364.

Hough, L. M. (1984). Development and evaluation of the 'Accomplishment Record' method of selecting and promoting professionals. *Journal of Applied Psychology*, **69**, 135–146.

Hough, L. M., Keyes, M. A. and Dunnette, M. D. (1983). An evaluation of three 'alternative' selection procedures. *Personnel Psychology*, **36**, 261–276.

Hulin, C. L., Drasgow, F. and Parsons, C. K. (1983). *Item Response Theory: Applications to Psychological Measurement*, Homewood, Illinois: Dav. Jones–Irvin.

Hunt, E. and Pellegrino, J. (1985). Using interactive computing to expand intelligence testing: a critique and prospectus. *Intelligence*, **9**, 207–236.

Hunter, J. E. and Hirsch, H. R. (1987). Applications of meta-analysis. In C. L. Cooper and I. T. Robertson, *International Review of Industrial and Organizational Psychology 1987*, Chichester: John Wiley.

Hunter, J. E. and Hunter, R. F. (1984). Validity and utility of alternative predictors of job performance. *Psychological Bulletin*, **96**, 72–98.

Janz, T. (1982). Initial comparisons of behaviour description interviews versus unstructured interviews. *Journal of Applied Psychology*, **67**, 577–580.

Karson, S. and Odell, J. W. (1975). A new automated system for the 16PF. *Journal of Personality Assessment*, **39**, 256–260.

Katz, L. and Dalby, J. T. (1981). Computer and manual administration of the Eysenck Personality Inventory. *Journal of Clinical Psychology*, **37**, 586–588.

Keenan, A. and Wedderburn, A. A. I. (1980). Putting the bott on the other foot. Candidates' descriptions of interviewers. *Journal of Occupational Psychology*, **53**, 81–89.

Kilcross, M. C. (1976). *A Review of Research in Tailored Testing Report No 9/76*, Farnborough, Hants: APRE, Royal Aircraft Establishment.

Knights, R. M., Richardson, D. H. and McNavry, L. R. (1973). Automated vs clinical administration of the Peabody Picture Vocabulary Test and the Coloured Programme Matrices. *American Journal of Mental Deficiency*, **78**, 223–225.

Kohn, M. L. and Schooler, C. (1982). Job conditions and personality: a longitudinal assessment of their reciprocal effects. *American Journal of Sociology*, **87**, 1257–1286.

Kraut, A. I. (1972). A hard look at assessment centres and their future. *Personnel Journal*, May, 317–326.

Latham, G. P. and Saari, L. M. (1984). So people do what they say? Further studies on the situational interview. *Journal of Applied Psychology*, **69**, 569–573.

Latham, G. P., Saari, L. M., Pursell, E. D. and Campion, M. A. (1980). The situational interview. *Journal of Applied Psychology*, **65**, 422–427.

Liden, R. C. and Parsons, C. K. (1986). A field study of job applicant interview perceptions, alternative opportunities and demographic characteristics. *Personnel Psychology*, **39**, 109–122.

Locke, E. A. and Henne, D. (1986). Work motivation theories. In C. L. Cooper and I. T. Robertson (eds), *International Review of Industrial and Organizational Psychology, 1986*, Chichester & New York: John Wiley.

Lumsden, J. (1976). Test theory. *Annual Review of Psychology*, **27**, 254–280.

McBride, J. R. (1979). *Adaptive Mental Testing: the state of the art*. US Army Research Institute for the Behavioral and Social Sciences, 5001 Eisenhower Av, Alexandria, Virginia 22333.

McBride, J. R. and Martin, J. T. (1983). Reliability and validity of adaptive ability tests in a military setting. In Weiss, D. (ed.), *New Horizons in Testing: Latent Trait Test Theory and Computerized Adaptive Testing*, New York: Academic Press.

Mayfield, E. C. (1964). The selection interview: A re-evaluation of published research. *Personnel Psychology*, **17**, 239–260.

Mobley, W. H. (1982). *Employee Turnover: Causes, Consequences and Control*, Reading, Mass.: Addison-Wesley.

Monahan, C. J. and Muchinsky, P. M. (1983). Three decades of personnel selection research: A state-of-the-art analysis and evaluation. *Journal of Occupational Psychology*, **56**, 215–225.

Motowidlo, S. J. (1983). Predicting sales turnover from pay satisfaction among sales representatives. *Journal of Applied Psychology*, **68**, 484–489.

Muchinsky, P. M. (1986). Personnel selection methods. In C. L. Cooper and I. T. Robertson (eds), *International Review of Industrial and Organizational Psychology, 1986*, Chichester and New York: John Wiley.

Murphy, K. R. (1988). Psychological measurement: abilities and skills. In Cooper, C. L. and Robertson, I. T. (eds), *International Review of Industrial and Organisational Psychology*, 3, London: John Wiley.

Nirtaut, D. J. (1977). Assessment centers: An examination of participants' reactions and adverse effects. *Journal of Assessment Center Technology*, **1**, 18–23.

Petty, M. M., McGee, G. W. and Cavender, J. W. (1984). A meta-analysis of the relationships between individual job satisfaction and individual performance. *Academy of Management Review*, **9**, 712–721.

Rasch, G. (1960). *Probabalistic Models for some Intelligence and Attainment Tests*, Copenhagen: Neilson & Lydiche.

Reilly, R. R. and Chao, G. T. (1982). Validity and fairness of some alternative employee selection procedures. *Personnel Psychology*, **35**, 1–62.

Robertson, I. T. (1986). Assessing managerial potential. In G. Debus and H. W. Schroiff (eds), *The Psychology of Work and Organization*, Elsevier Science Publishers BV (North Holland).

Robertson, I. T. and Downs, S. (1979). Learning and the prediction of performance: development of trainability testing in the United Kingdom. *Journal of Applied Psychology*, **64**, 42–50.

Robertson, I. T., Iles, P. A., Gratton, L. and Sharpley, D. S. (in preparation). The psychological impact of personnel selection methods on candidates.

Robertson, I. T. and Kandola, R. S. (1982). Work sample tests: Validity, adverse impact and applicant reaction. *Journal of Occupational Psychology*, **55**, 171–182.

Robertson, I. T. and Makin, P. J. (1986). Management selection in Britain: a survey and critique. *Journal of Occupational Psychology*, **59**, 45–57.

Sackett, P. R. (1987). Assessment centres and content validity: Some neglected issues. *Personnel Psychology*, **40**, 13–25.

Samejima, F. (1969). *Estimation of latent ability using a response pattern of graded scores*. Psychometric Monograph No 17.

Sands, W. A. (1985). An overview of the accelerated VAT-ASVAB program. *Proceedings of the 27th Annual Conference of the Military Testing Association*, pp. 19–22.

Schmitt, N. and Coyle, B. W. (1976). Applicant decisions in the employment interview. *Journal of Applied Psychology*, **61**, 184–192.

Schmitt, N., Ford, J. K., Stults, D. M. (1986). Changes in self-perceived ability as a function of performance in an assessment centre. *Journal of Psychology*, **59**, 327–335.

Schmitt, N., Gooding, R. Z., Noe, R. A. and Kirsch, M. (1984). Meta-analysis of validity studies published between 1964 and 1982 and the investigation of study characteristics. *Personnel Psychology*, **37**, 407–422.

Schmitt, N. and Ostroff, C. (1986). Operationalizing the 'behavioral consistency' approach: Selection test development based on a content-oriented strategy. *Personnel Psychology*, **39**, 91–108.

Smith, C. A., Organ, D. W. and Near, J. P. (1983). Organizational citizenship behavior: Its nature and antecedents. *Journal of Applied Psychology*, **68**, 653–663.

Smith, J. M. (1978). Computer produced vocational guidance reports. *Journal of Occupational Psychology*, **51**, 109–115.

Smith, M. (1982). Patsy's gift for spotting programming skill. *Practical Computing*, **5**, 108–114.

Sneath, F., Takur, M. and Medjuck, B. (1976). *Testing People at Work*, London: Institute of Personnel Management.

Steege, F. W. (1986). *Computer Assisted and Adoptive Testing as Part of a System of Measures of Personnel Psychology*. Paper presented at 21st International Congress of Applied Psychology, Jerusalem.

Stettgan, D. A., Gray, G. C. and Wasmundt, K. C. (1979). Development of a low-cost stand alone microterminal for support of testing and instruction. *Catalog of Selected Documents in Psychology*, **9**, 1–32.

Teel, K. S. and Dubois, H. (1983). Participants' reactions to assessment centers. *Personnel Administrator*, March, 85–91.

Tenopyr, M. L. and Oeltjen, P. D. (1982). Personnel selection and classification. *Annual Review of Psychology*, **33**, 581–618.

Tuller, W. L. and Barrett (1976). The future autobiography as a Predictor of Sales Success. *Journal of Applied Psychology*, **61**, 3, 371–373.

Ulrich, L. and Trumbo, D. (1965). The selection interview since 1949. *Psycological Bulletin*, **53**, 100–116.

Vale, D. C., Keller, L. S. and Bentz, V. J. (1986). Development of a computerized interpretation system for personnel tests. *Personnel Psychology*, **39**, 525–542.

Wildegrube, W. (1985). News about CAT in the German Federal Armed Forces. *Proceedings of the 27th Annual Conference of the Military Testing Association*, 96–1–1.

Wright, C. R. Jr (1969). Summary of research on the selection interview since 1964. *Personnel Psychology*, **22**, 391–413.

Wernimont, P. F. and Campbell, J. P. (1968). Signs, samples and criteria. *Journal of Applied Psychology*, **52**, 372–376.

9

Comments on Personnel Selection Methods

ROBERT M. GUION
Bowling Green State University, Ohio

Very plaintively, Robertson and Smith asked, 'why do employers persist in using poor methods?' One reason might be that, after hearing the public debates about the quality of our tests (Cronbach, 1975), they think poor methods are what we have to offer. Perhaps some of them even know something about our own dissatisfactions; for example, some psychologists have criticized general mental ability tests for not tapping the most critical intellectual skills that might be tapped by experimental procedures (Weinman and Cooper, 1981). Problems of ethnic bias resulted in massive and sometimes acerbic discussion (Jaeger, 1976), and continuing debates about testing issues abound (e.g. Landy, 1986; Lawshe, 1985).

At a different level, the reason might be that we have not adequately preached the virtues of our best selection methods to the heathen—or that the habits of the ages, and the exhortations of the charlatans, have more influence than science. After all, interviewing and star-gazing are ancient rites of decision, whereas the more effective modern forms of employment testing are relatively new. Can technical merit, or improvement of it, influence the palatability of the predictor choices of the ultimate users? Can their choices be improved technically? Perhaps this commentary should begin with a reconsideration of some technical concerns.

Advances in Selection and Assessment. Edited by M. Smith and I. T. Robertson
© 1989 John Wiley & Sons Ltd

CHARACTERISTICS OF PREDICTORS

A quarter of a century or more ago, the evaluation of a potential predictor was fairly simple. Predictors, at least the ones evaluated, were usually tests. In choosing tests, practical considerations came first: cost and availability (mentioned by Robertson and Smith in their (Figure 8.2), testing time, probable acceptability to candidates, and ease of administration. Test manuals were examined (if choosers of tests were relatively well informed) for information about reliability coefficients, norms, and prior evidence of validity. If a test passed these preliminary hurdles, it could then be validated using a few local applicants or employees. Validity was simply the correlation between test scores and a criterion, usually supervisory ratings on a 5-point scale. When the validity coefficient was known, the evaluation of the predictor seemed complete.

Problems and ramifications of validity

The raw empiricism implied in that description is a vanishing aspect of the *zeitgeist* for employment psychologists. The brief list of evaluative standards or predictor characteristics presented in Figure 8.2, in today's *zeitgeist*, seems excessively *ad hoc* and atheoretical. Only a few of them seem concerned with understanding what is happening when the predictor is used. As we approach the end of a century of employment testing (treating the work of Münsterberg, 1913, as the start of modern employment testing), we need more understanding; our evaluative standards should be more theory-based.

As Robertson and Smith have said, validity is—at least in the older sense— an 'old friend'. However, without a clearer, more theoretical understanding of what validity information should tell us, and what information should help us evaluate validity, I cannot agree with their assertion that its 'problems and ramifications are well known.' To begin the commentary, I shall pursue some issues and implications that, in my opinion, have not been adequately considered in evaluating personnel selection methods.

For one thing, it has long been clear that validity is not a characteristic of a test; rather, it is a characteristic of an inference drawn from scores (Cronbach, 1971). As a matter of fact, validity is itself an inference. It is an inference of the confidence one can have in attributing meaning to scores, an inference drawn from a variety of kinds of evidence. Useful evidence may consist of a variety of validity coefficients using various criteria, but it may also consist of judgments about test construction procedures, about structural properties of the test (content, form, instructions, scoring procedures, graphics or other stimulus properties, and the like), about psychometric properties of sets of responses to individual items or to the test as a whole, about the support for the intended meaning of the scores (so-called construct validity), and the freedom of those scores from contaminating sources of variance (American Educational Research Assn. *et al.* (AERA) 1985; Messick, in press; Society for Industrial and Organizational Psychology [SIOP], 1987). Indeed, Messick (in press) has indicated that consideration of the social consequences of testing, as well as the consequences for the individual tested, must be considered in a complete assessment of the validity of score inferences. From this broader view of what validity means, Robertson and Smith do, in fact, give special attention to two aspects of validity—the influence of change, in jobs or persons, and the possibility of unintended side-effects of testing on the meaning of testing and of test score interpretation. Nevertheless, I should like to offer some further comment on the 'problems and ramifications' of validity before moving on to the other issues.

The role of reliability in validity

Statistically, reliability has long been known to be a limiting factor in the computation of validity coefficients. High reliability does not assure good validity coefficients, but low reliability assures low ones.

This limiting role of reliability (more accurately, of unreliability) also limits the meaning that can be attached to scores; it is as important as evidence for inferences of construct validity as for criterion-related evidence of validity. Consider, for example, estimates of internal consistency. If a test is considered a measure of something—some one thing—responses to its various components (items) should stem from a single source of variance, that is, be internally consistent. A high level of internal consistency does not tell us that the scores are valid measures of the attribute, but a low level of internal consistency tells us rather clearly that they are not.

Similarly, the logic of prediction calls for stable attributes measured with stable or consistent scores. A high-stability coefficient does not tell us that the characteristic being measured will predict future behavior, but a low-stability coefficient is fairly decent evidence that the characteristic, as measured, will not. Or, if a test requires judgments in scoring, a similar limiting function is played by the consistency or agreement among observers or scorers. High levels of consistency among scorers may indicate nothing more valuable than a commonly held bias or stereotype, but low levels of agreement indicate that test scores are likely to be badly contaminated by individual differences in evaluative judgments about test responses; indeed, the scores may say more about an observer than about the person taking the test. In short, the first evidence that valid inferences are possible is evidence of high reliability expressed by the operations (internal consistency, stability, equivalence, agreement) appropriate for the intended inferences, and evidence of low reliability is an immediate warning that, despite any other data, only a slight level of validity can be inferred, if any.

Classical reliability theory has been extended by generalizability analysis (Cronbach, Gleser, Nanda and Rajaratnam, 1972) to examine further sources of error, hence of invalidity in the intended inferences from scores. Generalizability theory permits the analysis of various facets of the test situation, including traditional considerations of unreliability and conditions of administration, different administrators, specifiable circumstances of testing, etc. The basic, limiting implication for validity remains: where one cannot generalize across facets or conditions of facets, the inferred meaning of scores is constrained to precisely defined, standard situations. Their implications for job performance may be similarly constrained.

Reliability may be expressed in terms of standard errors of measurement as well as (some would say in preference to) by reliability coefficients. With the standard error of measurement one is evaluating an individual score rather than an entire distribution; indeed, the standard error may differ at different points in the distribution (AERA *et al.*, 1985, cf. Std. 2.10). It provides a measure of the precision of a score; if a score is imprecise (i.e. has a large standard error of measurement and therefore a substantial interval around a true score in which obtained scores might lie), that score can hardly be a valid indicator of the attribute being measured for the person who gets it. Modern item response theory (IRT) (Hulin, Drasgow and Parsons, 1983; Lord, 1980) replaces conventional notions of reliability and standard errors of measurement with an information function; it shows the precision of measurement at every level of the attribute measured. It also provides a formal, mathematical model of the attribute such that a given set of items satisfying the conditions of the model is likely (unless things went badly awry from the outset of test development) to provide generally valid scores. If the model works well, the full set of items in an IRT-developed test is unidimensional (i.e. measures some one thing). If the original item pool was developed with insight into the nature of the attribute to be measured, it is reasonable to infer that the scores can be validly interpreted as measures of that one attribute; the more precise the score, the more valid the inference about the attribute. Thus, a high information level (unlike a high-reliability coefficient) can be treated as positive evidence of validity. With low information, we cannot draw an inference about the attribute with much precision at all, which is tantamount to saying that virtually no inference about the attribute implied by the score is likely to be valid.

The role of content and test development

Valid inferences are possible from haphazardly developed tests, but it is not likely. Judgments of validity, or at least of the likelihood of validity, may be based in part on the procedures used in test development. A first, simple question is whether there is any evidence that the test developer had a clear idea of the attribute to be measured. At the very least, the evidence would be a coherent, semantic definition of the attribute, but more useful evidence of clarity of intent stems from clearly articulated statements of the relations of the attribute to other attributes or experiences. A subsequent question is whether the mechanics of the measurement method fit the concept of the attribute. Suppose, for example, that one wants or is developing a test of problem-solving ability, defined in part as the ability to define problems and to identify alternative potential solutions. There would be good reason to question the validity of an inference of this ability from a score on a test where every item poses a specific problem and seeks the one correct answer to it. In Guilford's (1967) terms, one is unlikely to get a valid measure of divergent thinking ability using convergent thinking items.

The content of the test is closely related. In the days when people still spoke of 'content validity' (e.g. Guion, 1977), the question was how closely the content of the test matched some *a priori* definition of the content domain. If one wants to be able to infer level of knowledge about spectroscopy in metallurgy, for example, then one expects the content of the test to be a sample of a larger domain of such knowledge. This remains even with the demise of content validity as a meaningful term (AERA *et al.*, 1985; Guion, 1980; Messick, 1975; SIOP, 1987), an important question to answer in judging validities of inferences from scores. The appropriateness of content is, however, more than just the sampling of a predefined domain. Is it at a level appropriate to the intended examinees? Has similar content defined the relevant factor in previous factor analytic research? Is the content logically relevant to the attribute to be measured? If the attribute is multifaceted, does the content reflect all major facets or is it restricted to some one or a few of them? In multiple choice items, is the content of the distractors plausible, is there more than one (if any) correct answer, are cues to the correct answer provided in the stem? Answers to all such questions are important factors in a judgment of the validity of possible inferences from scores on the test.

Evaluation of validity may also include an evaluation of the structural properties of the test. This term (not to be confused with Loevinger's, 1957, more important concept of structural fidelity) encompasses matters such as the test length in time or in items, the operational independence of the items, the forms of item response required (e.g. open-end vs multiple choice), the psychometric properties of item responses and the distributions of such properties throughout the test, the evidence for any parallel forms that might be claimed, the nature of the distributions of scores in different samples, etc. Such structural properties tell a user how well the test developer defined or met intended test characteristics and, more importantly, how effective the test might prove to be in the intended uses.

The roles of correlates

The conventional correlate of interest in discussions of validity of selection tests is the correlation with a job-related criterion; the inference of interest is the probable level of performance on that criterion. If the correlation is high, the inference of effective performance from a relatively high score is considered valid; if the correlation is low, the inference of effective performance from the same score is considered to have little validity if any.

Such an inference, however, is *not* an interpretation of the *meaning* of the score; it is a statistical inference, not a measurement inference. The prediction (inference) of future performance can be done as well—usually better—with a composite of uncorrelated components that has little meaning if any beyond its ability to predict a specific criterion. I prefer to restrict my idea of validity to the inferential meaning of the test score as a measure of an attribute of examinees and to use a different term, job relatedness (or relevance), to refer to the inference based on statistical prediction. I shall have more to say about this in the next section.

Here, in my more restricted use of the term *validity*, the correlates of interest are those that contribute to the clarity of the meaning of a score on the test. This use of the term is most closely related to the meaning many writers have when they refer to construct validity (e.g. Guion, 1980; Loevinger, 1957; Messick, in press). I need not dwell on the various aspects of construct validity, but I will offer two comments before moving on. First, constructs are ideas, products of thought and imagination. They may be new ideas or old ones that have been widely studied. Because constructs may be new, even vague ideas, it is inappropriate to say that construct validation involves the testing and validation of an entire, firmly developed nomological network (Cronbach, 1987).

Second, at least some evidence should confirm the intended interpretations. In part, such confirmation comes from the logic of the articulated intention, the appropriateness of the measurement operations, and the appropriateness of test content; these are judgments that may provide initial but relatively weak confirmation or, if the judgments are essentially negative, provide rather profound disconfirmation. Confirmation also comes from empirical evidence that scores correlate with other variables in expected ways, either confirming intended interpretations or disconfirming competing ones.

Understanding the validity of inferences from test scores depends on the amount and kinds of evidence collected. So long as a test continues to be used in practice or in research, new evidence will accumulate. More evidence is better than less; strong evidence is better than weak; consistent evidence is better than inconsistent or contradictory evidence. Despite these truisms, at the time a decision must be made about a test, it is the preponderance of the accumulated evidence that determines the judgment of validity.

Job relatedness

A criterion-related validity study with a job-related criterion provides evidence of the job relatedness of the test. In this sense, in my usage of the terms *validity* and *job relatedness*, the evidence will coincide or overlap, that is, the same validity coefficient gives evidence both of validity and job relatedness. There are, however, other operations for demonstrating job relatedness that require a clear interpretation of scores in terms of attributes being measured—i.e. validity.

One reason for insisting on a distinction between these terms is the fact that this traditional merger of them through criterion-related validation is not feasible nearly so often as we used to think. There are two reasons. One is that the number of cases needed for a validation study to have adequate power is much larger than once thought (e.g. Schmidt, Hunter and Urry, 1976), and there are relatively few selection problems where the numbers of cases, the validity of criterion measurement, and range of available distributions of predictors and criteria will support the traditional validation study. The other is that the interest in selection is moving to filling single positions, where by definition there is but one opening to be filled regardless of the number of potential candidates. Even where there are several similar positions to be filled, if the number to be filled is quite small relative to the number of available applicants, the resulting restriction of range renders the traditional computation of a validity coefficient infeasible. An example at Rowntree Mackintosh reported by Andrew Harley (personal communication, 22 May 1987) consisted of openings for 40 people for which there were some 5000 applicants. The example identifies not only a problem with traditional validation models but a practical problem of how to process such a large number of applicants. Some logical procedure is needed to reduce the number to manageable size without denying opportunity to meritorious applicants or denying the company the opportunity to consider their merits.

The alternative to traditional validation is a two-step process for judging the job relatedness of predictors. The first step involves an analysis of the position, its responsibilities, and its relationships to other positions within the organization. From such analyses, one can draw some inferences about the attributes a successful candidate should have; valid measures of such attributes may then be considered job-related (Guion, 1987).

The considerations discussed here can also be used for evaluating other potential predictors with only slight modifications of language. It is a theme to which I shall return.

THE SEARCH FOR BETTER PREDICTORS

Can we provide better predictors? Surely we can achieve still greater levels of validity and job relevance, and perhaps these achievements will be more easily recognized by employers as truly great. Knowing the flaws in our best efforts, we may be quite skilled in looking for still better ones.

It would be unreasonable to suppose that any potential predictor could ever be devised that would merit a near-perfect score on all possible evaluative characteristics; the best one can ask is that the intended uses be supported by most of the important kinds of evidence. One need not be terribly cynical, however, to suspect that most predictors now used would not measure up well. Even in validity coefficients, as Robertson and Smith have said, we have no reason to believe that the maximum validity coefficient for a single predictor, estimated at 0.50, is any better now than it was sixty years ago (Hull, 1928). Although tests, specifically work sample tests and composites of mental ability and psychomotor tests, may offer the best available predictions (cf. Figure 8.5), the search for better predictors, like hope, springs eternal.

New constructs and methods

Robertson and Smith have summarized progress in computer-assisted testing, one of the uses of new technology. Computerized testing seems to be more than just another way to measure the same constructs we have measured in other ways; it may point the way to measuring constructs hitherto not measured at all. That is, the use of the microcomputer can permit inferences about the *processes* examinees use in reaching their final responses; instead of an overall score on, for example, spatial ability, one may be able to develop and interpret scores for the several ways spatial information can be processed in achieving that overall score. Inferences about the mental processes would surely be an aid to understanding resulting test scores. It does not necessarily follow that they would provide greater job relatedness of either the overall scores or scores for the component processes. If, as Frederiksen (1986) pointed out, format, personal characteristics, and testing situation can influence such processes, the generalizability from process in computer-assisted testing to process in job performance is currently not known. It is an empirical question whether knowledge of process will add predictability to knowledge of outcome (i.e. total score, however achieved).

Other uses of new technology can be suggested as sources of potentially new, improved predictors, but similar empirical questions remain to be answered for them. Many of these stem from measures developed from the constructs and methods of other research fields in psychology and education. Effective use of microcomputers in such research suggests a variety of new ideas for predictors. Work requires the processing of information; measures of effectiveness in basic information processing should be relevant to work of nearly all kinds and may lead to job-related composite measures predicting job performance better than traditional mental ability tests. Employment selection testers should be familiar with studies of individual differences in modern cognitive research (e.g. Dillon, 1985; Dillon and Schmeck, 1983; Sternberg and Wagner, 1986); many of the measures reported in them may provide the basis for a new era in selection test research. Cognitive measures beyond simple reaction time are potentially valuable for predicting such job activities as accuracy or speed of inspection, cleverness in forming hypotheses in troubleshooting (electronic, financial, or whatever), or classifying events, materials, or ideas.

Stress research has studied variables that might be, or might lead to, useful predictors of performance at work. Studies of the stress induced by tasks requiring divided attention could well lead to the development of job-related predictors either of health-related criteria or performance; quite possibly, ability to perform such jobs effectively may determine the level of stress experienced. Another potential example is the use of the evoked potential as an indicator of fatigue or of drug effects (Rizzuto, 1985); by using tasks that reflect or sample the nature of the attention-demanding jobs, and measuring changes in evoked visual or auditory potentials while performing these tasks, one may be able to predict which candidates for demanding jobs will be able to maintain alertness for long periods of time, i.e. have some resistance to fatigue or boredom. In both examples, of course, we are star-gazing; empirical data are needed before any enthusiasm erupts.

Computer-managed learning, using interactive video disks, has been reported in use in British Telecomm (B. Stewart, personal communication, 22 May 1987) for training interviewers. The technique could be adapted to develop tests of social skills for the selection of interviewers or others whose work requires a substantial level of interpersonal contact. New technology has also aided the old practice of obtaining self-appraisals. Dr D. Aris (personal communication, 22 May 1987) reported that self-appraisals have been found useful in a number of Dutch companies when done with microcomputer aid. Apparently, a sense of privacy in working with the computer seems to reduce the social desirability component.

Over the last several decades, many good ideas have emerged and have seemed promising for new kinds of selection testing—and have not kept the promises. Some failures may have been due only to failure to do the necessary intermediate development research. Perhaps other new ideas simply were not good enough, that is, were little more than novel ways to measure things that were already measured reasonably well by more conventional means. Some of the new technology may also fail to result in new, improved prediction of work performance; we will not know unless the development research is done.

Improving existing predictors

Perhaps the search for better predictors would be better served by improving those that will be used anyway. Robertson and Smith reported that interviews and references are the most frequently used predictors, and similar findings have been reported elsewhere (American Society for Personnel Administration

[ASPA], 1983). References and interviews rank rather low in the list of mean validity coefficients. Can they be made better?

I suspect, without any data at all, that any improvement made in the use of references will come about by treating the reference check as a structured interview, albeit by telephone; I hold little hope for written references. Reliance on the integrity, motivation, knowledge, and willingness of letter writers seems so doomed as to merit no comment. But improvement by turning the reference check into an interview? After all we know about the problems of the interview? Have I gone daft?

If we consider the conventional wisdom about interviews, the idea of using interviewing procedures in reference checks would be daft indeed. The conventional wisdom, however, deserves to be questioned. It is based on a research body, and a series of research reviews, that have been based on an erroneous assumption: the assumption that there is an entity called 'the interview', that validation studies on the interview have been done just as they have been done on entities such as 'the' general mental ability test, and that the results of such studies have persistently shown little or no reliability or validity for the interview (e.g. Mayfield, 1964; Schmitt, 1976; Ulrich & Trumbo, 1965; Wagner, 1949; Wright, 1969), although some of the reviews have culminated in suggestions for ways to 'fix' the interview to make it more valid. The fixes have not fared particularly well. Mayfield advocated studying and improving small components, but five years later, the judgment was that no 'fix' had been achieved: 'It is possible to sympathize with Mayfield's call for more microanalytic research and yet deplore the preciosity that characterizes so much of this style of research on the selection interview. Much microanalytic research is so contrived as to approach a level of patent sterility that precludes replication or extension of the line of investigation' (Wright, p. 409). The culprit in all this seems to be the monolithic assumption of 'the' interview—that one interview, or one interviewer, is pretty much like another. A more recent review (Arvey and Campion, 1982) held out more hope (although it was anticipated in some earlier reviews) for structured as opposed to unstructured interviews, i.e. a structured interview is *not* pretty much like an unstructured interview. More recently, Arvey and his colleagues backed up the suggestion by demonstrating in a replicated, large-sample study that structured interviews, across interviewers, can have validity coefficients at least as high as those ordinarily expected from mental ability tests or even test batteries (Arvey, Miller, Gould and Burch, 1987). A particular form of structured interview, the situational interview, has been held out as a most promising approach to interview improvement by Robertson and Smith.

I have at least as much hope for improvement through studying individual differences among interviewers as for various structures of interviews. Consider three different studies. First, in 1973, Valenzi and Andrews contrived a set 243 paper people, each representing a secretarial applicant, each judged independently by four experienced interviewers. The interviewers used the information in markedly different ways, resulting in markedly different judgments about these 'applicants'. Of course, this study, like so many of the microanalytic studies, was contrived, and there are serious questions about the generalizability of the paper people paradigm to real-life interviews (see Gorman, Clover and Doherty, 1978).

Second, in 1983, Zedeck, Tziner, and Middlestadt had 412 candidates for officer training interviewed by one of ten experienced interviewers. Candidates were rated on nine dimensions and on an overall scale representing acceptance or rejection of the applicant. Those admitted to the training program were subsequently evaluated by the school faculty, and those evaluations were regressed on the nine interview ratings. Despite some similarities in the regression weights, and despite uniformly high multiple correlation coefficients, there were pronounced differences among them in the judgment strategies reported. Correlations of overall ratings with school evaluations, combining all data, were essentially zero. Numbers were too small for individual correlations, but a novel analysis suggested validity differences among interviewers.

Third, in 1986, Dougherty, Ebert, and Callender studied three experienced interviewers who rated 120 job applicants; noteworthy differences were found in the correlations of interviewer ratings with subsequent criteria; moreover, training in the use of three key rating dimensions showed improvements in validity for all raters. These studies differ markedly, but all call attention to the not-surprising fact that different interviewers see candidates differently. Moreover, some interviewers are better than others in predicting the future behavior of candidates, as Dougherty et al. (1986) found. All things considered, it seems likely that structured interviews, based on clear understanding of the nature of the work to be done and conducted by well-trained interviewers whose judgment policies have been adequately modeled, can be as valid as other selection procedures.

The operations that distinguish a test from test score interpretations will not be closely matched by operations distinguishing an interview *per se* from the judgments reached, yet clearly it is the judgments reached that may be evaluated for validity. The analog of the test is not the interview but the interviewer. Meta-analysis across interviewers may serve a function similar to meta-analysis across different tests of similar purpose, but it is premature to assume a generalization of validity, even of validity coefficients, across all interviewers willy-nilly.

Consider the broader concept of validity in the context of the validities of an interviewer's judgments. The judgments surely must be reliable to be valid, but this requirement takes on further meaning in the context of reliable judgments: the policy for reaching the judgments must be exercised consistently, as indicated by the high multiple correlations for predictions of overall judgments in the three policy-capturing studies. Interview content is defined by the questions posed and the information given; the content will necessarily contribute to validity if it is informed by sensible job analysis and systematized in a sensible planned structure. The judgments can be evaluated for confirmatory evidence, as Dougherty *et al.* (1986) did in having supervisors rate the employees who had been interviewed on the same scales used by the interviewers. They can be evaluated for evidence of contaminating influences, such as the proportion of the time the interviewer (rather than the interviewee) does the talking (Daniels and Otis, 1950). In short, multiple pieces of evidence can be developed for validating and determining the job relatedness of judgments of interviewers, just as can be done for test score interpretations, and some, if not all, interviewers will be found to make valid judgments about job candidates. The research should be done.

The plaintive question will remain, however. Even if evidence that the interviewers' decisions are valid and job-related does indeed result from the research, will employers and interviewers do the necessary job analyses, structure the interviews appropriately, validate the judgments, and provide really relevant training so that valid interviewer judgments become commonplace? History gives no reason for optimism.

Before leaving the topic, return momentarily to the reference check. Can one analyze the job for which a candidate is being considered; formulate job-related questions that former employers, teachers, or others can answer; structure such questions in a sensible sequence; arrive at judgments; and be trained to make those judgments systematically and reliably? If these things can be done for interviews with candidates, they can be done for interviews with references; if they can be shown to result in more valid and job-relevant interviews with candidates, they can probably be shown to result in more valid and job-relevant reference checks. The popular, widely used predictors *can* be made better. It remains to be seen whether the improved versions will be more widely used.

CHANGE AND THE IMPACT OF SELECTION

We train people because we know people can change. In selecting people, we tend to forget their modifiability and concentrate instead on their stabilities, the fact that the characteristics present at the time of hire will continue to characterize them for a long time and will influence their behavior at work. Perhaps the most exciting part of the Robertson and Smith chapter is its insistence that change and the impact of selection deserve to be more widely considered in research and practice in employee selection.

Not only people change; jobs change, too. Some of the change in jobs is induced by changes in products or changes in technology, but part of it is induced by changes in the people who do them. Several people may be hired simultaneously to do virtually identical work; after time, some of those in the group will come to specialize in one aspect of the job, others will emphasize other aspects, and their jobs will no longer be quite the same. In part this may be adaptation to one's own abilities, interests, and limitations; in part it may be adaptations to the abilities, interests, and limitations of others in the work group. Whatever the source, people and their jobs change, and those involved in selection need to face the fact. One suggestion for facing it, and for considering the effect of the selection process itself on the candidate for employment, is to make selection more a joint decision process. Being candid with the candidate, as in realistic job previews, gives the selection process an aura of job or career development counseling. The result may be a kind of 'investment model' for job applicants—and a more dynamic, less static, individualistic process. Perhaps such tailoring will weaken the standardization of the process and, consequently, its validity. (In testing, however, 'tailored' testing has led to redefinition of standardization and to improved testing.) Maybe one implication of an individualized process is that old models of validation may be inadequate. If so, we may rejoice in the insight and move on to newer ones. Program evaluation models come to mind as likely candidates.

Another implication of the fact of change is that one may need to consider two quite different criteria in the hiring process. It may continue to be advisable to hire for the position at hand, as we typically do now, and also for the ability to learn and to adapt to change. The latter presents problems. In the United States, equal employment opportunity regulations tend to discourage attempts to predict for unknown conditions; moreover, there is a need to develop a theory of how and why people change and of the individual worker's influence in changing jobs.

Research in selection has generally focused on the interests and values of the organization. Robertson and Smith in their chapter, and Messick (in print) elsewhere, have argued that selection research must consider the interests and values of the individual and of the larger society. For testing, indeed, Messick has included the existence of possibly unintended side-effects within his concept of validity. Whether subsumed under validity or singled out for special attention, the wider effects of selection and of individual components of the selection process need to be understood. Figure 8.7 in Robertson and Smith's chapter identifies an ambitious and needed research program, and we ought to be getting on with it.

REFERENCES

American Educational Research Assn, American Psychological Assn, and National Council on Measurement in Education (1985). *Standards for Educational and Psychological Testing*. Washington: American Psychological Association.

American Society for Personnel Administration (1983). *Employee Selection Procedures* (ASPA-BNA Survey No. 45). Washington DC: Bureau of National Affairs.

Arvey, R. D. and Campion, J. E. (1982). The employment interview: a summary and review of recent research. *Personnel Psychology*, **35**, 281–322.

Arvey, R. D., Miller, H. E., Gould, R. and Burch, P. (1987). Interview validity for selecting sales clerks. *Personnel Psychology*, **40**, 1–12.

Cronbach, L. J. (1971). Test validation. In R. L. Thorndike (ed.), *Educational measurement*, 2nd edn. Washington: American Council on Education.

Cronbach, L. J. (1975). Five decades of public controversy over mental testing. *American Psychologist*, **30**, 1–14.

Cronbach, L. J. (1987). Five perspectives on validation argument. In H. Wainer and H. Braun (eds), *Test Validity*. Hillsdale NJ: Erlbaum.

Cronbach, L. J., Gleser, G. C., Nanda, H. and Rajaratnam, N. (1972). *The Dependability of Behavioral Measurements: Theory of Generalizability for Scores and Profiles*. New York: Wiley.

Daniels, H. W. and Otis, J. L. (1950). A method for analyzing employment interviews. *Personnel Psychology*, **3**, 425–444.

Dillon, R. F. (ed.) (1985). *Individual Differences in Cognition*, vol. 2. Orlando FL: Academic Press.

Dillon, R. F. and Schmeck, R. R. (eds) (1983). *Individual Differences in Cognition*, vol. 1. New York: Academic Press.

Dougherty, T. W., Ebert, R. J. and Callender, J. C. (1986). Policy capturing in the employment interview. *Journal of Applied Psychology*, **71**, 9–15.

Frederiksen, N. (1986). Toward a broader conception of human intelligence. *American Psychologist*, **41**, 445–452.

Gorman, C. D., Clover, W. H. and Doherty, M. E. (1978). Can we learn anything about interviewing real people from 'interviews' of paper people? Two studies of the external validity of a paradigm. *Organizational Behavior and Human Performance*, **22**, 165–192.

Guilford, J. P. (1967). *The Nature of Human Intelligence*. New York: McGraw Hill.

Guion, R. M. (1977). Content validity—the source of my discontent. *Applied Psychological Measurement*, **1**, 1–10.

Guion, R. M. (1980). On trinitarian doctrines of validity. *Professional Psychology*, **11**, 385–398.

Guion, R. M. (1987). Changing views for personnel selection research. *Personnel Psychology*, **40**, 199–213.

Hulin, C. L., Drasgow, F. and Parsons, C. K. (1983). *Item Response Theory: Application to Psychological Measurement*. Homewood IL: Dow Jones-Irwin.

Hull, C. L. (1928). *Aptitude Testing*. Yonkers-on-Hudson NY: World Book.

Jaeger, R. M. (1976). On bias in selection [Special issue]. *Journal of Educational Measurement*, **13**, 1–99.

Landy, F. J. (1986). Stamp collecting versus science: validation as hypothesis testing. *American Psychologist*, **41**, 1183–1192.

Lawshe, C. H. (1985). Inferences from personnel tests and their validity. *Journal of Applied Psychology*, **70**, 237–238.

Loevinger, J. (1957). Objective tests as instruments of psychological theory. *Psychological Reports*, **3**, 635–694. (Monograph Supplement 9)

Lord, F. M. (1980). *Applications of Item Response Theory to Practical Testing Problems*. Hillsdale NJ: Erlbaum.

Mayfield, E. C. (1964). The selection interview: a re-evaluation of published research. *Personnel Psychology*, **17**, 239–260.

Messick, S. (1975). The standard problem: meaning and values in measurement and evaluation. *American Psychologist*, **30**, 955–966.

Messick, S. (in press). Validity. In R. L. Linn (ed.), *Educational Measurement*, 3rd edn. New York: Macmillan.

Münsterberg, H. (1913). *Psychology and Industrial Efficiency*. Boston: Houghton-Mifflin.

Rizzuto, A. P. (1985). *Diazepam and its effects on psychophysiological and behavioral measures of performance* (Doctoral dissertation, Bowling Green State University). Bowling Green OH.

Schmidt, F. L., Hunter, J. E. and Urry, V. W. (1976). Statistical power in criterion-related validation studies. *Journal of Applied Psychology*, **61**, 473–485.

Schmitt, N. (1976). Social and situational determinants of interview decisions: implications for the employment interview. *Personnel Psychology*, **29**, 79–101.

Society for Industrial and Organizational Psychology (1987). *Principles for the Validation and Use of Personnel Selection Procedures*, 3rd edn. College Park MD: Author.

Sternberg, R. J. and Wagner, R. K. (eds) (1986). *Practical Intelligence: Nature and Origins of Competence in the Everyday World*. New York: Cambridge University Press.

Ulrich, L. and Trumbo, D. (1965). The selection interview since 1949. *Psychological Bulletin*, **63**, 100–116.

Valenzi, E. R. and Andrews, I. R. (1973). Individual differences in the decision process of employment interviewers. *Journal of Applied Psychology*, **58**, 49–53.

Wagner, R. (1949). The employment interview: a critical summary. *Personnel Psychology*, **2**, 17–46.

Weinman, J. and Cooper, R. L. (1981). Individual differences in perceptual problem-solving ability: a response analysis approach. *Intelligence*, **5**, 165–178.

Wright, O. R. Jr (1969). Summary of research on the selection interview since 1964. *Personnel Psychology*, **22**, 391–413.

Zedeck, S., Tziner, A. and Middlestadt, S. E. (1983). Interviewer validity and reliability: an individual analysis approach. *Personnel Psychology*, **36**, 335–370.

10

A Case Study Examining the Accuracy of Predictors

CLAUDE LEVY-LEBOYER
Université René Descartes, Paris

THE ISSUE

Insurance company X had difficulty in recruiting new agents to run agencies in the provinces, selling life insurance, as well as more traditional products (car insurance, dwelling insurance and the like). The difficulty arose from the fact that the company did not wish to increase the number of the agencies, only to replace retired agents. These retired agents usually created and developed their agency, they owned their business and had a contract with the company—implying that they were allowed to sell it to a newcomer provided he was accepted in the company. This no longer worked, as candidates able to buy the agency were more and more difficult to find. The company is now setting up a system of loans for 'good candidates'. Thus it needs, more than before, to have a valid predictor of candidate's achievement.

METHOD

Job analysis

A job analysis was performed with three well-established agents in a small, a medium size and a large agency. It showed that the main activity of the agent was devoted to contacts with his clients in selling contracts and managing

Advances in Selection and Assessment. Edited by M. Smith and I. T. Robertson

them. This involved a thorough understanding of the products the agent was selling and social skills in dealing with clients, persuading them or helping them to complete a file when they applied for reimbursements. The administrative part of managing the contracts was mostly in the hands of the company.

After discussion with the personnel department, it was decided to test an experimental battery of selection tools against production and supervisors' ratings after one year. Production was measured through a percentage of the assigned quotas. Ratings did not exist previously in a shape which could be used for an experimental procedure: supervisors (*inspecteurs*) usually visited new agents twice in the first year and wrote a narrative report based on their observations. Moreover, the supervisors' activities as help for the new agent or as rater were not clearly separated: reports were both an account of the agent's behaviour and results of the supervisor's action in trying to correct what was considered as a faulty behaviour.

The experimental battery

This was composed of:
  (i) a leaderless group test where the group was in charge of writing a paper on '*Les 10 commandements*' of the insurance agent;
 (ii) two general intelligence tests, one verbal, one non-verbal;
(iii) two verbal abilities tests;
 (iv) the Guildford–Zimmerman personality questionnaire.

The 'subjective' criterion

This was developed using four steps: (1) a list of behaviour considered important for success was generated by a first group of supervisors; (2) these behaviours were rated for importance by a second group of supervisors; (3) the list was edited after discarding behaviours with a high variance of the rating, and after a work session with the company executives on these behaviours in order to clarify their sale policy; (4) each behaviour of the final list received a positive or a negative weight between −2 and +2 based on the mean ratings of importance given in step (2).

A group of 483 subjects was tested during a period of 6 months. The mean age of the subjects was 30 with a standard deviation of 5.3. Their level of education was fairly homogeneous, most of them having had secondary education; their occupational experience was largely in the tertiary sectors, either in office jobs or in selling jobs. Among these 483 candidates, 125 were chosen by the company, using the current procedure based on interviews with two members of the production department and one member of the personnel department. None of these people participated in the leaderless group test and no data from the experimental battery was made available to them.

RESULTS

(1) *Analysis of the actual selection process*: no subject under the 4th decile in one or the other test of general intelligence was recruited; otherwise there was no significant difference betwee the 145 recruited and the 358 not recruited. Age was higher in the recruited group but not significantly so (32.4 against 29.2).

(2) *Interrelations among test results*: various correlations were calculated between the different results; the most interesting relationships being observed between the LGD ratings and the test results. A general rating of activity was given to each subject after the LGD on the following scale: no participation—some participation—active participation—very active participation. Moreover a rating was given by the raters on a 5-point scale on the social quality of the subjects as shown during the LGD.

Relationships between the participation scale and the intelligence scores, on one hand, and the participation scale and the verbal test scores on the other hand were not significant (rbis = 0.17 and −0.05).

Between the 4 tests and the ratings of 'social quality', there is a clear relationship, as shown by the variance analysis (Snedecor F all significant for $p > 0.1$).

(3) *Validity*: after one year of work as insurance agents, the 145 agents were rated by their supervisors on the check list prepared as described above. No significant relationship was found between these ratings and any of the tests described above. But when we classified the subjects according both to their intelligence and verbal scores and to their participation rates, subdividing each category of the participation scale in two groups of 'gifted' and 'less gifted', we obtained a classification of the subjects in 8 subgroups. Among these 8 subgroups, the rate of success, as indicated by the check list scores, was significantly different:

		N	% successful after 1 year
No participation	gifted	12	8%
	less gifted	14	86%
Some participation	gifted	22	54%
	less gifted	21	86%
Active participation	gifted	24	54%
	less gifted	23	69%
Very active participation	gifted	15	26%
	less gifted	14	71%
		145	48%

These research results still belong to the insurance company; we are not allowed to publish more specific figures. But the table above shows clearly that when a subject does not participate in the LGD and belongs to the 'gifted' group, the low rate of participation is due not to cognitive and verbal deficiency but to problems in social relations skill—which explains why the prediction of success in sales activity is very poor. On the other hand, the 'less gifted' who overcome their own deficiencies and manage to be active in the LGD have excellent prospects. The same trend emerges in the intermediate ranking.

11

Fairness in Employment Selection

NEAL SCHMITT
Michigan State University

The primary reason for developing personnel selection procedures and conducting personnel selection research has always been the prediction of employee performance and selection of those individuals whose predicted performance was best. Recent work on utility measurement (Boudreau, 1983a,b; Cascio, 1982a; Schmidt, Hunter, McKenzie and Muldrow, 1979) indicates that valid selection procedures can add substantially to organizational productivity.

At least since the passage of the Civil Rights Act of 1964, American society has demanded the consideration of a second goal: equal employment opportunity for various subgroups (minorities and women) in our society. In 1965, President Johnson issued Executive Order 11246 which prohibited discrimination in a manner similar to the Civil Rights Act but also required that all Federal contractors and subcontractors take *affirmative action* to ensure that employees are treated without regard to race, color, sex, religion, or national origin. Affirmative action has taken on various meanings for those minority groups underrepresented in the workforce (Ledvinka, 1982, pp. 118ff.) including (a) special recruitment efforts directed at applicants from minority groups, and (b) special treatment in hiring decisions or training programs for minority group members. This order plus subsequent court cases which have been tried under Title VII of the Civil Rights Act have used as a minimum standard the goal of approximately equal hiring rates for majority and minority groups. In fact, the determination of the degree to which different proportions of individuals from subgroups are hired is the initial step in equal employment cases (Arvey, 1979a; *Griggs* vs *Duke Power*, 1971). Because of the unique legis-

Advances in Selection and Assessment. Edited by M. Smith and I. T. Robertson
© 1989 John Wiley & Sons Ltd

lative background of this problem, nearly all of the research we cite in this chapter will have been generated in American workplaces. It turns out that these two goals—organizational productivity and affirmative action—are frequently in conflict. While the American political and legal systems have forced consideration of this conflict, it is likely an examination of selection procedures in other multicultural societies such as is now occurring in Israel would yield evidence of a similar conflict.

In this chapter, we begin with a brief summary of the literature on subgroup differences in performance on various selection instruments and differences in validity of selection instruments for members of different subgroups. We then describe the use of test-criterion relationships to make optimal predictions (Cleary, 1968) about individual job performance and the implications of such use for minority hiring. The practical significance of the conflict between organizational productivity goals and the goals of representational employment of various cultural/ethnic groups is then described. In a final section, we describe recent work on item bias which has resurrected some earlier issues regarding the 'problem' of test bias.

SELECTION INSTRUMENTS: SUBGROUP DIFFERENCES

Tests represent an attempt to objectify the employment process and to make the employment of persons on nonjob-relevant bases less possible. However, proponents of equal employment opportunity and affirmative action have correctly noted that many of the commonly used employment tests produce lower scores for members of minority groups than for majority group members. Further, use of tests has been attacked because these tests are usually developed using members of the majority group only. The position of these proponents of Equal Employment Opportunity is that tests are likely to be inappropriate (or nonvalid) for use with minority group members. The passage of the Civil Rights Act of 1964 and subsequent legal charges of the discriminatory use of tests prompted the examination of the differential validity of tests across subgroups. Differential validity refers to the possibility that predictions of job performance are more or less valid for a given subgroup than for other subgroups. In this section, we summarize evidence concerning both subgroup differences in means and validities of various selection instruments (see Schmitt and Noe, 1986, for a more detailed discussion of these differences). As will become obvious in subsequent sections, this evidence does not necessarily mean (1) the test is biased; or (2) that appropriate uses of the test are impossible.

Differential validity

Early discussions concerning whether tests were of different predictive value concluded that differential validity existed when the predictor-criterion relationship was significantly different from zero for one subgroup only (single group validity). Boehm (1972) and Humphreys (1973) argued effectively that the concern with single group validity was irrelevant and misdirected. Evidence of differential validity was present when a significant difference between subgroup validity coefficients was observed.

Further, Schmidt, Berner, and Hunter (1973) provided an analysis of the single group validity hypothesis using data from several hundred validity studies on black and white subgroups and concluded that the frequency of single group validity did not exceed that which would be expected if the subgroup population validities were equal. Using a much more powerful and direct test of the differences between racial subgroup validities, Hunter, Schmidt, and Hunter (1979) found a significant difference between black and white validities for 866 pairs of validity coefficients. The difference, however, was only 0.02 and in most practical instances, it would likely be trivial.

While there have been at least two series of papers arguing various issues concerning differential validity analyses (see April 1977, and February 1978, issues of *Journal of Applied Psychology*), the current professional consensus appears to be that validity coefficients are not significantly different across subgroups. In critiquing the two series of studies mentioned above, Linn (1978) states that 'sample correlations are consistent with the belief that the differences in population correlations are near zero' (p. 511). A similar statement has been incorporated in professional guidelines (Society for Industrial-Organizational Psychology, American Psychological Association, 1987) and it would appear that at least at the level of predictor-criterion correlations, there is little evidence of a black-white difference in validity coefficients at least for cognitive ability tests. After reviewing data from standard tests used for selection and prediction in schools and colleges, specialized training programs in the armed forces, and employment settings, Jensen (1980) concluded that differential validity was a nonexistent phenomenon.

Similar findings seem to occur when other ethnic groups are compared as well. In over 1000 comparisons of Hispanic-majority group validity coefficients from 19 different studies, Schmidt, Pearlman, and Hunter (1980) found no evidence for differential validity of employment tests. Zeidner (1987) has also provided data regarding scholastic aptitude tests for three Israeli ethnic groups: (a) Ariental (Asian/African), (b) European/American, and (c) Israeli. Analyses indicated little evidence of differential validity of aptitude test scores as a function of ethnic group membership.

Results of studies comparing male and female validities are less conclusive and suggest that women may be more predictable than men. Schmitt, Mellon, and Bylenga (1978) found statistically significant differences in validity coefficients for male and female subgroups. The differences between male and female groups were small (approximately 0.04) and most validity comparisons came from educational, not employment tests. More recently, Hirsh and

McDaniel (1987) conducted a meta-analysis of 59 male-female pairs of validity coefficients obtained during revalidation of the General Aptitude Test Battery. Results indicated that women's job performance was slightly more predictable (validity differences ranged from 0.04 to 0.10) than was the performance of men for cognitive, psychomotor, and perceptual ability measures. These male-female differences in validity coefficients were greatest for low complexity jobs.

Differences in validity and subgroup means for various predictors

While there appear to be no differences in validity coefficients for various subgroups, use of a selection procedure in a mixed group may still result in the selection of a small number of minority individuals if the minority group mean score on the predictor is substantially lower than the mean score of the majority group. With corresponding differences on the criterion, test use is not necessarily *unfair* to the *individual*, though very few members of the lower-scoring group will be selected. The important consideration is whether the *predictions* of subgroup differences in performance on some criterion match the *actual* subgroup differences on that criterion. It is obvious, then, that the predictor differences are important only relative to criterion differences. It is also true that tests of high as opposed to low validity produce greater proportions of hiring among lower scoring groups when separate regression equations are used (see Jensen, 1980, pp. 512–514). Hence, our attention in a recent paper (Schmitt and Noe, 1986) centered on subgroup mean differences on various predictors and the relative level of validity of these predictors. This previous review is summarized qualitatively in Table 11.1. For the purpose of

Table 11.1   Level of validity and subgroup mean differences for various predictors

Predictor	Validity	Subgroup mean difference
Cognitive ability and special aptitude	Moderate	Moderate
Personality	Low	Small
Interest	Low	?[a]
Physical ability	Moderate-High	Large[b]
Biographical info.	Moderate	?
Interviews	Low	Small(?)
Work samples	High	Small
Seniority	Low	Large(?)
Peer evaluations	High	?
Reference checks	Low	?
Academic performance	Low	Moderate(?)
Self-assessments	Moderate	Small
Assessment centers	High	Small

[a] Indicates either a lack of data or inconsistent data.
[b] Mean differences largely between male and female subgroups.

interpreting Table 11.1, *low* validity means less than 0.20, *moderate* validity means between 0.21 and 0.40, and *high* validity means above 0.40. Subgroup mean differences greater than 1.00 are classified as *large*; differences between 0.50 and 1.00 are described as *moderate*; and those less than 0.50 as *small*. In examining this table it is important to note that in nearly all cases, there are significant reported exceptions and that none of the figures cited are corrected for range restriction or criterion unreliability. In the next sections, we illustrate the effect of the level of validity and subgroup mean differences on the predictor on differential prediction, affirmative action, and organizational productivity.

DIFFERENTIAL PREDICTION

To summarize, there appears to be an absence of differences in subgroup validity coefficients, but sizable differences in means of minority and majority groups for most types of selection instruments. Both sets of data are relevant to the fair use of tests, but the real issue is the evaluation of differential prediction which includes consideration of validity coefficients *plus* standard errors of estimate, and the regression line that describes the predictor-criterion relationship (Linn, 1978; Jensen, 1980; Bartlett, Bobko, Mosier and Hannan, 1978). Criterion-related validation studies serve to provide regression equations whereby predictions of subsequent job applicants' job performance can be made. In this section, we examine the implications of the use of these regression equations. As indicated above, and as we will develop in this section, literature indicates that these regression equations are fair to the individual in the sense that her/his predicted job performance is not affected by subgroup status. The Cleary (1968) approach to test fairness involves use of separate subgroup regression equations when those equations are significantly different. Use of these regression equations to produce a single rank order of applicants based on their predicted scores will produce the best qualified set of employees; but they will not result in the selection of equal proportions of members of various subgroups when subgroup mean performance differs.

Test bias issues attracted a great deal of research attention in the 1970s. Earlier researchers agreed that the position which defines a test as fair only if there are no mean score differences between population subgroups was untenable (Guion, 1966). Such a definition assumes *a priori* a lack of real group differences on psychological traits which is not consistent with most empirical evidence. Cleary (1968) presented a definition which has become accepted by most psychometricians. It reads as follows:

A test is biased for members of a subgroup of the population if, in the prediction of a criterion for which the test was designed, consistent nonzero errors of prediction are made for members of the subgroup. In other words, the test is biased if

the criterion score predicted from the common regression line is consistently too
high or too low for members of the subgroup. (p. 115)

Cleary's definition and subsequent alternative, statistical definitions (Cole,
1973; Darlington, 1971; Linn, 1973; Thorndike, 1971) have been compared
repeatedly (Peterson and Novick, 1976; Schmidt and Hunter, 1974; Hunter
and Schmidt, 1976; Jensen, 1980). These comparisons have led to the view
that the most easily applied and rationally consistent model is Cleary's
approach. Her definition, as alluded to above, implies that if the regression
lines for blacks and whites or any other subgroup are not equal, then each
person will receive a statistically fair predicted criterion score only if separate
regression lines are used for the two groups. We return to this fairness issue
only to illustrate that the presence of subgroup mean differences on selection
tests is not terribly important if we adopt Cleary's definition of fair test use.
*What matters is the bias, or lack of bias, present in the criterion against which the test
has been validated.* This latter possibility has received relatively little attention,
as we will see below.

Using Cleary's definition, most research evidence indicates a slight overpre-
diction of minority group performance when a single or common regression
equation is used. However, use of different regression equations produces
average predicted performance for subgroups which is identical to the actual
difference, hence unbiased by the Cleary formulation.

When using separate regression equations, it does not make any difference
that predictor mean differences are equal to, less than, or greater than criterion
mean differences. Such differences can be corrected by a simple arithmetic
procedure based on separate regression equations. In making the corrections,
however, we assume that the criterion against which the test has been validated
is itself unbiased. Schmidt and Hunter (1974) as well as others (Guion, 1966;
Cleary, 1968; Thorndike, 1971) have cautioned that no meaningful analysis of
test fairness issues can be undertaken without an unbiased criterion. Given the
recognized criticality of the criterion, it is surprising that most of the attention
in the test bias literature, or in the courts for that matter, has been directed
to predictor rather than to criterion measurement.

A final critical point for affirmative action considerations should be made
about the use of separate regression equations for subgroups. Use of separate
regression equations will result in the selection of relatively few members of
the lower-scoring group. Consider the case in which the minority and majority
group means differ by one standard deviation for both predictor and criterion
measures. The proportion of minority group persons selected given various
levels of the selection ratio (proportion of applicants selected) and using
separate regression equations as prescribed by Cleary (1968) would always be
much lower than the proportion of majority persons selected and would justify
a claim of adverse impact in American courts. Actual proportions of minority

members hired for various situations are presented in Table 4 of Schmitt and Noe (1986).

Low validity and low selection ratios produce the most severe adverse impact. The crux of the conflict between affirmative action goals and productivity goals is the following. A procedure which produces the best possible potential employees and which is fair to the individuals of both groups in the sense that the expectation or prediction of their job performance matches their actual performance, will result in the hiring of a very small proportion of the minority group members.

In analyzing test fairness issues, we alluded to the critical assumption that the criterion against which tests are validated is unbiased. Only recently has much research attention been directed to criterion bias as it relates to minority-majority performance differences. In the next section of our chapter, we attempt to summarize research and research issues regarding measurement of minority and majority job performance.

CRITERION RESEARCH

Various researchers have continued to note the importance of the criterion and have indicated the need for more research on relationships among criteria of job performance (Tenopyr and Oeltjen, 1982; Zedeck and Cascio, 1984). Bias, as traditionally defined, assumes a lack of congruence between job performance measures (actual criteria) and an ultimate criterion defined as a person's true organizational worth for the purposes of this chapter. Bias is systematic or consistent measurement of something other than the ultimate criterion. Examination of differences in subgroup performance on various criteria, as well as studies of the relationship among criteria, will not provide absolute answers to the bias problem since we do not have *the* ultimate criterion. However, such studies will provide greater understanding of various criteria and may also tell us when to expect large differences among various subgroups. Looking at the correlates of these subgroup differences may also yield hypotheses and understanding concerning reasons for subgroup differences.

Both laboratory and field studies of the relationship between objective and subjective criterion measures have been reported. While laboratory studies typically report a high degree of relationship (Bigoness, 1976; Borman, 1978; Schmitt and Lappin, 1980), field studies typically report objective-subjective correlations that are close to zero (e.g. Seashore, Indik and Georgopoulos, 1960; Kirchner, 1960; Bass and Turner, 1973). Recently, Heneman (1983) reported that the median correlation across 14 studies of cost or profit-related criteria and subjective ratings of overall effectiveness was 0.28.

Of more direct relevance to the issue of bias in criterion measurement has been the work of Ford and Kraiger (Ford, Kraiger and Schechtman, 1986;

Kraiger and Ford, 1985). They have begun to study the degree to which race effects are present in various types of criteria. In their first analysis, Kraiger and Ford reviewed the results of 74 studies in which black raters rated both subgroups. Using meta-analytic procedures (Hunter, Schmidt, and Jackson, 1982) to combine data from different studies, they found that corrected mean correlations between ratee race and the performance ratings were 0.18 for white raters (who rated white ratees higher) and negative 0.22 for black raters (who rated black ratees higher). Estimates of d, a standard deviation measure of race effect size (Glass, 1976) were 0.37 and −0.45 respectively. Note that these differences are substantial and statistically significant, but not as large as the mean differences we usually observe for various kinds of selection instruments which were reviewed above. Kraiger and Ford also examined the degree to which five moderator variables either enhanced or restricted the extent of racial differences in the performance rating criteria. Race effects were larger in field than laboratory studies. Further, race effects declined as the percentage of blacks in the work group increased (a similar effect was found for women and men candidates in assessment center groups) (Schmitt and Hill, 1977). No differences in the race effect were found for different rating scales (trait versus behavioral rating scales) rating purposes (administrative versus research purposes), or when rater training was or was not undertaken.

In their second meta-analysis, Ford, Kraiger and Schechtman (1986) studied race effects in both subjective and objective indices of performance. In the 53 studies they identified which reported objective and subjective performance indices for different race subgroups, 44 different objective criteria were used. These 44 criteria were grouped into three categories of performance indicators (productivity and accuracy measures, as well as accidents and service complaints), absenteeism or tardiness, and cognitive criteria (training and job knowledge tests). In each of the 53 studies, ratings of overall effectiveness on the particular objective criterion measured were also available. Overall, race effects were strikingly similar for objective (point-biserial correlation of 0.21) and subjective criteria (point-biserial correlation of 0.20). Separate analyses of differences among the three criterion categories were conducted for both objective and subjective performance indices. While there were no significant differences among the three types of criteria for subjective performance ratings, the cognitive performance criteria ($r = 0.36$) exhibited a significantly higher race effect than did the absenteeism ($r = 0.16$) or performance indicator ($r = 0.11$) categories. The cognitive criteria were written tests similar to the cognitive paper and pencil tests for which we usually observe relatively large racial differences.

In summary, the Ford–Kraiger research suggests that white workers perform better than black workers on most job performance criteria, the only exception being the instance in which black raters rate black and white employees. Further, their research indicates that race differences may be larger when the number of minority members in the group being rated is small. Differences between race subgroups on subjective performance indices are closely mirrored by differences on objective indices. For objective indices, the greatest difference between racial groups occurs with cognitive performance measures. Differences in subgroups' criterion performance are at most one-half standard deviation.

Clearly this research can help to answer questions which are central to the conflict between organizational goals in personnel selection and affirmative action considerations. Understanding when and how racial differences in subgroup performance occur will allow more definitive answers regarding whether those differences are job-relevant or bias. An important consideration, however, is that we have only begun to examine the presence and meaning of subgroup differences on criteria and given their importance in the issue of fair employment, this seems to be a critical deficiency in research data. Studies of which criterion elements are related to demographic variables and to predictor variables would contribute to knowledge regarding the bias issue, and more broadly, the construct validity of criteria.

AGE DIFFERENCES IN JOB PERFORMANCE

Most previous discussions of fair employment issues have centered on sex or race subgroups. However, at least in the USA, hiring practices with respect to members of different age groups have also been of some concern. Recently, a meta-analysis by Waldman and Avolio (1986) provides some data on the relationship between age and job performance, though the studies are few, and involve relatively few subjects, especially when any type of explanatory moderator analyses is employed. The data did indicate that older workers performed better when productivity indices were considered while age was negatively related to supervisory ratings. Moderator analyses revealed that performance and age were positively related with performance ratings for professionals but negatively related to nonprofessionals' performance ratings.

Given the existence of subgroup differences (at least for racial subgroups) on various selection instruments and on various criteria and the fact that tests do not appear to underpredict minority performance, the last question that arises concerns the practical consequences for productivity and affirmative action when we attempt to maximize one goal at the expense of the other. We saw evidence of the impact on minority hiring through our examination of the test fairness literature. In the next section, we review literature which has specified the expected productivity gain/loss under various circumstances and with various approaches to affirmative action and the fair use of tests.

TEST UTILITY AND AFFIRMATIVE ACTION

In assessing the impact of selection procedures on organizational productivity and minority hiring rates, several situational characteristics are important: the base rate or proportion of minority individuals in the applicant pool, the selection ratio or the proportion of the applicant pool which is selected, the validity of the test, and the standard deviation of job performance in dollar terms. The first researchers to draw the implications of various combinations of these variables for minority hiring and organizational productivity were Hunter, Schmidt, and Rauschenberger (1977).

We present a portion of the Hunter *et al.* (1977) tables (1, 2, 5, and 6) as our Table 11.2 to use as an example. Their calculations assumed a criterion difference between minority and majority group equal to one-half standard deviation which is slightly larger than that reported by the Ford and Kraiger research cited above; therefore, the data reported in Table 11.2 may be a slight overestimate of the conflict between productivity and affirmative action goals. In parentheses in the body of the table are the portion of minority candidates

Table 11.2   Relationship between validity, minority base rate, and selection ratio for optimal organizational productivity and quota hiring[a]

Selection ratio	Base rate	Model	Validity .20	.40	.60
.10	.90	OP	.504(.030)[b]	.770(.067)	1.095(.080)
	.90	Q	.351(.100)	.702(.100)	1.053(.100)
.50	.90	OP	.192(.445)	.340(.458)	.493(.469)
	.90	Q	.160(.500)	.319(.500)	.479(.500)
.10	.70	OP	.569(.005)	.827(.030)	1.137(.052)
	.70	Q	.351(.100)	.702(.100)	1.053(.100)
.50	.70	OP	.246(.296)	.369(.364)	.513(.404)
	.70	Q	.160(.500)	.319(.500)	.479(.500)
.10	.50	OP	.522(.003)	.822(.016)	1.139(.035)
	.50	Q	.351(.100)	.702(.100)	1.053(.100)
.50	.50	OP	.270(.106)	.380(.266)	.520(.338)
	.50	Q	.160(.500)	.319(.500)	.479(.500)
.10	.30	OP	.463(.001)	.786(.010)	1.116(.026)
	.30	Q	.351(.100)	.702(.100)	1.053(.100)
.50	.30	OP	.246(.025)	.369(.183)	.513(.277)
	.30	Q	.160(.500)	.319(.500)	.479(.500)
.10	.10	OP	.390(.001)	.733(.007)	1.077(.019)
	.10	Q	.351(.100)	.702(.100)	1.053(.100)
.50	.10	OP	.192(.009)	.340(.126)	.493(.225)
	.10	Q	.160(.500)	.319(.500)	.479(.500)

[a] Q = Quota hiring; OP = optimal organizational productivity strategy; i.e. Cleary model selection.
[b] Numbers in parentheses are the portion of minorities hired. Decimals represent the average improvement over random selection in criterion standard deviation units. A difference between minority and majority group criterion means of 0.5 standard deviations is assumed.

hired using both a quota strategy under which the proportions of both majority and minority members hired equals the overall selection ratio and the Cleary regression-based strategy which maximizes expected organizational productivity. Decimal numbers not in parentheses are average standard scores of persons selected under both of these strategies.

Looking first at the minority hiring rate, we can draw the following conclusions:

(1) A lower proportion of minority candidates is selected as validity for the combined group decreases. Both minority hiring and organizational productivity increase as a function of increases in validity.

(2) *Lower* proportions of minority candidates in the applicant pool (base rate) are associated with *lower* rates of hiring from the minority group.

(3) A larger selection ratio results in a greater proportion of minority hiring, though large differences in minority hiring between the Cleary model and a quota model occur at most levels of selection ratio.

(4) While not presented in Table 11.2, computation of adverse impact ratios indicated a violation of the 4/5 rule (Uniform guidelines on employee selection procedures, 1978) for all circumstances represented in the table using the regression strategy.

If we consider the standard score performance of those selected under the two models, the following observations are possible:

(1) The relationship between expected organizational productivity and base rate is complex. The largest absolute gains in expected organizational productivity occur at intermediate levels of minority base rate and the largest differences in expected productivity between quota and Cleary models occur at intermediate levels of minority base rate.

(2) As was obvious from earlier treatments of utility (Taylor and Russell, 1939; Brogden, 1946), the selection ratio and test validity have significant impact on utility.

(3) The largest differences in expected productivity between quota and Cleary models occur at low levels of validity.

(4) The largest differences in expected productivity between Cleary and quota models generally occur at low selection ratios though this difference becomes smaller as the minority base rate decreases.

(5) Over a wide range of the situations depicted in Table 11.2, we see little difference in organizational productivity between Cleary and quota models. The word 'little' is used advisedly, however, and is dependent on the standard deviation of employees' worth to the organization.

With information on the size of the standard deviation of employees' performance in economic terms, one can examine the tradeoffs between affirmative action and profitability. For instance, consider the case in which validity is 0.40, selection ratio is 0.50, and the minority base rate is 0.30. In this circumstance, the difference between the Cleary and quota models in organizational productivity (measured in standard deviation units) is 0.05. If the average salary for the position for which we are hiring is $25,000, the standard deviation of employees' worth to the organization may very likely be $10,000. The $10,000 figure is a rough estimate based on recent work in utility estimation which indicated that the standard deviation of job performance is typically 40 percent of the annual salary (Schmidt, Mack, and Hunter, 1984). If the organization hires 100 new employees, the expected financial difference between application of Cleary and quota models in one year's time is $50,000 ($10,000 × 0.05 × 100). At this same level, application of the Cleary model would result in hiring 5 or 6 (30 × 0.183) minority employees while the quota model would dictate the employment of 15 (30 × 0.5) minority group members. Hence, the employment of 10 additional minority members must be balanced against an annual difference in productivity equal to approximately $50,000. This productivity difference can also be projected beyond the first year to the average tenure of an employee. Though such projections may be more problematic than the first year estimates (Boudreau, 1983a,b), they will obviously produce much larger economic gain. *How to equate the economic gain with social and political concerns about reverse discrimination or the obligation to right past discrimination is a much more difficult problem* which has received no attention to our knowledge. Another aspect of the situation which researchers have not examined is the organization's legal cost in the event of a discrimination suit. These costs are frequently substantial and there is some evidence that companies have abandoned some testing procedures because of the threat of adjudication (American Society of Public Administrators, 1983).

Cronbach (Cronbach and Schaeffer, 1981) and his colleagues have developed formal mathematical models of the tradeoffs between affirmative action and equal opportunity for various subgroups on the one hand and maximal profit on the other. Their models are consistent with the work of Hunter *et al.* (1977) but, in addition, they consider the implications of using minimum cutoff scores for hiring. The quota models against which the Cleary model was compared in producing Table 11.2 and similar tables in Hunter *et al.* (1977) assumed that the top-scoring individuals in both the minority and majority group were selected. When the average predicted performance of the two groups is different, however, this involves setting a different cut score for hiring minority and majority applicants. Because this solution is often politically, legally, and socially undesirable, many organizations instead set a cutoff score at a point which represents a minimally acceptable level of predicted job performance. Above this level, selection according to quotas may be made on the basis of an interview or even by random selection. Cronbach and Schaeffer (1981) showed that the quality of the workforce is not seriously diminished when the top-ranked applicants in both groups are selected according to some quota system. However, if an employer hires individuals from majority and minority groups who meet some minimal cutoff disregarding individual differences above that cutoff, a great deal of potential utility is lost. Using this approach, the greatest sacrifice accrues from the selection of majority individuals who are not the best qualified. If the minority group is 20 percent of the applicant pool and hypothetical minimum cutoffs and ranking are used to hire individuals, four times as many majority individuals as minority individuals are hired. In addition, the range of individual differences above the cutoff is greater for majority people than for minority candidates; consequently, the greatest utility loss accrues not from the selection of minority members who are less qualified than majority candidates, but rather from the selection of less than the best qualified majority candidates. The selection ratio, mean differences between groups, the size of the majority and minority applicant group, and the within-group regressions all affect the tradeoff between quota and Cleary models and between the two approaches to setting cutoff scores. Cronbach and Schaeffer (1981) and Hunter *et al.* (1977) have developed the quantitative tools to make the tradeoffs explicit.

Recently, Schmidt *et al.* (1984) have presented an example of the utility implications of different forms of test use. Three modes of test use were compared: (a) top-down selection; (b) minimum required test scores equal to the mean; and (c) minimum score at one standard deviation below the mean. Assuming a selection ratio of 0.10, top-down selection using a test versus a structured interview resulted in an increase in average productivity of about 13 percent. With a minimum test score set at the mean of the test, dollar value of output gains was only 45 percent as large as the dollar value for top-down selection. Percentage increase in output was less than 6 percent. When the cutoff score was set one standard deviation below the mean increase in output was only about 2 percent and the dollar value of output gains was only 16 percent of the top-down figure. Clearly, use of the minimum cutoff score method results in substantial loss.

Further complicating the assessment of utility under any strategy of selection is the imposition of hiring quotas for protected groups. Kroeck, Barrett, and Alexander (1983) developed a computer algorithm to predict the necessary recruitment and performance outcomes for organizations under different subgroup quota constraints. They concluded that the joint probability of locating enough qualified applicants so as to exceed by a small percentage the subgroup representation in the population may require extensive recruitment and perhaps result in substantial performance differential between the subgroups selected into the organization. That is, the mean scores of the protected subgroup are likely to be lower than under circumstances with no recruitment pressure, and the majority group mean scores are likely to be higher.

Another factor which complicates the evaluation of tradeoffs between affirmative action and profitability goals is the fact that not all top-ranking candidates will accept job offers. It may be that minority candidates are heavily recruited and it is extremely difficult to attract them to one's organization. Alternatively, one may be able to minimize the negative impact of use of quotas by more vigorous recruiting efforts with both minority and majority applicants. Murphy (1986) attempted to quantify the effect of differential acceptance rates on utility. He maintains that a high rejection rate will actually produce utility losses when compared with random selection, because the organization will be forced to select applicants of increasingly lower ability. As Murphy notes, comparison with random selection is inappropriate since applicants may be selected at random, but they almost certainly will not accept at random. The higher ability applicant is likely to get multiple job offers. Regardless, Murphy's primary message is correct: utility is very likely less than usually estimated because of differences in acceptance rates for high and low ability applicants. The probability that affirmative action will lead to a net gain or loss in utility relative to the figures in Table 11.2 and similar utility analyses will depend on:

(1) the overall acceptance rate;
(2) the acceptance rate among minority and majority members;
(3) the correlation between the probability of accepting a job offer and ability for subgroups; and
(4) the difference between minority and nonminority criterion performance, assuming a Cleary-based definition of fairness.

As Murphy pointed out, we have little information about any of the first three parameters and are only beginning to develop an integrated body of information about the fourth. Further, we noted at the beginning that one of the multiple meanings 'affirmative action' has acquired is the degree of effort organizations expend in recruiting.

A related issue is the failure on the part of job candidates to pursue a job when selection involves several hurdles. Arvey, Gordon, Massengill, and Mussio (1975) examined applicant records for openings in 70 entry-level jobs in a large city. They found that time lags between candidates' initial application and the organization's certification that they were valid job candidates, and any subsequent selection hurdle produced larger dropout rates among minority than majority applicants. Hunt and Cohen (1974) reported that over half of the white candidates for a patrolman job who passed the first written exam did not continue to the point where they had completed all the selection hurdles. There is no evidence that those who dropped out in these studies were more or less qualified; in any event, their omission from subsequent steps in the selection process will certainly impact the utility of these steps if for no other reason than the fact that the selection ratio is larger. Whether it makes the affirmative action–organizational productivity conflict more severe depends on the relationship between ability and dropout probability. If the more qualified job applicants drop out or, as Murphy suggests, fail to accept jobs, then the effect on overall utility will be negative. Obviously, recruitment practices play a critical role in dropout and acceptance rates and little current research exists on effective minority recruiting (for a summary, see Heneman, Schwab, Fossum and Dyer, 1983).

Finally, separate treatment of subgroups of job applicants may result in claims of reverse discrimination from members of a higher scoring subgroup who are not hired. A quota model, even one based on separate subgroup regression equations, will always produce the potential for reverse discrimination claims. This issue has been discussed in two US Supreme Court cases (*Regents of the University of California* vs *Bakke* (1978) and *United Steelworkers of America* vs *Weber* (1979) with no real resolution (see Cascio, 1982b, pp. 27–28 for a discussion).

ITEM BIAS STUDIES

The issue of test bias has taken a new turn in the American context at least primarily as a result of two recent court cases. In the first case, Golden Rule Insurance Company (1984) filed suit against the Illinois Department of Insurance and the Educational Testing Service when the insurance company found that blacks failed the Illinois insurance licensing exams at a greater rate than whites. To end the litigation, the Educational Testing Service agreed to use items for which the passing rates of all subgroups were greater than 0.4. In addition, they agreed to select items for which the proportions of correct answers for whites and blacks differ by no more than 0.15 when such items are available. In the other case (*Allen* vs *Alabama State Board of Education*, 1985), the defendant agreed to select items for which the proportions of black and white examinees who answered the item correctly differed by no more than 5 percent. These legal/political solutions to the bias issue obviously ignore the issue of whether these test items relate to any external criterion though the solution does specify that replacement items come from the same content domain. Their concern with internal measurement bias is correct only if there are no subgroup performance differences. This definition of bias is the same one dismissed by Guion (1966) over two decades ago.

However, Drasgow (1987) has demonstrated that even when one is concerned only with internal criteria of bias that the proportion difference between subgroups is an inappropriate index of bias. Using item response theory to define item bias (Hulin, Drasgow and Parsons, 1983) is more defensible (Humphreys, 1986). In this approach one holds constant the score on the latent trait (what the test as a whole measures) and examines the probability of a right answer across subgroups. The estimates of the slope and difficulty parameters for items represent the nonlinear regressions of the items on the hypothetical trait. When these parameters differ across subgroups, an item is said to be biased. In a study of English and Mathematics tests, use of measurement bias methods designed to minimize methodological artifacts identified many 'biased' items. However, the size of these effects for the tests as a whole was negligible. The negligible effects on overall test scores are partly due to the fact that the tests of significance employed to identify these items are very powerful.

As stated above, these internal bias estimates are irrelevant anyway. Humphreys (1986) has argued convincingly that there is nothing a test constructor can do (short of bad psychometric practice) to reduce intercept bias by manipulating items that differ from the rest of the item pool in difficulty level. Discarding such items reduces the predictive and construct validity of the total test score and distracts attention from the causes of differences in criterion performance. This, of course, is the position espoused in the section on criteria in this paper. Linn and Drasgow (1987) state that application of the Golden Rule procedure will reduce reliability because it will favor items with poor discriminating power and it will lessen validity because it is those items that best measure the underlying attribute being measured that are most likely to be eliminated using the Golden Rule criteria. Predictor differences are largely irrelevant in discussions of predictive bias; the attention should be directed to understanding the criterion.

Roznowski (1987) provides an example in which two tests comprised of items with large differences between male and female subgroups provided equally good validities for either group as measured by correlations with general intelligence. She argues, like Humphreys, that eliminating items from a test because their content capitalizes on experience of, or knowledge more likely attained by one group or culture, may actually decrease the test's predictive power. She argues that it is actually best to combine items with a wide diversity thereby increasing contributions from relevant sources and decreasing the overall impact of systematic irrelevant sources.

SUMMARY AND CONCLUSIONS

Our discussion of personnel selection and equal employment opportunity began with a summary of subgroup differences in mean scores and validity coefficients of various selection instruments. We then examined statistical issues—including differential validity, test fairness, and differential prediction—and ended that discussion by pointing to the key role of criterion measurement. Literature on subgroup differences in job performance was next reviewed. The impact of various factors on, and the extent of, the conflict between demands for organizational productivity and the number of minority individuals hired was discussed and finally, we referred to some research on item bias which is relevant to the fairness issue.

This discussion leads us to the following conclusions:

(1) Sizable subgroup differences in mean performance exist on many selection instruments. Black-white differences on aptitude tests are usually close to one standard deviation. Female-male differences on physical ability tests are at least one standard deviation. Smaller differences occur on most other instruments.

(2) There is little evidence for significant differences in subgroup validity coefficients.

(3) The Cleary model of test fairness has been accepted by psychometricians and in legal circles. Use of the Cleary formulation directs attention to the importance of an unbiased criterion.

(4) Job performance differences between majority and minority groups are between one-third and one-half standard deviation although they may be slightly larger or smaller depending on the type of criterion.

(5) In the presence of subgroup job performance differences, there will always be a conflict between organizational goals associated with the selection of persons whose expected performance is highest and the selection of persons from a lower performing subgroup.

(6) High test validities minimize the conflict referred to in (5) above, as do high selection ratios, and to a lesser degree, high proportions of minority group members in the applicant pool.

(7) Using utility analyses to obtain estimates of the expected standard deviation of job performance in economic terms, one can estimate the tradeoff between hiring increased numbers of minorities and organizational productivity. This tradeoff is likely to be smallest when top-down selection from a list of applicants takes place as opposed to some minimal qualifications strategy. Estimates of organizational costs of quota strategies are further complicated when recruitment costs and the effects of increased recruitment pressure on the likelihood that subgroup members will accept a job are considered.

(8) More recent focus on item bias also ignores the criteria being predicted. As such, we are likely to resurrect the same controversies which were debated in the test bias literature in the 1970s.

While the temptation always exists to compile a large list of areas requiring additional research, we will emphasize only a reorientation of research effort. While there are exceptions, most of the research reviewed in this paper focused on the documentation of individual differences. In research on both predictor and criterion subgroup differences, more attention should be directed toward construct validity considerations. Increased effort should be directed toward an understanding of the constructs underlying both predictor and criterion differences and what, if any, remedial action is likely to minimize those differences. Use of miniaturized training sessions (Siegel, 1983) may provide information on the trainability or modifiability of lower scoring individuals. The work of Hunter and Hunter (1984) using GATB validity coefficients and information on job complexity is another example of this type of effort. The work of Kraiger and Ford cited earlier also leads to construct considerations.

REFERENCES

Allen vs *Alabama State Board of Education*, No. 81-697-N (consent decree filed with United States District Court for the Middle District of Alabama Northern Division, 1985).

American Society of Public Administrators (1983). ASPA-BNA Survey No. 45: Employee selection procedures. Washington, DC: Bureau of National Affairs.

Arvey, R. D. (1979a). *Fairness in Selecting Employees.* Reading, MA: Addison-Wesley.

Arvey, R. D., Gordon, M. E., Massengill, D. P. and Mussio, S. J. (1975). Differential dropout rates of minority and majority job candidates due to 'time lags' between selection procedures. *Personnel Psychology*, **28**, 175–180.

Bartlett, C. J., Bobko, P., Mosier, S. P. and Hannan, R. (1978). Testing for fairness with a moderated multiple regression strategy: an alternative to differential analysis. *Personnel Psychology*, **31**, 233–242.

Bass, A. R. and Turner, J. N. (1973). Ethnic group differences in relationships among criteria of job performance. *Journal of Applied Psychology*, **57**, 101–109.

Bigoness, W. J. (1976). Effect of applicant's sex, race, and performance on employer's performance ratings: some additional findings. *Journal of Applied Psychology*, **61**, 80–84.

Boehm, V. R. (1972). Negro-white differences in validity of employment and training selection procedures: summary of research evidence. *Journal of Applied Psychology*, **56**, 33–39.

Borman, W. C. (1978). Exploring upper limits of reliability and validity in job performance ratings. *Journal of Applied Psychology*, **63**, 135–144.

Boudreau, J. (1983a). Effects of employee flows on utility analysis of human resource productivity improvement programs. *Journal of Applied Psychology*, **68**, 396–406.

Boudreau, J. (1983b). Economic considerations in estimating the utility of human resource productivity improvement programs. *Personnel Psychology*, **36**, 551–576.

Brogden, H. E. (1946). On the interpretation of the correlation coefficient as a measure of predictive efficiency. *Journal of Educational Psychology*, **37**, 65–76.

Cascio, W. F. (1982a). *Costing Human Resources: The Financial Impact of Behavior in Organizations.* Boston, MA: Kent.

Cascio, W. F. (1982b). *Applied Psychology in Personnel Management.* Reston, VA: Reston Publishing Co.

Cleary, T. A. (1968). Test bias: prediction of grades of negro and white students in integrated colleges. *Journal of Educational Measurement*, **5**, 115–124.

Cole, N. S. (1973). Bias in selection. *Journal of Educational Measurement*, **10**, 237–255.

Cronbach, L. J. and Schaeffer, G. A. (1981). *Extensions of personnel selection theory to aspects of minority hiring* (Project Rep. No. 81-A2). Palo Alto, CA: Stanford University.

Darlington, R. B. (1971). Another look at 'cultural fairness'. *Journal of Educational Measurement*, **8**, 71–82.

Drasgow, F. (1987). Study of the measurement bias of two standardized psychological tests. *Journal of Applied Psychology*, **72**, 19–29.

Ford, J. K., Kraiger, K. and Schechtman, S. (1986). Study of race effects in objective indices and subjective evaluations of performance: A meta-analysis of performance criteria. *Psychological Bulletin*, **99**, 330–337.

Glass, G. V. (1976). Primary, secondary, and meta-analysis of research. *Educational Researcher*, **10**, 3–8.

Golden Rule Insurance Company et al. vs *Washburn et al.*, No. 419-76 (stipulation for dismissal and order dismissing cause, Circuit Court of the Seventh Judicial Circuit, Sangamon County, IL 1984).

Griggs vs *Duke Power Co.* (1971). *Fair Employment Practices*, 175.

Guion, R. M. (1966). Employment tests and discriminatory hiring. *Industrial Relations*, **5**, 20–37.

Heneman, H. G., III, Schwab, D. P., Fossum, J. A. and Dyer, L. D. (1983). *Personnel/ Human Resource Management*. Homewood, IL: Richard D. Irwin.

Heneman, R. (1983). *The Relevance of Supervisory Ratings to Measures of More 'Ultimate' Criterion: A Metaanalytic Investigation*. Presented at the Fourth Annual Industrial Organizational Psychology and Organizational Behavior Student Convention. Chicago, IL.

Hirsh, H. R. and McDaniel, M. A. (1987). Differential validity by gender in employment settings. Paper presented at the Annual Conference of The Society for Industrial-Organizational Psychology, Atlanta, GA.

Hulin, C. L., Drasgow, F. and Parsons, C. K. (1983). *Item Response Theory: Application to Psychological Measurement*. Homewood, IL: Dow–Jones–Irwin.

Humphreys, L. G. (1973). Statistical definitions of test validity for minority groups. *Journal of Applied Psychology*, **58**, 1–4.

Humphreys, L. G. (1986). An analysis and evaluation of test and item bias in the prediction context. *Journal of Applied Psychology*, **71**, 327–333.

Hunt, I. C. and Cohen, B. (1974). *Minority Recruiting in the New York City Police Department*. New York: Rand Institute.

Hunter, J. E. and Hunter, R. (1984). Validity and utility of alternative predictors. *Psychological Bulletin*, **96**, 72–98.

Hunter, J. E. and Schmidt, F. L. (1976). Critical analysis of the statistical and ethical implications of various definitions of test bias. *Psychological Bulletin*, **83**, 1053–1071.

Hunter, J. E., Schmidt, F. L. and Hunter, R. (1979). Differential validity of employment tests by race: a comprehensive review and analysis. *Psychological Bulletin*, **86**, 721–735.

Hunter, J. E., Schmidt, F. L. and Jackson, G. B. (1982). *Advanced Meta-analysis: Quantitative Methods for Cumulating Research Findings Across Studies*. Beverly Hills, CA: Sage.

Hunter, J. E., Schmidt, F. L. and Rauschenberger, J. M. (1977). Fairness of psychological tests: implications of four definitions for selection utility and minority hiring. *Journal of Applied Psychology*, **62**, 245–260.

Jensen, A. R. (1980). *Bias in Mental Testing*. New York: Free Press.

Kirchner, W. E. (1960). Predicting ratings of sales success with objective performance information. *Journal of Applied Psychology*, **44**, 398–403.

Kraiger, K. and Ford, J. K. (1985). A meta-analysis of ratee race effects in performance ratings. *Journal of Applied Psychology*, **70**, 56–65.

Kroeck, K. G., Barrett, G. V. and Alexander, R. A. (1983). Imposed quotas and personnel selection: A computer simulation study. *Journal of Applied Psychology*, **68**, 123–136.

Ledvinka, J. (1982). *Federal Regulation of Personnel and Human Resource Management*. Belmont, CA: Wadsworth.

Linn, R. L. (1973). Fair test use in selection. *Review of Educational Research*, **5**, 20–37.

Linn, R. L. (1978). Single group validity, differential validity, and differential predictions. *Journal of Applied Psychology*, **63**, 507–514.

Linn, R. L. and Drasgow, F. (1987). Implications of the Golden Rule settlement for test construction. *Educational Measurement Issues and Practice*, **6**, 13–17.

Murphy, K. R. (1986). When your top choice turns you down: effect of rejected offers on the utility of selection tests. *Psychological Bulletin*, **99**, 133–142.

Peterson, N. S. and Novick, M. R. (1976). An evaluation of some models for culture-fair selection. *Journal of Educational Measurement*, **13**, 3–29.

Regents of the University of California vs *Bakke*. 17 Fair Employment Practices Cases, 1000 (1978).

Roznowski, M. (1987). The use of tests manifesting sex differences as measures of intelligence: implications for measurement bias. *Journal of Applied Psychology*, **72**, 480–483.

Schmidt, F. L., Berner, J. G. and Hunter, J. E. (1973). Racial differences in validity of employment tests: reality or illusion? *Journal of Applied Psychology*, **58**, 5–9.

Schmidt, F. L. and Hunter, J. E. (1974). Racial and ethnic bias in psychological tests. *American Psychologist*, **29**, 1–9.

Schmidt, F. L., Hunter, J. E., McKenzie, R. C. and Muldrow, T. W. (1979). Impact of valid selection procedures on work-force productivity. *Journal of Applied Psychology*, **64**, 609–626.

Schmidt, F. L., Mack, M. J. and Hunter, J. E. (1984). Selection utility in the occupation of U. S. park ranger for three modes of test use. *Journal of Applied Psychology*, **69**, 490–497.

Schmidt, F. L., Pearlman, K. and Hunter, J. E. (1980). The validity and fairness of employment and educational tests for Hispanic Americans: a review and analysis. *Personnel Psychology*, **33**, 705–724.

Schmitt, N. and Hill, T. E. (1977). Sex and race composition of assessment center groups as a determinant of peer and assessor ratings. *Journal of Applied Psychology*, **62**, 261–264.

Schmitt, N. and Lappin, M. (1980). Race and sex as determinants of the mean and variance of performance ratings. *Journal of Applied Psychology*, **65**, 428–435.

Schmitt, N., Mellon, P. M. and Bylenga, C. (1978). Sex differences in validity for academic and employment criteria and different types of predictors. *Journal of Applied Psychology*, **63**, 145–150.

Schmitt, N. and Noe, R. A. (1986). Personnel selection and equal employment opportunity. In C. L. Cooper and I. Robertson (eds), *International Review of Industrial and Organizational Psychology*. London: Wiley.

Seashore, S. E., Indik, B. P. and Georgopoulos, B. S. (1960). Relationships among criteria of job performance. *Journal of Applied Psychology*, **44**, 195–202.

Siegel, A. I. (1983). The miniature job training and evaluation approach: additional findings. *Personnel Psychology*, **36**, 41–56.

Society for Industrial and Organizational Psychology, Inc. (1987). *Principles for the Validation and Use of Personnel Selection Procedures*, 3rd edn. College Park, MD: Author.

Taylor, H. C. and Russell, J. T. (1939). The relationship of validity coefficients to the practical effectiveness of tests in selection. *Journal of Applied Psychology*, **23**, 565–578.

Tenopyr, M. L. and Oeltjen, P. D. (1982). Personnel selection and classification. *Annual Review of Psychology*, **33**, 581–618.

Thorndike, R. L. (1971). Concepts of culture fairness. *Journal of Educational Measurement*, **8**, 63–70.

Uniform guidelines on employee selection procedures (1978). *Federal Register*, **43**, 38,290–38,309.

United Steelworkers of American vs *Weber*. 99 S. CT. 2721 (1979).

Waldman, D. A. and Avolio, B. J. (1986). A meta-analysis of age differences in job performance. *Journal of Applied Psychology*, **71**, 33–38.

Zedeck, S. and Cascio, W. F. (1984). Psychological issues in personnel decisions. *Annual Review of Psychology*, **35**, 461–518.

Zeidner, M. (1987). Test of the cultural bias hypothesis: some Israeli findings. *Journal of Applied Psychology*, **72**, 38–48.

12

Fairness in Employment Selection: a Comparison of UK and USA Experience

M. A. PEARN
Pearn Kandola Downs, Oxford

Neil Schmitt begins his chapter by drawing attention to the fact that personnel selection research and the validation of selection procedures had, in the past, focused almost exclusively on the prediction of job performance. With the advent of Civil Rights legislation in the United States, another concern was added, viz. that there should also be equality of employment opportunity for various subgroups, with the emphasis on women and ethnic minorities. The focus of selection research in the past was primarily on validity (however defined), but in the last fifteen to twenty years the concern has shifted to validity *and* fairness.

As Guion (1976) has pointed out, both academics and practitioners thought, until the late 1960s, that validation of selection procedures was an established technology which was not worthy of serious innovative research or, for that matter, conceptual debate and analysis. The pressures of equal opportunities legislation, particularly in the United States, and the resultant guidelines of law enforcement agencies, stimulated considerable debate on the nature of validity and *the* validation process as well as with definitions of fairness (Pearn, 1978). The consensus must now be that there is no such thing as the validation of a selection procedure but that there are as many validities as there are sources of evidence, from whatever source, which make one inference about subsequent job performance based on performance on a selection device, more reasonable than another. The explosion of debate and re-

Advances in Selection and Assessment. Edited by M. Smith and I. T. Robertson

search in the USA on fairness and selection generally was not paralleled in the UK.

Throughout the late 1960s and the mid-1970s, legislative developments in the UK closely followed the example being set in the United States. The 1968 Race Relations Act made direct discrimination in employment unlawful for the first time, but it was not until 1975 that the Sex Discrimination Act made direct and also indirect discrimination on grounds of sex and married status unlawful. The Race Relations Act of 1976 repealed the 1968 Act and created a law virtually identical with the Sex Discrimination Act. The new equal opportunities legislation incorporated a definition of discrimination in effect which was inspired by the United States Supreme Court in the *Griggs* vs *Duke Power* case of 1971. In the United Kingdom, discrimination in effect is referred to as indirect discrimination, and has a complex statutory definition which in practice makes it very difficult for an applicant to prove discrimination.

For many years now, observers in the United Kingdom have watched with envy (and sometimes bewilderment) the public and academic debates, the controversies over guidelines, regulations, and codes of practice, and the massive amount of selection research on test fairness, validation, validity generalisation, and adverse impact. Before extracting some of the lessons for the UK from the American research, particularly as summarised in Neil Schmitt's paper, it is necessary to draw attention to the significant differences that exist between the United States and the United Kingdom in the context of equal opportunities, and which may explain the high level of interest and activity in the United States by contrast with the comparatively small impact within the UK.

Table 12.1 attempts to summarise the key differences. In the United States, the ethnic minority black population is mainly the historic product of several centuries of the importation of slave labour, mostly from West Africa, which terminated in the nineteenth century. As a result, the vast majority of black people in the United States today were born and educated in the United States. There is, of course, an ethnic minority immigrant population, perhaps the most significant section of which is the Hispanic-surnamed group, for whom recent immigration and language differences combine to compound socio-economic disadvantage. This is more akin to the situation in the United Kingdom where the ethnic minority population is frequently regarded as immigrant, since most black immigration (from the Caribbean and the Indian subcontinent) into the UK occurred in the early 1960s and 1970s. Immigration control in the UK has virtually brought primary immigration from (non-white) New Commonwealth countries and Pakistan to an end. Although the public image of Britain's black population is that of immigrants, well over half the black population are born in the United Kingdom, and the vast majority of those under 30 are UK-born (Brown, 1984).

Table 12.1   Comparisons between the USA and the UK

	USA	UK
History	Slavery/immigration	Immigration
Population	18–20%	5%
Legislation	1964/72	1965/75/76
Judges	Informed	Uninformed
Appeals	Spirit	Letter
Political will	High/declining	Low
Class action	Yes	No
Contract compliance	Yes	Yes, but not enforced
Penalties	Punitive	Low
Representational employment	Yes	No
Employer response	Energetic	Passive
Strategy	Regulatory	Advisory/conciliatory

The size of the two groups differs enormously. In the United Kingdom the black population is estimated at between 4 and 5 per cent, whereas the ethnic minority population of the United States is nearly 20 percent. Women represent about half the total population in both countries, primary interest has been in women and ethnic minorities. Discrimination on grounds of age, disability, sexual preference, or even social class is not unlawful in the UK. Only in Northern Ireland is discrimination on grounds of religious or political belief unlawful.

The evolution of equal opportunities legislation in both countries has been somewhat similar, with the United States taking a lead in definitions of discrimination, etc., which were followed in the UK. On the whole, the United States is a more litigious society than the United Kingdom, and there has been considerable emphasis in the UK, from the mid-1960s onwards, on conciliation, and the application of 'good sense' and moderation, rather than on punitive sanctions applied by the courts.

The enforcement of the laws in the two countries is completely different. In the United States the laws are enforced through the courts where the judges (with notable exceptions) have tended to adopt a sympathetic attitude stemming from an understanding of the issues involved. The posture of the courts resulted from the very high profile that civil rights acquired in the 1960s and 1970s, mainly as a result of the civil rights movement. By comparison, discrimination cases involving employment issues in the UK are brought before industrial tribunals which are informal courts where only the chairperson is legally qualified, and who is assisted by lay members who are nominated by the CBI and the TUC (the employers' and unions' representative bodies in the UK). The tribunals are intended to be informal and cannot award punitive damages.

There are other important legal differences between the two countries. When a case is appealed in the United States, ultimately to the Supreme Court, the judges for the most part interpret the law according to the spirit and intentions of Congress rather than the letter of the law, and many important cases have been brought under the US Constitution. It must be recognised that the appointment of judges by an administration will inevitably influence the interpretation of, and sympathy for, a piece of legislation. In Britain, legal appeals tend to focus on the letter of the law, with the result that narrow rather than far-sighted judgements and decisions are made. By contrast, the European Court of Justice tends to make judgements more on the basis of the spirit and intent of the law rather than its letter. UK sex discrimination and equal pay law is subject to ultimate appeal to the European Court of Justice, though this is not the case under the Race Relations Act. This arises from the Treaty of Rome, which governs membership of the European Common Market. Britain is required to have legislation on sex discrimination, though not on race relations, as a condition of membership of the Common Market.

Other important differences between the two countries are that very powerful mechanisms exist in the United States for persuading employers to take the legislation seriously. These include punitive damages and compensation on a scale which clearly frightened many employers into action and which can only be regarded with astonishment in the UK. In addition, there is the existence of effective Federal contract compliance regulations which affected up to one-third of the total labour force of the United States, and class actions where an individual can bring a case on behalf of any number of similarly affected people are powerful mechanisms for change. None of these powerful remedies and mechanisms for change has operated in the United Kingdom. Contract compliance provisions exist within the Race Relations Act only, but have never seriously been applied in the UK (Institute of Personnel Management, 1987).

The main reason why powerful mechanisms were created for bringing about change in employers' practices and policies was that a high degree of political will existed in the United States, especially during the administrations of Johnson and Nixon, to combat race and sex inequality in the United States. Although this political will is probably now declining in the United States, it lasted long enough to allow significant machinery to be put in place to facilitate change. This degree of political will and associated enforcement strategies has never existed in the United Kingdom.

Although successive governments in the UK have upheld the principle of non-discrimination and equality of opportunity, there has never been a high level of public funding and government action to make employers respond energetically with a results-orientated approach to equal opportunity issues. In the United States, government strategy has tended to focus on a regulatory pattern of intervention, with very powerful legal and financial sanctions, whereas in Britain the strategy has tended to rely on exhortation and advice, with the law having little impact on employers. The positive results-orientated strategies in the United States contrast strongly with the more passive processes-orientated approach in the UK. There is virtually no concern with representational employment whereby the *under-representation* of one sub-group by comparison with another is *prima facie* evidence of discrimination. Again, it is only in Northern Ireland that serious attention is paid to representational employment.

It is not surprising, therefore, that in the UK there has not been a corresponding amount of research on selection and fairness to that in the United States. In Britain the interest does not lie in representational employment as such, but in selection procedures and processes which result in adverse impact. Most *prima facie* cases of adverse impact are judged to be 'justifiable' under the law. None the less, the lessons that can be drawn from the United States experience are still very relevant to the UK, though many of the problems and some of the solutions are very different.

Much of the research in the United States has focused on the validity of selection instruments and their impact on different subgroups. The vast majority of this work has been carried out on ethnic minority groups and, to a lesser extent, on male/female groups. Assessment centres, self-assessments and work-samples appear to have the best combination of moderate to high validity combined with small subgroup differences. These techniques (particularly work-samples and assessment centres) are not always feasible, but self-assessment techniques which are widely applicable clearly warrant further investigation, particularly as a promising aid to short-listing. Ability and cognitive tests offer a combination of moderate validity and moderate subgroup differences. Biodata and peer evaluation also offer promising validity, but further research needs to be done to investigate subgroup differences.

The implication of this research for employers is clear: they should not base selection decisions solely on interviews, nor should short-listing be based on unstructured and unsystematic procedures. On balance, the employer can optimise both validity and fairness by using appropriate cognitive and ability tests in the selection process, especially as an alternative to relying on interviews alone. Paradoxically, employers in the UK often express concern about the fairness of tests, mainly because quantitative data are yielded which can be analysed and averaged, and yet there is far less concern about the fairness and validity of selection interviews, even though there is considerable evidence of bias and discrimination in the interview process, and little evidence of validity (Arvey, 1979). This point was strongly made in the report of a case-study research project on the effects of testing on the career opportunities of women and men (Pearn, Kandola and Mottram, 1987). The authors concluded that, on balance, employers should use tests, especially if the alternative was sole reliance on interviews or other instruments of low validity.

The debate and research on the reality of differential validity attracted a degree of interest in the UK (BPS, 1980). It is now reasonably certain, from research in the United States, that validity coefficients are not significantly different across subgroups. Once again, most of this research has been based on ethnic minority groups in the United States, and to a much lesser extent on sex groups. However, concern over differential prediction still exists. Subgroup differences on predictors lead to worries about the impact of the selection procedure on subgroups. If the "criterion" truly reflects and represents job performance in a meaningful and important way, and the measurement of performance on that criterion is itself free of bias, then it would be reasonable to assume that subgroup differences on the predictor do in fact reflect subgroup differences in performance. Thus, the use of the selection instrument would result in proportionately fewer members of the lower scoring subgroups being selected. In the UK this would not present a legal problem if the selection procedure could be justified, though only a few employers who have a results-orientated strategy on equal opportunities express concern at this situation.

On the whole, the best strategy for employers is to use selection instruments which combine moderate to high validity with small or moderate subgroup differences. The choice of criteria, and the fairness of criterion measurement, is still a relatively neglected area of selection research. The role of job analysis in establishing the construct validity of the criterion is critical, and may well alter the interpretation of what is or should be happening when someone is assessed for a job.

As Schmitt reports, the extensive debates about, and empirical evaluation of, the various models of test fairness appear to have come down in favour of the early formulation by Cleary (1968). This is somewhat paradoxical for the use of the model means that separate regression equations should be used for subgroups where these equations are significantly different. This results in the prediction being fairest to individuals but will probably result in a smaller proportion of the lower scoring subgroup being hired. Ironically, in this situation, not using separate regression equations results in a tendency to overpredict the job performance ratings of the lower performing subgroup. Consequently the chances of an individual from a lower performing subgroup are greater when separate regression equations are not used. In their report, Pearn, Kandola and Mottram (1987), described a case history in which significant subgroup differences on a selection test did not correspond to differences in measures of job performance. The employer developed separate norms for the two subgroups, and increased the number of lower scoring subgroup members who were called for interview but did not reduce the frequency with which the majority group members were being selected. The lesson of this example is that test users should always evaluate the impact of a selection instrument on key subgroups in a given situation. Similar advice has recently been offered by Toplis, Dulevicz and Fletcher (1987).

In Britain, it is rare rather than common for selection tests to be used with regression equations. It is far more common for tests to be used in a descriptive way, and frequently not even with a cut-score. When cut-scores are used, they are only rarely backed by a validation study. Consequently, the issues of test fairness and differential prediction do not arise as a serious problem for employers, with some notable exceptions, especially in the public sector. Similarly, the conflict described by Neil Schmitt between goals of affirmative action and organisational productivity do not arise, as the UK places little emphasis on representational employment, though large differences in selection-rates between subgroups can trigger a legal requirement to justify the procedure. In practice, this occurs only rarely, and damages cannot be awarded.

Neil Schmitt devotes a large part of his survey of research on selection fairness to the apparent conflict between affirmative action and organisational productivity. The assumption is made that the highest scoring candidates on a predictive selection instrument should be hired. It can be argued that it is not always necessary for an employer to select from the top down in terms of predicted job performance. Instead the employer could define a minimum standard of suitability based on a thorough understanding of what is involved in doing a job. If selecting from the top down would result in only a very small proportion of minority groups being selected, and this was judged to be not in the long-term interests of the organisation, then alternative strategies could be explored. A minimum standard as first hurdle, could be followed by a structured random formula so that the proportions of subgroups in the applicant and selected groups are unaltered. In the absence of any other systematic or structured selection instrument (biodata, self-assessment), the use of randomised selection formulae could be fairer than subjective unstructured examination of application forms with ill-defined criteria, or none at all (Pearn and Banerji, 1987). The role of randomised procedures or lotteries for short-listing or for reducing the pool of candidates who have already met a minimum standard of suitability warrants serious research, particularly when the alternative is to rely on procedures which have known biases.

The focus of American research on selection fairness has been on instruments, regression equations, and prediction of organisational productivity. The social process of selection and the cognitive strategies of selectors when interpreting candidate information have received much less attention. The vast majority of employers in the UK do not use sophisticated selection instruments and it is likely that only a minority will be persuaded to use tests, biodata, self-assessment, etc., particularly as aids to short-listing. Most employers are likely to rely on a paper sift of application forms using ill-defined criteria which invariably are not even systematically applied. The problem for many employers is the reduction of very large numbers of application forms, frequently in the thousands, to smaller numbers to be interviewed. Biodata and self-assessment questionnaires are the only form of selection device which can be sent to candidates in very large numbers and at relatively low cost. Cognitive and ability tests involve inviting the candidate to the employer's establishment for testing and therefore involve considerably more expense and time. The only other form of selection device which has the convenience and advantages of biodata and self-assessment, is a form of random structured pre-screening based on a formula to maintain the proportions of various subgroups in the applicant group, particularly after a minimum standard or criterion has been met.

In addition, research on the social and cognitive processes involved in selection decision-making will greatly assist employers in devising procedures which will minimise unfairness in selection. Thinking-aloud studies of selectors doing paper sifts, of the kind carried out by Herriot and Rothwell (1983), would provide valuable insights into how conscious or unconscious race or sex bias can influence the assessment of candidates. Analysis of transcripts of real interviews would also reveal invaluable data that could be analysed by the methods of discourse analysis (Dijk, 1987).

Employers in the UK are currently investing a great deal of time and resources in the training of interviewers with special emphasis on avoiding sex and race bias in the interview. There is a need for systematic research to evaluate the effectiveness of the training in terms of how interviews are conducted before and after the training. Discourse analysis of interview transcripts would provide an effective measure of the impact of such training.

Further research is needed into how selectors interpret and evaluate application forms, references and CVs. For example, Oliphant and Alexander (1982) revealed sex effects in the ratings of CVs by personnel professionals. Ideally, research should be based in real rather than laboratory or artificial settings. Failure to do so oversimplifies or distorts the processes being studied, and reduces the applicability of the findings to real situations. In terms of fairness in selection, future research should focus much more on the interpretive and decision-making processes in hiring and promotion, rather than on selection instruments. Serious consideration should be given to the evaluation of structured randomised procedures for short-listing, as an alternative to reliance on subjective interpretation of application forms or resumes. Randomised short-listing after passing minimum hurdles should be fairer than any alternatives with known biases.

REFERENCES

Arvey, R. D. (1979). *Fairness in Selecting Employees*. Reading, Mass: Addison-Wesley.

British Psychological Society (1980). *Discriminating Fairly: a Guide to Fair Selection*. London: The Runnymede Trust and Leicester: The British Psychological Society.

Brown, C. (1984). *Black and White Britain: The Third PSI Survey*. London: Heinemann.

Cleary, T. A. (1968). Test bias: prediction of grades of negro and white students in integrated colleges. *Journal of Educational Measurement*, **5**, 115–124.

Dijk, T. A. van (1987). *Communicating Racism: Ethnic Prejudice in Thought and Talk*. London: Sage.

Guion, R. M. (1976). Personnel selection and placement. In M. Dunnette (ed.) *Handbook of Industrial and Organisational Psychology*. Chicago: Rand McNally.

Herriot, P. and Rothwell, C. (1983). Expectations and impressions in the graduate selection interview. *Journal of Occupational Psychology*, **56**, 303–314.

Institute of Personnel Management (1987). *Contract Compliance: The UK Experience*. London: IPM.

Oliphant, V. N. and Alexander, E. R. (1982). Reactions to resumes as a function of resume determinateness, applicant characteristics and sex of raters. *Personnel Psychology*, **35**, 829–842.

Pearn, M. A. (1978). *Employment Testing and the Goal of Equal Opportunity: The American Experience*. London: The Runnymede Trust.

Pearn, M. A. and Banerji, N. (1987). *The Use of Educational Qualifications to Short-list Candidates for Clerical Jobs: Eight case studies*. Report to the Home Office Research Unit. Oxford: Pearn Kandola Associates.

Pearn, M. A., Kandola, R. S. and Mottram, R. (1987). *Selection Tests and Sex Bias*. Equal Opportunities Commission Research Series. London: HMSO.

Quinn, R. P., Tabor, J. M. and Gordan, L. K. (1968). *The Decision to Discriminate*. Ann Arbor: Institute of Social Research, University of Michigan.

Toplis, J., Dulevicz, V. and Fletcher, C. (1987). *Psychological Testing: A Practical Guide*. London: Institute of Personnel Management.

13

Case Study on Fairness

RICHARD S. WILLIAMS
The Management College, Henley-on-Thames

BACKGROUND

The material described here arose out of an investigation into 'standards of reporting', in other words a concern over the distributions of appraisal form ratings. Also, the opportunity was taken to examine gender differences in ratings.

DESCRIPTION OF THE APPRAISAL SCHEME

At the time of the study the core of the scheme was an appraisal form completed annually by the appraisee's immediate supervisor whose manager ('grand-parent' to the appraisee), in turn, countersigned the form. An appraisal inter-view was expected to take place between the appraisee and the 'grandparent'.

The appraisal form was an eight-page document. The first page contained identifying and other biographical information. Page 2 required a description of the duties performed during the year under review, and a narrative assess-ment of the performance of these duties was found on page 3 along with an overall evaluation of performance on a six-point scale ranging from 'outstanding' to 'unsatisfactory'. Pages 4 and 5 comprised so-called 'aspects of performance', for example oral expression, acceptance of responsibility, which were rated on a six-point scale, with the end points of the scale having behavi-oural definitions for each 'aspect'. On page 6 there were sections for commenting on training and development needs, and for rating promotability

Advances in Selection and Assessment. Edited by M. Smith and I. T. Robertson

according to a three-point scale: 'well fitted', 'fitted', 'not fitted for promotion'. A rating of long-term potential (on page 7) was made on a four-point scale: 'unlikely to progress further', 'to have potential to rise one grade but probably no further', 'to have potential to rise two or three grades', 'to have exceptional potential'. This page also included a narrative 'pen-picture' by the appraiser, and the final page was for the countersigning manager's narrative report.

The completed appraisal form itself was not shown to the appraisee but it formed the basis of performance feedback which was conveyed via the appraisal interview. The emphasis tended to be on the backward aspects of appraisal with little attention, in practice, being paid to work planning. The appraisal form was used by personnel staff in identifying training and development needs. It was used also when job transfers were being considered but, to all intents and purposes, it had no impact on salary determination. So far as rewards were concerned the main purpose of the appraisal form was in influencing promotion decisions. Typically, a certain number of 'well fitted' or 'fitted' promotability ratings would be required during the previous three or four years in order to be considered for promotion. Those selected for consideration then would be interviewed (a panel interview) and appraisal form assessments would be taken into account by the panel in arriving at a promotion decision. For this reason 'standards' of appraisal ratings clearly are important.

DATA COLLECTED

The data collected came from three British government departments of different sizes and from three grade levels. Department A was large, B medium-sized, and C small. The three grade levels were clerical, first-level supervision and second-level supervision. The three levels (indeed, any one level) embraced a wide variety of jobs. The age range, level of educational qualifications, and length of service of the employees all were very wide.

Initially, data were collected from the appraisal forms for small samples of staff; the tables give overall performance (Table 13.1), promotability (Table 13.2), and long-term potential (Table 13.3) ratings. It later became possible to collect a larger data base from Department A as this Department transferred certain appraisal form information to a computer record. The computerised data available are overall performance and promotability ratings and these are shown in the tables under the heading 'A2'.

The figures in Table 13.1 show the well-established positive bias in the distributions of overall performance ratings; this has been taken as 'leniency' in standards of rating and can be looked on as a manifestation of raters' reluctance to rate. However, given the difficulty of obtaining an independent criterion against which to compare such ratings there always will be some uncertainty about how far they depart from being 'true' assessments of

Table 13.1 Overall performance ratings by department, grade and sex

	A Second level		B First level		B Clerical level		C Second level		C First level		A2 Second level		A2 First level	
	M	F	M	F	M	F	M	F	M	F	M	F	M	F
Outstanding	23	1	3	3	1	4	8	1	6	2	107	10	135	93
Very good	272	36	54	56	15	63	86	29	62	45	1206	171	1625	936
Good	146	16	51	38	19	96	42	14	66	41	613	72	1160	569
Fair	15	2	17	7	14	29	0	2	18	6	98	9	187	92
Not quite adequate	1	0	2	0	0	1	0	0	1	0	5	0	15	7
Unsatisfactory	0	0	0	0	0	0	0	0	0	0	1	0	3	0

Table 13.2 Promotability ratings by department, grade and sex

	A Second level		B First level		B Clerical level		C Second level		C First level		A2 Second level		A2 First level	
	M	F	M	F	M	F	M	F	M	F	M	F	M	F
Well fitted	125	11	3	0	0	2	18	3	7	1	596	68	741	321
Fitted	167	16	43	45	12	38	52	13	40	27	780	91	1167	598
Not fitted	161	27	81	59	37	153	65	30	105	66	654	103	1217	778

Table 13.3 Long-term potential ratings by department, grade and sex

	A Second level		B First level		B Clerical level		C Second level		C First level	
	M	F	M	F	M	F	M	F	M	F
Unlikely to progress further	55	12	20	22	17	103	29	13	34	23
Potential to rise about one grade	218	28	49	51	19	87	52	18	49	31
Potential to rise two or three grades	181	15	57	31	13	3	54	15	69	40
Exceptional potential	1	0	1	0	0	0	1	0	1	0

performance. The influence of non-performance factors on performance ratings is well-documented (Landy and Farr, 1983) and it is highly likely that such factors have an impact on the promotability and potential ratings also. Indeed, the fact that appraisal ratings play a significant part in determining promotion decisions is itself one pressure towards inflation.

Inflated ratings consequently become devalued as a means of identifying those to be considered for promotion. Take Department A, for example, where more than 60 per cent of employees are rated as being 'outstanding' or 'very good' and where roughly the same proportion are seen as being promotable. In absolute terms this means that something like 3000 people are regarded by their line managers as being suitable for promotion to the next higher level. Promotion opportunities for such a large number do not exist. So, whether or not these ratings are 'true' the department is left with a number of problems: reducing the 3000 to a more manageable number; managing the disappointment of those who believe they are promotable but are not in fact promoted; reducing the positive bias in the ratings.

There is some variability across departments. This may partly be explained by 'true' performance variability but it is possible that the 'culture' of the department has some influence also. In particular the guidance and instructions provided by Personnel (which may have the effect of creating a particular 'response set') have a bearing on this.

The sex of the appraisee is another non-performance factor which has been shown to affect the ratings given (see Williams and Walker, 1985). As with the present data the findings overall are not clear-cut. The figures given here show no consistent sex difference. But where there are differences the direction of the difference is particularly interesting. For overall performance the differences found here are in favour of women; for promotability and potential the differences are against women.

The fact that in any one year disproportionately fewer of one sex than the other receives 'well fitted' and 'fitted' promotion ratings does not in itself necessarily constitute indirect discrimination as defined in British law. However, given that promotability ratings have a part to play in determining consideration for promotion it clearly is possible that one sex or the other may be disadvantaged. And it is possible that indirect discrimination may result. Take Department A2 in the present case, for example. At the first level significantly more women than men receive 'not fitted' ratings. If the same pattern were found for the previous three years, say, then indirect discrimination may be taking place in that a disproportionately higher number of women (as compared to men) would not be considered for promotion. Thereafter, the 'success' rate of the women may be greater than that of the men given the former's superior overall performance ratings. This assumes, of course, that performance ratings are given due weight by promotion boards but the possibility of further disadvantage creeping in at this stage cannot be ruled out.

Where a significant disparity (defined in statistical terms) is found it should be regarded as a warning sign that further investigation of the differences may be required. For example, a difference against women in, say, promotability ratings may prompt a scrutiny of appraisal forms to check for internal consistency, adequacy of supporting evidence, and the like. A study of appraisers' attitudes may be appropriate; the view that women are less promotable than are men may simply be a reflection of a stereotype that women will marry and leave to have children.

Data of the kind presented thus may be used to monitor equal employment opportunity and in this regard they may also be useful for training purposes.

Though it has to be conceded that the observed differences may be 'true' performance differences they nonetheless may be used on training courses as a vehicle for discussing gender differences in performance, sex stereotypes, expectations of men and women at work, and performance management more generally.

Since these data were collected the appraisal scheme has been substantially changed, both in philosophy and procedure. Study of the phenomena described here is continuing but it is too early yet to report any results.

REFERENCES

Landy, F. J. and Farr, J. L. (1983). *The Measurement of Work Performance*. New York: Academic Press.

Williams, R. S. and Walker, J. (1985). 'Sex differences in performance rating', *Journal of Occupational Psychology*, **58**(4), 331–337.

14

Selection as a Social Process

PETER HERRIOT
Birkbeck College, London

1 THEORETICAL ORIGINS

Applied psychologists have consistently treated social processes as intrusions into the assessment process. They have been considered as subjective interpersonal elements which interfere with objectivity and decrease reliability and validity. Research into social processes has treated them as a cause of bias, and the practical outcome has been the effort to reduce their influence. Hence, for example, interviews are devised which consist of a predetermined series of job sample or personal history questions; or training programmes are conducted in order to minimise the effects of interviewers' implicit personality theories upon their judgements of applicant suitability.

An alternative view starts from an entirely different premise. It suggests that recruitment and selection procedures constitute the initial episodes in the developing relationship between individual and organisation. Selection is not the gate through which applicants must pass before they can relate to the organisation; it is itself part of that relationship. Social psychology then becomes a means of understanding the nature and development of this relationship, rather than the analysis of intrusive interpersonal behaviour.

Applied psychologists in the field of selection have largely concentrated their efforts upon assessment. They have developed tools of assessment, demonstrated their validity and utility, and, with the aid of meta-analysis, are beginning to develop general theories of aptitude for work. However, organisations continue in the main to ignore these efforts. Robertson and Makin (1986), for example, showed that the frequency of use of various mainstream techniques

Advances in Selection and Assessment. Edited by M. Smith and I. T. Robertson
© 1989 John Wiley & Sons Ltd

for managerial selection in the UK is inversely related to their known validity (Hunter and Hunter, 1984; Schmitt *et al.*, 1984). One response to such findings on the part of psychologists has typically been to attribute their cause to organisations; for example, that every interviewer believes him or herself to be the exception to the general rule regarding the low validity of interviews. However, attributions of responsibility might more profitably be directed inwards. It is conceivable that psychologists have over-emphasised the importance of assessment within the context of the overall selection procedure. We have failed to provide an adequate theoretical account of the recruitment and selection process as a whole. Organisations are aware from their experience that the process involves a relationship between organisation and applicant in the context of the job market. Their emphasis on the interview as their favoured instrument of selection indicates their felt need to meet the applicant face-to-face. Psychologists need to provide a socially based theory in order to understand the relationship within which assessment tools are used. What follows is a first attempt at such a theory.

Concepts which feature in the theory proposed here are derived from a variety of social psychological sources. The first is the idea of *role-making* (Katz and Kahn, 1978). Katz and Kahn deploy their role-making model to describe the relationship between organisation and employee. They suppose that the organisation sends messages regarding its role expectations of the employee. For the rest of this chapter the organisation will be referred to as having expectations, attitudes, etc. This usage is shorthand for the employee's organisational role-set. These expectations are both prescriptive, in the sense that they relate to actions which the employee should carry out; and predictive, in the sense that the organisation thinks it likely that the employee will behave in the expected way. The messages may be implicit or explicit, and may be accurately perceived or be misperceived by the employee. The employee will also hold role expectations of herself. 'Each individual has a conception of the office he or she occupies, and a set of attitudes and beliefs about what should and should not be done by an occupant of that office' (Katz and Kahn, 1978, p. 194). As a consequence of the perceived organisational expectations and her own role expectations of herself, the employee will act in response.

However, Katz and Kahn point out: 'To list the concepts in this order emphasises one direction of causality—the influence of role expectations on role behaviour. There is also a feedback loop; the degree to which a person's behaviour conforms to the expectations of the role-set at one point in time will affect the state of those expectations at the next moment' (1978, p. 195). To sum up, Katz and Kahn consider the relationship between organisation and employee to be one in which expectations held by the organisation of the employee are communicated, perceived, matched with the employee's own expectations of her office, and acted upon. Such actions affect organisational expectations, . . . and so on, in a cyclical process.

One noteworthy omission from this theory is the concept of reciprocity. The employee may not merely have expectations of herself; she may also have expectations of how the organisation should and will act towards her. This reciprocity is captured in the idea of the *psychological contract* (Argyris, 1960; Levinson, 1962; Schein, 1965). At any given point in time, the relationship may be characterised by the extent to which the expectations each party holds of the other are congruent. However, it is *perceptions* of the other party's expectations of oneself together with one's own expectations of the other party which predict the state of the relationship. Congruence is therefore likely to be different for each party, since it is defined as the proportion of a party's own expectations and *perceived* other's expectations which are the same.

The idea of the *episode* has been developed by Argyle *et al.* (1981) to describe self-contained sequences of events in social situations. For example, an employment interview can be construed as an episode. Argyle *et al.* emphasise that each episode has its own rules, explicit or implicit, which the participants need to know and be practised in, in order to play their roles acceptably.

Another theoretical approach which will contribute to a social psychological account of the selection process is that of Bandura (1977, 1978, 1986). He argues that:

> A global view of what people think of themselves cannot possibly account for the wide variations they typically show in their self-reactions under different situational circumstances, on different activities, and at different times. . . . In social learning theory, a self system is not a psychic agent that controls behaviour. Rather, it refers to cognitive structures that provide reference mechanisms and to a set of subfunctions for the perception, evaluation, and regulation of behaviour. (Bandura, 1978, p. 348)

People observe their own actions and their consequences; evaluate them in terms of their standards, others' expectations, and whether they attribute their actions to themselves or others; and respond by evaluating themselves and acting in consequence. Hence in a relationship with an organisation an employee might bring to the relationship initially a self-concept possessing a considerable degree of *self-efficacy*. Self-efficacy implies the belief that one is capable of achieving one's objectives in specific situations; it differs from the concept of internal locus of control, in the sense that the latter implies the tendency to attribute all outcomes oneself rather than to situational constraints. It also differs from the concept of (positive) self-esteem, in the sense that self-esteem is a more global concept relating to the self-concept in general rather than to effectiveness in particular. Such a concept of the self-system and of self-efficacy is necessary if we are to understand employees' decisions that they are capable of acting in accord with organisations' expectations; whether to try to modify them; and what expectations to hold of the organisation for themselves.

Finally, we cannot ignore the concept of *power* in a social relationship. Labour market factors *may* give power to the applicant, if the selection ratio is high. However, where it is low, the organisation holds the power, since it can always find other qualified applicants. The organisation, furthermore, manages the selection procedure, determining what selection tools are used and in what order. It expects the applicant to disclose information about herself as of right, but treats disclosure about itself as optional. It retains the right not to disclose to the applicant information it has obtained about her (e.g. the results of psychological tests which she has undergone).

2 THEORETICAL PROPOSITIONS

2.1 Selection is a role-making social process

Katz and Kahn's model of the relationship between the organisation and the employee is also applicable to all those events which occur before the employment contract is entered upon. That is, in the recruitment and selection process also, the organisation communicates its expectations which are perceived accurately or inaccurately, related to the self-system, and acted upon. The applicant's actions affect subsequent organisational expectations; the organisation may accommodate its expectations in the light of this feedback.

2.2 The role-making process is reciprocal

As the idea of the psychological contract suggests, the applicant also has expectations of the organisation. Hence at any one point in time, the organisation will have a perception of the applicant's expectations of it. The converse is true of the applicant; as indicated in 2.1 (above), she will have a perception of the organisation's expectations of her.

2.3 Expectations are of two types

First, each party holds expectations of the other regarding their behaviour during the selection procedure itself. For example, the applicant might expect the organisation to spend a lot of time answering questions about the nature of the work and the life-style involved in working for the organisation. The organisation might expect the applicant to answer questions about the organisation in order to demonstrate that she was motivated enough to find out about it.

The second type of expectation relates to the future job; how the applicant expects the organisation to treat her, and how the organisation expects the applicant to behave when an employee. For example, the applicant may be willing to take early responsibility but want a supervisor available for support, while the organisation may say it expects the applicant to be mobile within the UK.

In all these cases, the other party's expectations may be misperceived. For instance in the examples above, the applicant may be misperceived as expecting to be excessively dependent, while the organisation may be misperceived as expecting to be able to move the applicant at a moment's notice.

2.4 The selection process consists of a sequence of episodes

Each episode consists of the communication of a set of expectations to the other party, who responds. Thus, for example, the sending of a blank application form to the applicant and the applicant's decision whether to complete it constitutes an episode. Each episode has its own specific rules, often implicit expectations about how the recipient of the message should behave. For example, the application form should be completed with respect to all the questions asked, and any open-ended questions should be completed in such a way that the space available is filled. Furthermore, expectations about the job are also communicated. For example, if there is a question regarding particulars of the applicant's degree, it is likely to be inferred by the applicant that the job requires degree-level skills. The applicant's response may be to exit from the relationship, in this case to decide not to complete the application form. It may be to respond, in the way expected. Or it may be to respond in a way not entirely in accord with the organisation's expectations, but not so as to cause the organisation to reject the application out of hand, merely to accommodate somewhat. For example, an applicant might leave blank a question enquiring whether she was married. Obviously, an episode may operate in the reverse direction, involving expectations communicated by the applicant to the organisation, and resulting in a similar range of decision options. Indeed, it is proposed that the selection process consists in the main of alternating messages with the response to one initiating the next message, as in a conversation. Figure 14.1 presents a model of the typical procedure used by organisations in the UK recruiting graduates.

It is important to note that the expectations communicated in different episodes may be different, for several reasons. First, different organisational representatives may be involved in each episode, and not present a consistent message. Second, the organisation may have accommodated its expectations of this applicant as a result of feedback. Third, the applicant may have accommodated her expectations for the same reason. Finally, expectations of immediate behaviour within each episode differ by definition, since each episode has its own rules.

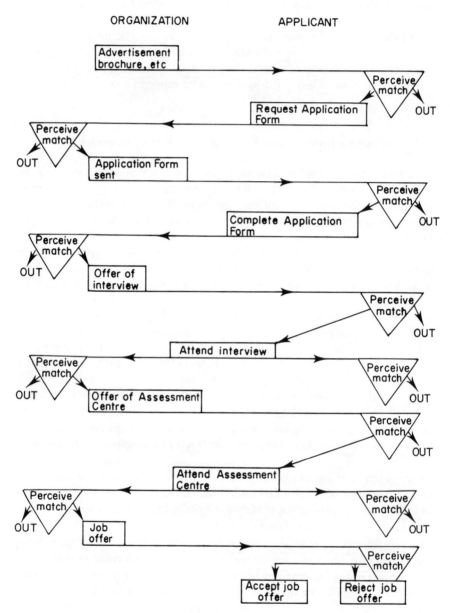

Figure 14.1   Episodes of a selection process

2.5 Response to the organisation's expectations is partly a function of the applicant's self-efficacy

An applicant with a high degree of self-efficacy may act in accordance with her belief in her capacity to respond as the organisation expects. For example, she will demonstrate confidence in her ability to acquire the new technical skills which she is told that she will need. Further, she will respond with the confidence that her own response will in turn affect the organisation's response in the way she desires; that is, she will believe that her own expectations will be met by the organisation. So, for example, she may respond to the organisation's expectation that she should be prepared to be mobile with the message that she will travel, but only so far as to be within reasonable distance of her aged parents. Or she may understand the implicit expectation that she should not ask questions at the interview until invited to, but respond by apologising before she asks one early in the interview. This latter example indicates that an applicant with a high degree of self-efficacy will believe herself able to meet the organisation's expectations during the selection procedure as well as in the job. Indeed, she may try impression management as a means to this end.

2.6 Response to the applicant's expectations is partly a function of the applicant's perceived efficacy

The applicant's mode of communication of her expectations and her presentation of herself will result in favourable or unfavourable judgements of her capability of fulfilling the organisation's expectations about job behaviour. For example, confident non-verbal behaviour and an account of her ambitions for career advancement will result in her being considered highly motivated to work for the organisation. Similarly, a really competently and tidily completed application form or a polite request for further detailed information will be likely to result in a continued relationship rather than the organisation withdrawing.

2.7 Each party is likely to perceive the other's expectations regarding the job to be more congruent with its own than is actually the case

In principle, misperceptions could operate in both directions, with, for example, applicants perceiving organisational expectations as being even *less* congruent with their own than they actually are. This is unlikely in practice, however, since organisations are concerned to present a favourable public image in general, and in particular to attract more applicants by glossy brochures and the like. Similarly, it might be argued that organisations will believe the applicant's expectations of work to be more similar to their own than is in fact the case. This is likely to be due to their inability to empathise with others whose experience is different.

2.8 Power in the relationship is partly related to the labour market

Where there is a high selection ratio, the organisation will compromise by accommodating its expectations to bring them in line with the applicant's. Where there is a low selection ratio, the applicant accommodates hers to conform. Alternatively, in the former case, the organisation accepts a higher degree of incongruence, while in the latter, the applicant does so.

3. PREDICTIONS

The key dependent variable used in many studies of social relations is the decision to remain in the relationship or to leave it. When the selection process is analysed as a social relationship, leaving the relationship by the applicant involves such actions as not completing a form, refusing an invitation to an interview, or rejecting a job offer. From the organisation's point of view, leaving the relationship implies not inviting the applicant for interview, and other forms of rejection. In terms of the present theoretical approach, the decision to stay or leave is taken by one or the other of the parties at the end of each episode. The pattern tends to be an alternating, cyclical one as demonstrated in Figure 14.1. After the employment contract has been entered into, withdrawal by the employee is characterised as voluntary turnover, by the organisation as involuntary turnover.

Hypothesis 1

The probability of a party's leaving the relationship at any one point in time during the selection procedure is negatively related to the current degree of congruence between the party's expectations of the job and their perceptions of the other's expectations of the job.

Hypothesis 2

Probability of exit is negatively related to the degree of congruence between a party's expectations of the selection procedure and their perceptions of the other's expectations of the selection procedure.

Hypothesis 3

Probability of exit is positively related to the degree of accuracy of one party's perception of the other's expectations of the job, since increased accuracy decreases false congruence (proposition 2.7 above). Hence, when expectations are made explicit, probability of exit increases.

Hypothesis 4

Probability of exit after employment (voluntary and involuntary turnover) will decrease when expectations have been made explicit during the selection procedure. Job performance will be improved, since the employee will have a clearer idea of what is expected of her.

Hypothesis 5

Probability of exit is negatively related to the level of job-related self-efficacy held of herself by the applicant, or her efficacy as perceived by the organisation.

Hypothesis 6

Probability of exit is positively related to the selection ratio in the case of the applicant, negatively in the case of the organisation.

Hypothesis 7

Degree of congruence of expectations will increase during the course of the selection process, as parties accommodate to their perceptions of the other's expectations.

Hypothesis 8

Degree of accuracy of perceptions of the other's expectations will also increase during the course of the selection process, as parties acquire more information about them. Hence the effect of accommodation in increasing congruence will be offset by the effect of accuracy in decreasing it. Aggregated congruence will increase, however, since parties with low congruence will exit.

Hypothesis 9

Where the selection ratio is high, organisations are more likely to change their expectations to achieve greater congruence than are applicants, and also are more likely to tolerate greater incongruence. When the selection ratio is low, the reverse is the case.

Hypothesis 10

Where congruence regarding selection procedures is low, satisfaction with them will be low. As a consequence applications will decrease in those cases where current and potential future applicants are in contact (e.g. in university).

Hypothesis 11

Where the selection ratio is low, organisations will place greater weight upon congruence of expectations regarding the selection process. This is because the other types of congruence (those regarding the job and efficacy) are unlikely by themselves to discriminate sufficiently between equally well-qualified applicants.

4 EVIDENCE

Evidence supporting this theory is sparse and scattered, and mostly refers to isolated episodes of the selection process. This is because most academic research has investigated the properties of selection instruments rather than of selection processes. It will therefore be presented under more general headings than the propositions and hypotheses outlined above.

4.1 Organisations' expectations regarding the selection process (see 2.3 and Hypothesis 2)

From the point of view of the present theoretical approach, this is an extremely important variable. Its presence in the theory suggests that the classical view of selection as the assessment of suitability for employment is a limited and partial approach. It is maintained here that the degree to which the applicant is considered likely to meet the organisation's expectations regarding job behaviour is only one of several predictors of organisational decisions to exit from the relationship. A major and hitherto neglected predictor is the organisation's expectations regarding the applicant's immediate behaviour in the selection procedure. In other words, it is suggested that present as much as predicted failure to meet expectations will determine whether the relationship is severed. The expectations held by the organisation of the applicant's behaviour in a particular episode are considered to be part of the rules of that episode (Argyle et al., 1981).

Hence failure to meet these expectations may be characterised as the breaking of social rules. Inferences will be drawn by the organisation from these violations regarding characteristics of the applicant; for example, poor spelling on an application form may be taken to imply lack of effort and therefore lack of motivation to join the organisation. Such inferences may be used subsequently to justify the decision to reject the applicant; but form-filling behaviour (as opposed to the content of the form) is certainly not a selection instrument derived from a job analysis.

In contrast to the previous research of Campion (1978), Wingrove et al. (1984) investigated both style and content of application forms in an effort to discover what predicted whether graduate applicants were rejected or selected for interview. Six organisations provided 792 application forms which were coded into 315 variables. Of these, 41 related to the mode of presentation of the form. Four interpretable factors emerged from analysis, which were:

(i)   The applicant wrote a lot, filling the spaces provided.
(ii) The writing was neat and legible, and included certain key words relating to ambition, responsibility, and career.
(iii) Forms were typed rather than handwritten with few spelling mistakes.
(iv) Forms were of scruffy appearance and included additional sheets.

Factors (i) and (ii) added significantly to the power of a logistic regression model in the case of two transport organisations; factor (iv) for a computer organisation. Further analysis (Herriot and Wingrove, 1984) was conducted upon think-aloud protocols of selectors as they read the application forms. Comments upon the presentation of the form were second only in frequency to comments about general areas such as academic achievements or work experience. It seems clear from these data that these organisations expected certain behaviour in the completion of the application form, and tended to reject applicants who failed to meet these expectations.

As far as the interview is concerned, it is clear that there are certain rules about what is acceptable behaviour in social situations in general, and that most people appreciate most of these (Price and Bouffard, 1974). However, applicants and organisations have significantly different expectations about how much each party will talk, and about what subject. Interviewers expect applicants to talk more about themselves than applicants expect to, while applicants expect interviewers to talk more about the organisation than interviewers expect to (Herriot and Rothwell, 1983). Indeed, the amount that the applicant talked about her education added to the predictive power of a regression model predicting judged suitability for employment. In an early use of Bales' interaction process analysis of the selection interview, Sydiaha (1962) showed that rejection was more likely when applicants asked for information, opinions, or suggestions, thus supporting the idea that interviewers do not expect applicants to behave in this way.

Much of the research on non-verbal communication in the interview may perhaps be explained in the same way. Generally, more active and aggressive non-verbal behaviour by the applicant is likely to result in selection (Dipboye and Wiley, 1977); it is also likely to result in an interview impression of self-confidence (Tessler and Sushelsky, 1978). Interviewers expect the applicant to demonstrate self-confidence where her record justifies it, and are more likely to reject a well-qualified applicant if she lacks confidence.

It follows from all this evidence that accurate information concerning the expectations of both parties regarding the selection procedure should prevent the organisation from rejecting an applicant for the invalid reason that she did not know the rules of the game.

4.2 Applicants' expectations regarding the selection process (see 2.3 and Hypothesis 2)

Recruiters' behaviour was the major reason for accepting a job offer in the case of one-third of Glueck's (1973) student applicants. In a review article, Rynes *et al.* (1980) wonder whether recruiter behaviour is so powerful because applicants use it to infer likely organisational behaviour, or because they guess from it how likely they are to receive a job offer. Certainly, the probability of interviewees' acceptance of a job offer is predicted by their perceptions of the interviewer's personality, her manner, and the adequacy of the job information which she provides (Schmitt and Coyle, 1976). In more recent work, Harn and Thornton (1985) found that the interviewer's listening skills are the only significant predictor of willingness to accept a job offer. This relationship was moderated by the extent to which the applicant saw the interviewer as typical of the organisation. Moreover, these effects do not seem to be limited to graduate level employees. Liden and Parsons (1986) found that applicants for seasonal employment in an amusement park were more likely to accept a job offer the more they liked the interviewer. This relationship was moderated by their perception of the alternative jobs open to them, thus supporting another element of the theory proposed here. However, in a study comparing the relative effects of attributes of the job and of recruiting practices on rated probability of accepting a job offer, Powell (1984) found no effect for practices.

The subsequent estimations of the interview held by MBA students were predicted by interested and concerned interviewer behaviour, by being asked technical questions in their area of expertise, and by discussing the careers of other MBAs in the organisation (Alderfer and McCord, 1979; Keenan and Wedderburn, 1980). Applicants also like to be asked open-ended questions (Jablin and McComb, 1984).

There are indications that applicants prefer some selection devices to others. Job sample tests are considered fairer, clearer, and more appropriate than paper and pencil tests (Schmidt *et al.*, 1977). Applicants may believe their privacy has been invaded if they have disclosed personal information during the selection process, especially if they consider themselves to have no control over how it will be used or what will be done with it (Fusilier and Hoyer, 1980).

While it may not be easy to relate all these findings to applicants' *expectations* of how the organisation will and should behave during the selection process, it is nevertheless clear that sympathetic interpersonal behaviour, the presentation of job information, and the use of selection procedures with face validity affect applicants' satisfaction with the process and their likelihood of accepting a job offer.

4.3 The role of self-efficacy (see 2.5 and Hypothesis 5)

Despite the considerable recent evidence on the wide-ranging effects of the self-concept on behaviour (Markus and Wurf, 1987), applied psychologists in the field of selection have paid little attention to this theoretical construct. Some early research showed that preference for organisations is closely related to applicants' self-concepts. Tom (1971) found that students looking for jobs held similar images of themselves and the organisation for those organisations which they preferred. However, Behling and Tolliver (1972) showed that this relationship was moderated by their self-esteem, and only held for those with high self-esteem. Indeed, self-evaluations of ability are more valid for people with an internal locus of control (Mabe and West, 1982).

Potential applicants may not apply in the first place if they believe that there is a low probability of their receiving a job offer (Rynes and Lawler, 1983). Certainly, they may self-select out by not taking up a job offer if they have found themselves unable to manage a trainability test (Downs et al., 1978). On the other hand, the more they see themselves as the prime agents in determining the course of their future life, the more successful are sales representatives (Tullar and Barrett, 1976). Positive relationships have been obtained between ratings by new recruits into the British army of their confidence in their ability to complete initial training, and actual completion rates (Winter and Herriot, in preparation).

Hence the self-efficacy of the applicant regarding their capacity to do a job and their ability to be selected have important consequences for whether they remain in the selection procedure or self-select out.

4.4 Applicants' expectations regarding the job (see 2.2, 2.7, and Hypotheses 3 and 4)

There is some disagreement in the research literature as to the extent to which organisations and applicants hold different expectations of the job. The MBA students of Ward and Athos (1972) found that recruiters matched for organisation only agreed $r = 0.56$ in terms of their descriptions of the job, while the students agreed $r = 0.48$ with the recruiters. Faculty, students, and recruiters largely shared the same beliefs about the relative importance of applicant characteristics to the recruiters (Posner, 1981). However, faculty and recruiters were poor judges of what students wanted from a job. Once employed, business school students change the expectations which they held before entering the organisation (Wanous, 1976). While their expectations of intrinsic rewards decrease markedly after 8 months, those of extrinsic rewards remain the same.

Extrinsic rewards may be easily communicated before entry, intrinsic ones less so. Such disappointment of expectations can have deleterious consequences; Mabey's (1986) engineering graduates experienced lower job satisfaction and organisational commitment the more unrealistically inflated their initial expectations, while Katzell's (1968) nurses were more likely to withdraw from training for the same reason.

To recapitulate on 2.7, if the employee has received a clear indication of the organisation's expectations before employment, then her perception of those expectations will become less congruent with her own expectations. This is because she will tend to hold inflated expectations about the job. Hence accuracy will increase and consequently congruence will decrease, with the probability that the applicant will exit during the selection process. On the other hand, if such realistic job previews have not been provided during the selection process, accuracy will only increase after the evidence of bitter experience in employment has been assimilated. Consequently voluntary turnover will *increase* in the absence of any realistic job preview. However, if a preview has been provided, individuals may be clearer about what the organisation expects of them, and so perform better when they are in employment. It is important to note that the preview should be provided *early* in the selection procedure. Otherwise (see Hypothesis 8) parties will have increased their congruence already by accommodation to the extent that increased accuracy will not decrease congruence sufficiently to cause exit. Overall, the research on realistic job previews supports this analysis. In their meta-analytic review of 20 studies, Premack and Wanous (1985) found that previews lowered applicants' expectations; increased the probability of exit before employment; decreased turnover; and increased commitment, job satisfaction, and performance.

It is worth emphasising that organisations have spent far less energy on discovering more accurately the other part of the congruence equation—the job expectations held by the applicants. Nor do they often explain what behaviour they expect of applicants in the selection procedure. Yet such effort would be well worth its costs, since faulty perceptions on either side might result in false congruence and consequent faulty decisions.

5 UTILITY

Research on utility has typically assessed the cost-benefit of specific psychometric instruments (see Boudreau, this volume), using the financial value of the individual's work to the organisation as the benefit, and the cost of the test or assessment centre as the cost. If we look at the selection procedure as a whole, and as it is actually carried out, these methods of utility analysis appear extremely limited in scope. Rather than evaluating instruments, we need to evaluate a process; the appropriate techniques appear to be those of programme evaluation. Rather than the prediction of individuals' work behaviour and its value, we will need to look at the organisational outcomes in terms of internal structure and external relations. For example, the consequences of a selection process which increases accuracy of perceptions of the organisation's expectations for the training department; the results of an intrusive personality test in terms of organisational image and recruitment success; the implications of appointing people with a high level of incongruence for placement and career development. It is interesting to note movement in this direction by utility theorists. It is when a theoretical analysis of the selection process is undertaken that the need for broad-ranging evaluation becomes clear.

REFERENCES

Alderfer, C. P. and McCord, C. G. (1970). Personal and situational factors in the recruitment interview. *Journal of Applied Psychology*, **54**, 377–385.

Argyle, M., Furnham, A. and Graham, J. A. (1981). *Social Situations*. Cambridge, Cambridge University Press.

Argyris, C. (1960). *Understanding Organisational Behaviour*. Homewood, Illinois, Dorsey.

Bandura, A. (1977). Self-efficacy: toward a unifying theory of behavioural change. *Psychological Bulletin*, **84**, 191–215.

Bandura, A. (1978). The self system in reciprocal determinism. *American Psychologist*, **33**, 344–358.

Bandura, A. (1986). *Social Foundations of Thought and Action*. Englewood Cliffs, Prentice-Hall.

Behling, O. and Tolliver, J. (1972). Self-concept moderated by self-esteem as a prediction of choice among potential employers. *Academy of Management Proceedings*, **32**, 214–216.

Campion, M. A. (1978). Identification of variables most influential in determining interviewers' evaluations of applicants in a college placement centre. *Psychological Reports*, **42**, 947–952.

Dipboye, R. L. and Wiley, J. W. (1977). Reactions of college recruiters to interviewee sex and self-presentation style. *Journal of Vocational Behaviour*, **10**, 1–12.

Downs, S., Farr, R. M. and Colbeck, L. (1978). Self-appraisal: a convergence of selection and guidance. *Journal of Occupational Psychology*, **51**, 271–278.

Fusilier, M. R. and Hoyer, W. D. (1980). Variables affecting perceptions of invasion of privacy in a personnel selection situation. *Journal of Applied Psychology*, **65**, 623–626.

Glueck, W. F. (1973). Recruiters and executives: how do they affect job choice? *Journal of College Placement*, **33**, 77–78.

Harn, T. J. and Thornton, G. C. (1985). Recruiter counselling behaviours and applicant impressions. *Journal of Occupational Psychology*, **58**, 57–65.

Herriot, P. (1987). The selection interview. In Warr, P. B. (ed.) *Psychology at Work* (3rd edn) Harmondsworth, Penguin.

Herriot, P. and Rothwell, C. (1983). Expectations and impressions in the graduate selection interview. *Journal of Occupational Psychology*, **56**, 303–314.

Herriot, P. and Wingrove, J. (1984). Decision processes in graduate pre-selection. *Journal of Occupational Psychology*, **57**, 269–276.

Hunter, J. E. and Hunter, R. F. (1984). Validity and utility of alternative predictors of job performance. *Psychological Bulletin*, **96**, 72–98.

Jablin, F. M. and McComb, K. B. (1984). The employment screening interview: an organisational assimilation and communication perspective. In Bostrom, R. (ed.) *Communication Yearbook*. Beverley Hills, CA: Sage.

Katz, D. and Kahn, R. L. (1978). *The Social Psychology of Organisations* (2nd edn) New York, Wiley.

Katzell, M. E. (1968). Expectations and drop-outs in schools of nursing. *Journal of Applied Psychology*, **52**, 154–158.

Keenan, A. and Wedderburn, A. A. I. (1980). Putting the boot on the other foot: candidates' descriptions of interviewers. *Journal of Occupational Psychology*, **53**, 81–89.

Levinson, H. (1962). *Men, Management, and Mental Health*. Cambridge, Mass.: Harvard University Press.

Liden, R. C. and Parsons, C. K. (1986). A field-study of job applicant interview perceptions, alternative opportunities, and demographic characteristics. *Personnel Psychology*, **39**, 109–122.

Mabe, P. A. and West, S. G. (1982). Validity of self-evaluation of ability: a review and meta-analysis. *Journal of Applied Psychology*, **67**, 280–296.

Mabey, C. (1986). *Graduates into Industry*. London, Gower Press.

Markus, H. and Wurf, E. (1987). The dynamic self-concept: a social psychological perspective. *Annual Review of Psychology*, **38**, 299–337.

Posner, B. Z. (1980). Comparing recruiter, student, and faculty perceptions of important applicant and job characteristics. *Personnel Psychology*, **34**, 329–340.

Powell, G. (1984). Effects of job attributes and recruiting practices on applicant decisions: a comparison. *Personnel Psychology*, **37**, 721–731.

Premack, S. L. and Wanous, J. P. (1985). A meta-analysis of realistic job preview experiments. *Journal of Applied Psychology*, **70**, 706–719.

Price, R. H. and Bouffard, D. L. (1974). Behavioural appropriateness and situational constraint as dimensions of social behaviour. *Journal of Personality and Social Psychology*, **30**, 579–586.

Robertson, I. T. and Makin, P. J. (1986). Management selection in Britain: a survey and critique. *Journal of Occupational Psychology*, **59**, 45–57.

Rynes, S. L., Heneman, H. G. and Schwab, D. P. (1980). Individual reactions to organisational recruiting: a review. *Personnel Psychology*, **33**, 529–542.

Rynes, S. L. and Lawler, J. (1983). A policy capturing investigation of the role of expectancies in decisions to pursue job alternatives. *Journal of Applied Psychology*, **68**, 620–631.

Schein, E. H. (1965). *Organisational Psychology*. Englewood Cliffs, Prentice Hall.

Schmidt, F. L., Greenthal, A. L., Hunter, J. E., Berner, J. G. and Seaton, F. W. (1977). Job samples versus paper and pencil trades and technical tests: adverse impact and examinee attitudes. *Personnel Psychology*, **30**, 187–197.

Schmitt, N. and Coyle, B. W. (1976). Applicant decisions in the employment interview. *Journal of Applied Psychology*, **61**, 184–192.

Schmitt, N., Gooding, R. Z., Noe, R. A. and Kirsch, M. (1984). Meta-analyses of validity studies published between 1964 and 1982 and the investigation of study characteristics. *Personnel Psychology*, **37**, 407–422.

Sydiaha, D. (1962). Bales' interaction process analysis of personnel selection interviews. *Journal of Applied Psychology*, **46**, 344–349.

Tessler, R. and Sushelsky, L. (1978). Effects of eye contact and social status on the perception of a job applicant in an employment interviewing situation. *Journal of Vocational Behaviour*, **13**, 338–347.

Tom, V. R. (1971). The role of personality and organisational images in the recruiting process. *Organisational Behaviour and Human Performance*, **6**, 573–592.

Tullar, W. L. and Barrett, G. V. (1976). The future autobiography as a predictor of sales success. *Journal of Applied Psychology*, **61**, 371–373.

Wanous, J. P. (1976). Organisational entry: from naive expectations to realistic beliefs. *Journal of Applied Psychology*, **61**, 22–29.

Ward, L. B. and Athos, A. G. (1972). Student expectations of corporate life: implications for management recruiting. Boston, Harvard University Division of Research.

Wingrove, J., Herriot, P. and Glendinning, R. (1984). Graduate pre-selection: a research note. *Journal of Occupational Psychology*, **57**, 169–171.

Winter, B. and Herriot, P. (in preparation). Aptitude, self-efficacy and situation as predictors of success in training.

15

Selection as a Social Process: from Scapegoat to Golden Hen?

R. J. Tissen
Management Studiecentrum, Stichtig de Baak

Although the title of Peter Herriot's chapter on selection as a social process may seem to the casual observer to suggest the self-evident, his contribution is, in reality, an important one, both for the furthering of theory-development as for actual practice: the continuous desire of organizations to be able to select the best possible candidates.

First of all Herriot's approach places the issue of selection in a much broader perspective, thereby rightfully distancing himself from the narrow focus of applied psychologists and of many practitioners on 'techniques' instead of 'process'. This is all the more interesting when one looks at the fact that many of the 'mainstream' selection techniques arre of varying—but generally low—validity. While for most of the alternative techniques as described in chapter 14, the question of their ultimate validity—and thus of their overall effectiveness—still needs to be firmly settled.

It is precisely here that Herriot poses his central concept, namely that it is highly unlikely that we will be able to develop effective tools of assessment, without at least taking social process variables explicitly into account, not to mention incorporating them in what could be the first step towards a more wholistic approach to selection.

It is within this context that Herriot argues 'the need for a socially based theory in order to understand the relationship within which assessment tools are used'.

Katz and Kahn's idea of role-making to describe the relationship between

Advances in Selection and Assessment. Edited by M. Smith and I. T. Robertson
© 1989 John Wiley & Sons Ltd

organization and employee is an interesting one as a starting point for such a theory. It, however, becomes even more interesting when this idea and Herriot's concept of a socially based theory are interpreted from a 'corporate culture' perspective, of which in the last years we have seen a proliferation of articles in both the popular and the scientific press. Thus the supposition that the organization sends messages regarding its role expectations of the employee really constitutes what is generally described, but hardly ever well defined, as corporate culture. Intra-organizational behaviour can, as a result, indeed be viewed as the match between expectations held by the organization of the employee and expectations of the employee as to how the organization will act towards him or her (p. 174). If the relationship between the organization and the employee can be characterized as above then the whole issue of corporate culture cannot be limited to the confinements of the organization as such, but must also include all those events that occur before an employment contract is entered into. Selection as a social process then becomes a vital instrument in sustaining or changing corporate culture, which underlines the importance of treating the selection procedure as more than applying a certain set of techniques.

It logically follows that 'managing' the external-internal flow process becomes an equally important issue for organizations, one which has up until now been underestimated and of which a relatively low degree of understanding exists.

Herriot's proposal to view the selection process as a series of episodes (p. 175), whereby each episode consists of the communication of a set of expectations to the other party, who then responds, serves as a first but fundamental stepping stone in the process of understanding the relationship between applicant and organization. It can indeed help to gain a clear understanding of the key dependent variable used in many studies of social relations, e.g. the decision to remain in the relationship or to leave it.

It however does not directly explain the decision of people either to enter a relationship or not unless one accepts the fact 'that corporate culture' functions as an initial episode in establishing a relationship. This explains the 'self-selecting mechanisms' which many organizations with a strong corporate culture refer to when addressing the question of establishing a relationship with potential employees. It also underlines the cyclical pattern of episodes: many cycles of consistent episodes and matched behavior between the organization and its employees may explain the strength of certain corporate cultures.

After establishing an initial relationship the organization's expectations regarding the selection process, the applicant's expectations regarding the selection process and the job, become important areas of attention, equal to or even beyond the use of specific tools both parties have available in the selection procedure.

Herriot is right to point out that in theory a major and hitherto neglected variable concerns itself with the organization's expectations regarding the applicant's immediate behavior in the selection procedure, an aspect of the whole process that is, in actual practice, widely recognized as being an issue of predictive value. He is also right in drawing the conclusion that accurate information concerning the expectations of both parties regarding the selection procedure is essential. This stresses the need for developing tools to prevent the organization from rejecting an applicant for the invalid reason that he or she did not know the rules of the game. It is interesting to note here that one of the largest Dutch (commercial) temporary work agencies sends out a leaflet to all of its applicants with information on exactly this element of the selection process. This, however, seems to be the exception to a general rule. The general rule is that it is 'not done' to provide applicants with this kind of information, since it may enable them to engage in 'artificial behavior', e.g. applicants preparing themselves to behave in a certain manner for only a short time during the selection process, in order to get the job.

As regards applicant's expectations of the selection process, Herriot observes that sympathetic interpersonal behavior of the interviewer, the presentation of job information and the use of selection tools with face validity affects an applicant's satisfaction with the process and increases the likelihood of their accepting a job offer. Although there is as yet not much research to rely upon, this seems to be somewhat in contrast with actual practice where selection in many cases is still predominantly seen as a routine activity, with little structural significance, that can be delegated to junior (staff) managers who need not have any real professional aptitude or training in this field. As for providing applicants with relevant job information, it can be argued that many organizations see this as 'added costs' instead of 'added value', thereby stressing an attitude that most applicants 'should be happy with the opportunity of a job'.

The role of self efficacy (p. 183) reflects back on what is earlier noted as the meachnism of self-selection that seems to benefit organizations with a strong corporate culture. The issue raised here is that applicants' self-concept is closely related to their preference for organizations. Hence it is important for organizations in each episode of the selection process to analyze an applicant's state of self-efficacy with the desired organizational state, in order to be able to influence the decision to remain in the selection procedure or to (self-) select out.

Finally Herriot raises an equally important issue when he points out that job previews tend to lower applicants' expectations and therefore increase the probability of exit before employment but also result in decreased turnover, increased commitment, job-satisfaction and performance. This again stresses the need to look at the selection process as more than the application of a set of psychometric instruments and for that matter—on utility analysis as typically assessing the cost-benefit of these instruments (p. 184).

16

Selection as a Social Process – Case-study

Donald McLeod
Civil Service Commission, Staines

The aim of this case-study is to provide the reader with a real-life example of an existing selection process, in some detail, in order to help relate the necessary abstractions of Herriot's chapter to something more concrete. The process to be described is that by which graduate entrants to the Civil Service are selected as 'high-flier' Administration Trainees. Cross-references will be made from time to time to the similar method by which graduates are chosen for training as specialist Inspectors of Taxes.

THE CIVIL SERVICE SELECTION BOARD (CSSB)

1 Publicity

Herriot omits an essential stage, one that precedes the first contact between the two parties to this prospective social relationship—the organisation and the applicant. This of course is establishing by job-analysis exactly what is to go into the advertising material, what the selection-assessment procedure is going to look like, what, indeed, new recruits will be expected to do and what knowledge, skills, and abilities they will be expected to bring to bear in the doing of it.

For the Administration Trainee entry, there will be regular discussion between the recruiting agency—the Civil Service Commission, of which CSSB is a part—and senior officials responsible for personnel management in the Service at large. The number of vacancies for the coming year's recruitment

Advances in Selection and Assessment. Edited by M. Smith and I. T. Robertson
© 1989 John Wiley & Sons Ltd

scheme will be fixed—typically, at the present time, at about 75–80. The 'prospectus' will be agreed.

Formal job-analyses have also been carried out from time to time (e.g. Dulewicz and Kennay, 1976; Paul, 1987). The brochure that goes to the prospective applicant covers a general description of the work and of expected career-progression; it sets out the demands in the form, broadly, of a person-specification; eligibility issues are detailed; so too are salary-scales; and a description of the selection procedure, with example test-items where appropriate, is also given. Advertising is placed in the national 'quality' press. The careers advisory services at universities and polytechnics can also play a large part in 'inaugurating' the social process proper between organisation and prospective applicant.

In deciding on whether or not to pursue an application there are, for the individual, one or two concrete issues of eligibility concerning nationality—it is, after all, an appointment with UK Government—and, for these training grades, age-limits. As a graduate entry a degree, or the prospect of a degree, with at least second-class honours is also a requirement. The rest of the decision will depend on the outcome of the individual's 'perceived match' exercise with respect to the prospects and demands of the job and his or her own needs and abilities.

2 Application form

It would be unusual for the organisation to exit at this point, as sending out an application form—or handing one over in a careers advisor's office—would be virtually automatic, unless the applicant had volunteered information that showed him or her to be clearly ineligible. The applicant, on the other hand, may very well exit before completing the form.

3 Pre-selection

For prospective administrators, the completed and returned application form results in an invitation to the formal pre-selection stage, known as the Qualifying Test (QT). This consists of a battery of seven purpose-designed aptitude tests covering verbal ability, numeracy, and logical problem-solving. The complete battery takes a day. The aim of the QT is to regulate numbers attending the assessment centre stage that follows and to do so in as predictively valid a way as is achievable. Developments are under way, at the time of writing, that aim at integrating a biographical score with the QT.

The degree of regulation required by this pre-selection stage is a direct function of the total number of applicants, the number of vacancies available, and the selection ratio typically required at the assessment centre stage—working to a fixed standard—in order to fill the vacancies. With about 120 places to fill, when the Diplomatic Service counterparts to Administration Trainee and one or two other smaller entries are included, then about 700 invitations are needed in order to secure 600 attenders at CSSB. From an applicant field of about 5000 this means that the pre-selection cut has to come somewhere in the region of the 85th percentile.

For the Tax Inspectorate the pre-selection stage is a Preliminary Interview Board (PIB). Invitation to the interview is determined by the score on purpose-designed biodata inventory. The minimum career-aim for this entry is one grade lower than for the administration entry, and the number of vacancies is higher—about 150 per year. This results in a slightly more generous selection ratio at CSSB, where four candidates seen will usually produce one success. Tracking the pre-selection regulator back to the typical 4000–5000 applications per year, and allowing for the reasonably stable proportions exiting voluntarily at each stage, means that with a PIB selection-ratio of about one success in three seen, the biodata cut has to reduce the initial field by about a third.

4 Assessment centre

Candidates come to CSSB, the assessment centre stage, in groups of five, where they are seen over a period of two days by a team of three assessors. There are perhaps four main facets to the assessment at CSSB. First, there is the background information that comes with the candidate, detailing for the most part his or her attainments. This is typically supplemented by referees' reports.

A distinctive feature of the assessment centre process, of course, is what in CSSB terminology is known as 'analogous exercises', but which is more commonly classed as job-simulation or work-sample testing. Here there are two major aspects—written work, broadly speaking of the 'in-tray exercise' variety, and group work, the main part of which comprises a 'committee exercise' in which candidates take it in turns to chair 15-minute sessions.

There are more cognitive tests. For the administration entry, scores are combined with certain of the QT test-scores and then standardised and normed on to the CSSB population, thus producing Verbal and Non-verbal Test Indices. Tax Inspector candidates will not have encountered cognitive testing at all before their arrival at CSSB. Again, their norms are calculated relative to the typical Inspectorate population met with at this stage.

Finally, there are one-to-one interviews with each of the three assessors. One of these, a professional psychologist of either an occupational or a clinical orientation, will be interested in what kind of a person this is, how he or she came to be like it, and where they might be headed. The second, a young high-flying administrator or Tax Inspector, will have come through the whole process him or herself only some five or six years previously. This so-called 'Observer's' aim will be to assess the applicant's intellectual ability in a somewhat more free-flowing and 'dynamic' way than anything provided by the cognitive tests. Finally, the Chairman—a recently retired Senior Civil Servant, say—will conduct an interview that aims at an understanding of the individual 'in the round'.

Informing the whole procedure is, of course, the specification and particularly its embodiment in a set of rating-scales—about a dozen dimensions covering intellectual, inter-personal, and personal abilities and qualities. All three assessors will have marked the job-simulation exercises independently and will have discussed their marks at the time. On the third morning, in final conference, they integrate these assessments with all the other information that has been produced or elicited, using the rating-scales as a framework and as a vehicle for discussing each individual's potential. A typical conference on five candidates will take two to three hours. After reaching a consensus decision the assessors write reports on each candidate.

The CSSB function is a permanent one, and requires a sophisticated management infrastructure, described in a certain amount of detail elsewhere (McLeod, 1988).

5 Final stages

For the Tax Inspectorate entry, CSSB is the last hurdle. For the would-be administrators there is a Final Selection Board—a panel interview lasting 30–40 minutes to which those deemed suitable at CSSB, together with the near-misses, are invited and which, if they accept the invitation, they attend some three to four weeks after CSSB. The interviewers are made up of representatives from Civil Service personnel and line management, an academic and a non-Service businessman or industrialist. The board is chaired by a Civil Service Commissioner and its main purpose is a moderating one.

For those declared successful, an offer will be made conveying the organisational decision about assignment—that is, to which particular government department he or she will be going. Even then there are final paper checks to be made, confirming eligibility and enquiring broadly into 'health and character'.

Then, those who have come through and who choose to, enter into another complex social relationship with their employing departments, one that for many will last them their working lives and which even allowing for those who leave before retirement, may extend on average for about twenty years.

SOCIAL-PROCESS ISSUES

Herriot organises his observations on the kind of evidence that would test his hypotheses, and thus his theoretical propositions, into four closely related subgroups—the organisation's and the applicant's respective expectations regarding the selection process, applicant self-esteem or 'self-efficacy', and the applicant's expectations regarding the job. He concludes with some reflections on utility.

The major expectation that the organisation has regarding the selection process in the CSSB case is that the applicant will apply him or herself to it seriously. Cognitive tests are, after all, often described as maximum performance tasks. To give as near a true reading as possible the applicant is expected to have understood this.

From the CSSB point of view—and that of the Commission more widely—there is another important assumption or expectation, one that centres on the direction in which information flows at various points in the sequence of clearly-defined episodes. This assumption is that the candidate will have grasped, from the explanatory literature, that once in the selection process the emphasis will be on the organisation assessing him or her. Opportunities for the candidate to assess the organisation are offered mainly outside this process. In addition to being provided with the recruitment literature, a major source of information for the prospective candidate not just about the job but about selection, he or she will also have been able to make use of careers advisory services, may have been put in touch with a liaison officer—a serving Civil Servant from the individual's own college, university, or polytechnic—and may also have had an opportunity to visit a government department. This last aspect is particularly important to the Inspectorate of Taxes, where a visit to a tax office at some point before arriving at CSSB will be expected of the candidate.

Such matters clearly impinge more on the applicant's expectations regarding the job than on those that concern the recruitment procedure itself. But they underline that aspect of the organisation's expectations with respect to selection just mentioned. The organisation, in other words, expects the *selection* process to be but a part of the wider recruitment process, and a part in which the information is to flow mainly one way—from candidate to organisation.

There is in fact a simple, practical basis to this. It is inappropriate for a selection agency such as CSSB to go into detail over job-prospects when the recruitment procedure is not targeted at filling, say, just one post. A general Service-wide entry of some 75–80 new recruits annually, assigned to departments after being declared successful, is a different issue.

Another expectation regarding the selection procedure that will be a strong feature of the organisational perceptions is that, in somewhat more classical terms, the process will be reliable and valid—trustworthy, that is.

As to some of the other organisational expectations, then it can be safely said that the amount of writing that covers the Application Form affects the pre-selection decision not at all. For Administration Trainee applicants, information on the form may very well be coded according to a carefully designed system, but it is the content rather than its form that is at issue. The same is of course true for the Tax Inspector's biodata inventory. In both cases, the organisation expects candidates to answer the questions put to them sensibly and truthfully. A point worthy of further examination is that the power of Herriot's 'scruffy appearance' factor (fourth of those emerging in the application-form analyses referred to in his section 4.1) may very well be reduced by formal scoring based on regression analysis.

There is a further related aspect. The greater the extent to which the organisation is working, as it were, at a remove from the candidate then the greater is the call on the organisation's expectations. Working at a remove calls for the organisation to be confident that the messages sent to prospective candidates will have been received without undue distortion. Put simply, it is important—in traditional psychometric terminology—for the decision-making process by which a prospective applicant becomes, or does not become, a substantive applicant to be reliable and valid. Realistic job-previews, as Herriot points out in his section 4.4, will contribute, but the idea also extends to expectations about how robust a biodata inventory may be. How susceptible is it to faking good, for instance?

For the job-simulation stages then again the underlying expectation—hope, maybe—is that they represent the kind of thing that candidates will be prepared to take seriously. And yet again, 'taking seriously' refers to some measure of expectation that their decision-making thus far has been reliable and valid, and that a measure of congruence regarding both job and selection-procedures has been achieved.

The dynamics of the simulation exercise are well worthy of exploration in Herriot's terms, however—particularly as both organisation and applicant, from their somewhat different standpoints, are dependent on those dynamics. The major piece of written work at CSSB, the Appreciation, is described when necessary as 'artificial but realistic'. The realism lies with the task's ability to simulate the kind of analytical and jugmental cognitive demands that a real-life task would present, compressed in time and stripped of interaction with others. For group exercises an even greater suspension of belief is asked, of assessors and assessed alike. Five candidates work at it while three assessors, interacting only to the extent of starting and stopping individual problems, look on, take notes, and form judgments. The judgments that they form, the assessments, rest on offering up the candidate's observed behaviour to the dimensions of the person-specification. The candidate is participating in a piece of group-work rendered more artificial than realistic by the presence of three explicitly non-participant observers. He or she also has perceptions of the true purpose of the task. Thus the construction that individual candidates may have placed upon the person-specification will determine to some extent how they approach the group-work. They will have been advised that the activity is not immediately competitive. That clearly poses an extra requirement, to get the balance between co-operation and competition right. But the applicant who has taken the requirement 'to work hard and quickly' as meaning 'to be dynamic' (in the popular and pejorative sense of that term) may actually disrupt the group task. Less visible to the assessors will be the individual who construes 'dealing with other people at all levels' as requiring an overly accommodating and emollient approach to his or her fellows, and for whom therefore only a hazy picture of ability emerges.

The self-efficacy dimension will also play an important part. The forming of candidates into their groups of five takes account not only of the likelihood of individuals knowing each other beforehand, and thus separating people from the same college or university say, but also seeks to ensure that individuals should not feel isolated in the group. As far as possible, for example, a very young candidate would not be grouped with four others at the top of the age-range. The underlying belief that informs this approach is, in essence, that the relativities that might form part of any notion of self-efficacy may intrude in a way that will interfere with the individual's ability to work effectively in the group.

The interviews clearly represent a point at which the discipline of the mainly one-way information flow must concentrate most attention. In training CSSB assessors in one-to-one interviewing they are told that a good interview may, to the casual observer, have much of the appearance of a fairly active conversation. Closer inspection should reveal, however, that the interviewer exerted far more control over the proceedings than would be the case in day-to-day social exchanges. This would have been achieved by asking questions that have to be answered, getting the interviewee to go far further into an area of discourse than he or she would feel natural about doing in those day-to-day social exchanges, and by refraining from involvement in the normal two-way exchange of facts, ideas, opinions, and beliefs. Clearly it should help to achieve effective elicitation of information appropriate to the task if the applicant as interviewee has some perception of this beforehand. Equally clearly, lack of congruence between interviewer's and interviewee's expectations need present no absolute barrier to the successful achievement of this aspect of assessment, though it may very well mean that the interviewer—as representative of the organisation—will have to work at establishing some acceptable level of congruence before the information starts to flow. Arguably, it should rest with the organisation's representative to detect whether or not the applicant does 'know the rules of the game'—as Herriot puts it. Maybe he or she should be particularly alert when prior hypotheses might suggest a very high probability of those rules not being shared, as may be the case, say, with applicants from cultural minority groups.

The sources of the applicant's expectations regarding the selection process are almost certainly worthy of investigation. In the present case, there is the information mentioned earlier that is contained in pre-application literature—brief descriptions of the procedure, and test-item examples. For those successful at pre-selection—administrator's Qualifying Test or tax inspector's Preliminary Interview—their invitation to attend the CSSB assessment-centre stage is accompanied by a booklet that describes this latter in some detail, complete with photographs of various parts of the process—group-exercises, interviews, and so on. For instance, the somewhat differing emphases of the three one-to-one interviews are described. And in preparation particularly for the interview with the young administrator or the tax inspector, the interview at which some assessment of the 'dynamics' of the candidate's intellectual ability is going to be attempted, then he or she is asked to offer two or three topics of current interest to discuss. Clearly, such a request is going to set up particular types of expectation and equally clearly these will depend on the individual's background. It is likely that the Oxbridge candidate will assume that the interview is going to take on the appearance of a familiar tutorial. Others may envisage something more akin to an oral examination. Neither is correct, as the intention—explained in the booklet, of course—is to provide material to work with at interview, where difficulties in assessing the candidate's abilities to deal with problems in 'real time' may well arise if something with which to work is not established early on. In a sense, it invites the candidate to participate, even if only to a very limited extent, in the design of part of the overall procedure and to have that part tailor made for him or her.

Other sources of the candidate's expectations will be the reasonably formal ones associated with careers advice—very much the same as for those concerning the job itself. But there will also be the informal or folk-loric networks, of old candidates at one's establishment of higher education, say.

Perceptions of the job itself, and of the selection and recruitment processes into it, will almost certainly share very similar sources, though the folk-loric might prove to be a little less powerful as far as job-expectations are concerned if the matter were to be put to the test. The Civil Service and civil servants have somewhat greater prominence in daily life, as conveyed say by the media, than is the case for the selection procedures. The message may, however, often be distorted.

The combination of perceptions of the job and of the selection procedures, no matter how imperfectly arrived at, will affect and interact with 'self-efficacy'—a relativistic term, as mentioned earlier—and will thus be likely to affect intentions and decisions concerning candidature. It seems likely that one of the most powerful influences on that combination may still be a belief that the senior administrative ranks of the Civil Service are the preserve of people of a particular socio-economic status and from a particular educational background—the so-called Oxbridge factor, for example. If recruitment were indeed restricted to middle-class graduates from Oxford and Cambridge, and thereby with a bias towards origins in the south-east of England, it could be argued that the country was not being as well served as it might be. A view that applying for Administration Trainee or Tax Inspector is pointless because such careers are an Oxbridge preserve, and that students elsewhere should set their sights on a lower-level entry, is almost certainly an example of inappropriate self-efficacy effects in action.

The candidate who gets as far as the assessment-centre stage does benefit from another source of impressions against which to refine perceptions of the job itself. To the extent that 'analogous exercises' do faithfully simulate important aspects of the work, then the candidates participating in them get to learn something that they might otherwise not have.

As to utility analysis, Herriot points out that concentrating on particular instruments or episodes may be too limited, and a program-evaluation approach to the whole process needs developing. What may strike one as interesting here is the echo of Dunnette's model for validation research (Dunnette, 1966). His model set out what was in essence a matrix—the 'true' variance in potential performance, the variance measured by selection instruments, variance in training and placement, performance-variance, and—as a kind of global dependent variable—variance in the outcomes for the organisation dependent upon relationships between all the others. This, a kind of systems-approach, has maybe not been all that easy to adopt, so it is only to be hoped that Herriot's even wider ranging proposals do not prove challenging to the point of intractability.

Finally, a steering committee of the British Psychological Society is, at the time of writing, drawing up plans for a new code of practice for tests and other 'portable' assessment instruments. In its action plan there is a clause that refers to the importance of approaching the individual being assessed as someone who is, after all, a constructor of his or her own meaning. Put another way, it reminds one of the well-established piece of advice to trainee interviewers—to remember that the interviewee is as hard at work trying to assess you as you are him. To view selection as a social process is to take this advice seriously.

Note Opinions expressed in this chapter are the author's own and should not be attributed to his employers.

REFERENCES

Dulewicz, Victor and Keenay, Gordon (1976). Job Classification of Senior Administration Posts. Behavioural Sciences Research Division Report No 22, Civil Service Department.

Dunnette, Marvin D. (1966). *Personnel Selection and Placement*, Wadsworth, Belmont.

McLeod, Donald (1988). Assessment Centres, in *Managing Recruitment* (ed. Elizabeth Sidney), Gower, Aldershot.

Paul, Sarah (1987). Assessment of Long-term Potential in the Administration Trainee Scheme. Recruitment Research Unit Report No 34, Civil Service Commission.

17

Meta-Analysis: Facts and Theories

JOHN E. HUNTER
Michigan State University
and
FRANK L. SCHMIDT
University of Iowa

INTRODUCTION

In 1977, we argued that massive errors had been made in the interpretation of validation study results in personnel selection research. We presented methods we called 'validity generalization' which would greatly reduce these errors (Schmidt and Hunter, 1977). In 1979, I (JH) noted that the same problems were found in virtually every area in psychology (Hunter, 1979). I recommended use of Glass' (1976) term 'meta-analysis' for use of our methods in more general contexts. I also argued that while meta-analaysis is not a theoretical tool in its own right, the use of meta-analysis would generate a rebirth of theoretical work in psychology. My argument was that theory cannot be constructed without facts and that meta-analysis is necessary to establish facts. We will now present theoretical work generated by meta-analysis to show that this promise is being realized. The area of application is the analysis of the relationships between general cognitive ability, job knowledge, job performance, and performance ratings. Recent findings have verified the theories of Edward Thorndike derived from research done in the 1920s: the major determinant of performance is knowledge and the major determinant of individual differences in knowledge is individual differences in general cognitive ability (which Thorndike called intelligence). In addition, differences in cognitive

Advances in Selection and Assessment. Edited by M. Smith and I. T. Robertson

ability also cause differences in performance due to differences in the immediate cognitive skills used directly in day-to-day work.

CUMULATIVE KNOWLEDGE AND THE NARRATIVE REVIEW

It is not possible in science to do perfect studies. This is especially true in field studies such as those in personnel selection and organizational psychology. Because of necessary study imperfections, science has always been suspicious of the results from isolated studies. Instead, facts are usually inferred from the cumulative findings across as many studies as possible.

Before meta-analysis, the process of deriving inferences from cumulative research had broken down. The traditional procedure for cumulative knowledge in psychology is now known as the 'narrative' review. A reviewer collects studies that bear on an issue such as the validity of cognitive ability tests predicting the performance of clerical workers. The reviewer tries to reconcile the findings of these studies and derive conclusions as to the strength and consistency of the studied relation. However, the research results in nearly every area appear to be contradictory. In an effort to deal with these contradictions, reviewers have been driven in one of two directions: (1) selective reviews with definite conclusions or (2) comprehensive reviews with vague conclusions of little use to either theoreticians or applied psychologists.

In *selective reviews* the reviewer speculates as to possible methodological problems with some of the studies. For example, the reviewer might argue that only the studies with a certain type of control group are worthy of attention. Once enough studies have been excluded on such methodological grounds, the remaining studies often yield definite results which form the basis of the reviewer's conclusions. There are two problems with this selective approach. One obvious problem is contradictory conclusions between reviewers. One reviewer selects a subset of studies which suggest that tests are good predictors while another reviewer selects a subset of studies that suggest the tests are poor predictors. Which reviewer is right?

The less obvious problem with selective reviews lies in how people treat 'methodological problems'. There is no aspect of study design which is always a problem. For example, lack of a control group in a test-retest design is a problem only if there would have been change in subjects even with no intervention. However if there were no such change, then there would be no need for a control group. The fact is that a 'methodological problem' is only a hypothesis. Yet reviewers do not typically challenge their own methodological hypotheses; they take the problem for granted. Actual empirical tests of hypothesized methodological problems have frequently found them to be nonexistent. Thus selective reviews are frequently based on entirely specious elimination of studies.

Which reviewer is right? Typically all selective reviews are wrong to some extent. Even if by chance, the reviewer selects the studies with results in the right direction, the study results are usually biased in a quantitative sense.

In *comprehensive narrative reviews* reviewers consider all or nearly all the studies. They reject only studies which have flaws that have been verified in other empirical research. Yet even comprehensive reviews typically draw false conclusions. The typical comprehensive review usually ends with a statement such as the following: 'Some studies have found that cognitive ability predicts clerical performance. However other studies have found no such relation. More research is needed to establish the properties of organizational settings that render cognitive ability irrelevant.' This vague and ambivalent conclusion kills theoretical development and drives applied psychologists to distraction. In nearly all research areas, continued research eventually produces contradictory results of this type. The resulting reviews produce a feeling of nihilism in researchers. Funding organizations also react negatively to such conclusions and cut off money to such areas. This research cutoff process is in part responsible for the apparent 'fads' in scientific research.

THE CONTRIBUTION OF META-ANALYSIS

Are these ambivalent review conclusions correct? Meta-analysis has shown that these vague and ambivalent conclusions are usually false. The apparently contradictory results are actually produced by sampling error. Since most psychological studies are done on samples far less than 1500 in size, most individual studies are subject to massive chance variation in results. To reviewers, that chance variation appears to be real variation. That chance variation is what produces most of the apparent contradictions between studies. To many psychologists, the results of meta-analyses have been a shock in this regard. They believed that the statistical significance test was supposed to solve the problem of sampling error. However, every mathematical statistician in the last 50 years has warned that this is false. Statisticians have noted that the significance test works only when the null hypothesis is true and often fails badly if the null hypothesis is false. However, statisticians have cast their argument in the arcane jargon of 'statistical power' and 'Type II error' and these arguments have not been widely understood.

One way to view meta-analysis is as a method for using cumulative research to escape the problems of sampling error. If the average sample size in individual studies were 68 (as in personnel selection research), then 25 studies would produce a cumulative sample size of 1950. If the underlying results are actually relatively uniform across studies, this sample size is large enough to draw fairly sharp conclusions. In research areas where there are large differences in results that are predicted by existing theories, the primary moderator variables can be verified and the main conclusions will be correctly drawn. Only in those unusual research areas where results vary in moderate amounts due to unknown causes will meta-analysis still be unsatisfactory with as many as 25 studies. However, with 100 studies it becomes possible to use meta-analysis to identify even minor moderator variables.

Meta-analysis can do more than just reduce the impact of sampling error on study results (Schmidt and Hunter, 1977; Hunter, Schmidt, and Jackson, 1982). Meta-analysis also makes it possible to reduce the impact of other study artifacts such as (1) attenuation of study results produced by error of measurement in the dependent variable; (2) attenuation of study results produced by error of measurement in the independent variable; (3) attenuation of results produced by dichotomization of the dependent variable; (4) attenuation of study results produced by dichotomization of the independent variable; (5) variation in results produced by range variation on the independent variable; and (6) attrition artifacts on the dependent variable (if there is no simultaneous range variation in the independent variable due to other causes). While these effects are systematic rather than unsystematic, the effects are very large in many research areas. Large quantitative errors can produce qualitative errors in theoretical interpretations based on those errors.

THE IMPACT OF STUDY ARTIFACTS ON STUDY OUTCOMES

We will illustrate the effects of study artifacts by considering one special research area: research on the validity of general cognitive ability predicting job performance. The typical validation study produces pairs of scores for each incumbent who works at some given job in some given setting: a cognitive ability test score and a measurement of job performance. Good (i.e. content valid) objective measurement of job performance is prohibitively expensive. Thus it is rarely done by companies and hence performance measurement for validation studies must be done by the researcher. Objective measurement is also almost always too expensive for the researcher. Thus researchers do the same thing as managers; they measure performance using supervisor performance ratings. How much is validity reduced? Meta-analysis (Hunter, 1986) has shown that whereas the validity of general cognitive ability predicting a content valid objective measure of job performance (i.e. content valid work sample performance measures) is 0.75, the study validity drops to 0.47 when ratings are substituted. Furthermore, this lower validity would only be observed in settings with ideal ratings conditions: consensus ratings by a population of raters. The correlation of 0.47 assumes that each person works under a variety of different supervisors who make independent observations of his performance. The rating measure then averages the judgements made by different supervisors and thus averages out the halo or idiosyncracy of their perceptions. In actual studies, there is usually only one supervisor who knows the worker well enough to rate him; the immediate supervisor. Meta-analysis has shown the reliability of a single rating to be only 0.47. This drops the study validity from 0.47 to 0.32. Furthermore, this reliability assumes that ratings were made on a summated rating scale (i.e. an average rating across several dimensions or across several behaviors). If only a global rating is observed, the study validity would be lower yet. Thus problems in measuring job performance drop validity from 0.75 to 0.32.

Employers have only limited time for testing. The typical measure of general cognitive ability has a coefficient of generalizability of about 0.80. This drops the study validity from 0.32 to 0.29.

In order to have a measure of job performance, the validation study can gather data only on those who work; i.e. incumbent workers. Yet the population of interest in personnel selection is the population of applicants. For a variety of reasons, the incumbents have a much narrower range of cognitive ability than do applicants. A meta-analysis of 415 validation studies done by the U. S. Employment Service shows that the mean standard deviation of incumbent workers is only 0.67 times as large as the standard deviation of applicants. This range restriction on cognitive ability reduces the study validity from 0.29 to 0.20.

The net impact of necessary study imperfections is to reduce the study population validity from 0.75 to 0.20. Sampling error then introduces non-systematic variation into the observed sample validity coefficient. The sampling error in a correlation of 0.20 depends on the size of the sample. The average sample size across 1500 validation studies was 68 (Lent, Aurbach, and Levin, 1971). For this sample size, the standard error of the correlation coefficient is 0.117. Thus only half the correlations will lie in a range of 0.11 to 0.29. About 5 percent of the observed correlations will actually be negative. About 5 percent of the correlations will be greater than 0.40. Thus we see why reviewers found an enormous range in validity in validation studies.

Many psychologists believe that the significance test solves the problem of sampling error. However, most psychologists have little understanding of Type II error. Consider the present situation. For a sample size of 68, a sample correlation must be 0.24 to be significant using a two-tailed test with an alpha of 0.05. Since the population correlation is only 0.20, this means that only correlations that are high by chance will be labeled 'significant'. The probability that the observed correlation will be significant is the probability that it will lie above 0.24; a probability of 44 percent. That is, only 44 percent of the significance tests will come out correctly. The error rate for the significance test in actual personnel selection studies of general cognitive ability is 56 percent.

Most psychologists believe that the error rate for the significance test is 5 percent. But that is the Type I error rate that applies if the population correlation is 0. When a test is valid, the relevant error rate is the Type II error rate. For a 0.05 level significance test, the error rate could be as high as 95 percent. The determining factors are sample size and the size of the correlation coefficient. Hunter and Hunter (1984) found an average population correlation of 0.10 for the interview. Given a sample size of 68, only 12 percent of sample correlations will be high enough to be significant. That is, for the interview, the error rate of the significance test has been 88 percent; very close to the 95 percent theoretical limit.

The low and sporadic observed correlations in validation research drove most comprehensive reviewers to turn normal science on its head. Whereas in the physical sciences, local studies are distrusted in favor of cumulative research, personnel researchers in 1976 believed in the law of situation specific validity. They believed that validity varied so much from one setting to the next that a researcher could only be assured of validity in a new setting if a local validation study showed validity in that setting. Thus local studies were preferred over cumulative research findings. Meta-analysis has now shown that the law of situation specific validity is false for most of the pedictors used in personnel selection. The comprehensive reviewers in personnel selection were the victims of sampling error (Schmidt and Hunter, 1981; Schmidt, Hunter, Pearlman, and Hirsh, 1985).

Similar problems have been found in other research areas. Hunter and Hirsh (1987) have reviewed most of the meta-analyses done in organizational psychology as of June 1986; including meta-analyses of interventions such as goal setting, participative decision making, etc. They found that in nearly every case, the inconsistency in direction of findings was due to sampling error. Sampling error has caused the false and ambivalent conclusions drawn by most comprehensive reviewers in most research areas in psychology.

However, sampling error is not the only problem. Other artifacts may be systematic, but they are still large in quantitative terms. In the cognitive ability literature, average observed validity was systematically dropped from 0.75 to 0.20 by artifacts of measurement and range restriction. There can be a qualitative error in conclusions that follow from a quantitative error that large. For example, the low observed validity of general cognitive ability caused most reviewers to reject the classic learning models of job performance. They concluded that if there were really significant learning on the job, then there should be a much higher correlation between intelligence and performance than 0.20. Their reasoning was right, but their facts were wrong. The low validity of 0.20 resulted from artifacts of the studies. When these artifacts are eliminated, the validity climbs to 0.75; the high value predicted by classic learning theories of performance.

COGNITIVE ABILITY AND JOB PERFORMANCE: APPLIED PERSPECTIVE

In this section, I (JH) will sketch the impact that meta-analysis has had on one area of research: research on the relationship between general cognitive ability and job performance. I will first sketch the impact from an applied point of view. Then I will review newer theoretical developments.

Meta-analysis has revolutionized our picture of personnel selection (Schmidt and Hunter, 1981; Hunter and Schmidt, 1983). Meta-analysis has enabled us to cumulate research findings on the validity of cognitive aptitude and ability tests, to assess the validity of alternative predictors of performance, to assess the fairness of tests, and to assess the extent of individual differences in job performance so as to provide the data needed for utility analysis. In a word, meta-analysis has finally allowed us to use 100 years of research to draw conclusions that go far beyond the possibilities of any single study. This work enables personnel selection programs to be based on cumulative research instead of on local validation studies. That is, meta-analysis has enabled personnel selection to make the transition from naïve empiricism to normal science.

In 1976, most personnel researchers believed in the law of situation specific validity. Meta-analysis has shown that hypothesis to be false. The validity of a given cognitive aptitude predicting performance in a given job does not vary across situations. In 1976, most researchers thought the average validity of general cognitive ability to be low. Meta-analysis has shown that the appearance of low validity was an artifact of the failure to correct for measurement error, range restriction, and other artifacts. Many researchers once thought that while cognitive ability would be relevant to complex jobs, it would not predict performance in simple jobs. Meta-analysis did show that in predicting performance ratings, the validity is lower for simple jobs than for complex jobs. But even for feeding/offbearing jobs, the validity is 0.23 on average; a value large enough to make selection on cognitive ability very useful. Furthermore, when objective measures of job performance are used, there is much less dropoff in validity for simple jobs. Thus meta-analysis has shown that general cognitive ability predicts performance on all jobs (Hunter and Hunter, 1984; Hunter, 1986; Schmidt and Hunter, 1981).

Many allegations of bias in cognitive tests have been made (short review in Schmidt and Hunter, 1981; a more extensive review in Hunter, Schmidt, and Rauschenberger, 1984). There was the hypothesis of single group validity: that even though a test might be valid predicting performance of majority workers, it would not predict the performance of minority workers. Meta-analysis showed this hypothesis to be false. There was the hypothesis of differential validity: that the validity of tests predicting minority performance would always be lower than the validity for majority workers. Meta-analysis showed the validity of cognitive ability and aptitude tests to be the same for majority whites, for blacks, for hispanics, for women and men, for different regions of the USA, etc. There was the hypothesis of underprediction: that the mean performance of minority workers would be higher than is predicted from majority regression lines. Meta-analysis showed the regression lines to be the same. In short, meta-analysis showed cognitive ability and aptitude tests to be fair to minority applicants.

There have been allegations that even if workers do differ in performance, the differences are so small that it does not matter to employers. Meta-analysis has shown this hypothesis to be false. Meta-analysis has shown that on objective ratio scale measures of performance, the standard deviation of performance is always at least 20 percent of mean performance (Schmidt and Hunter, 1983; Hunter and Schmidt, 1986). Even on the simplest jobs, workers in the top 5 percent will outperform workers in the bottom 5 percent by 2 to 1. In more complex jobs, the range of performance differences is much greater. This shows massive potential for increasing average productivity by using wise selection. Companies selecting the top 10 percent of applicants can increase productivity by more than 10 percent using a good measure of general cognitive ability.

There have been allegations that other predictors such as interviews or reference checks predict performance as well as cognitive ability. Meta-analysis has shown this allegation to be false. Meta-analyses have been performed for all the common predictors used in personnel selection (Hunter and Hunter, 1984; Hunter and Hirsh, 1987). There are two cases: (1) lateral transfer jobs where the applicant has already done the same or very similar work and (2) jobs where the applicant must be trained to do the job. If the applicants have already worked at the same job, then a good measure of current performance predicts future performance ratings at the same high level of validity as does general cognitive ability. However, poor measures of performance such as amount of experience or experience ratings predict much more poorly than does cognitive ability. If the applicant needs training to do the new job, then there is no predictor that works nearly as well as general cognitive ability.

The cumulation of the results of the thousands of studies done on personnel selection has now shown that a good test of general cognitive ability meets all the requirements for fair, valid selection. There is no need to do local validation studies to check out allegations against such tests. Indeed, power analysis has shown that local validation studies are much inferior to cumulative research findings; a result consistent with normal science.

ABILITY, KNOWLEDGE, AND PERFORMANCE: THE THEORETICAL PERSPECTIVE

Cumulative analysis of validation research provides a perfectly adequate basis for the use of general cognitive ability to select workers. However, many people are loathe to accept findings if there is no theoretical underpinning. However, recent meta-analyses have provided just this underpinning. Meta-analysis has now provided enough interlocking facts to allow testing of the classic performance theories. A full test pitting Thorndike's learning theory against behaviorist theories was presented in Hunter (1986). Since my purpose here is only to illustrate the manner in which meta-analysis promotes theoretical analysis, I will only sketch the use of meta-analysis to test the learning theory.

Learning and performance

The classic theory of job performance was derived from early research findings by Edward Thorndike (see Brolyer, Thorndike and Woodyard, 1927). This theory relating ability to performance derives its predictions from the learning process. Learning may take place in a formal training environment or it may take place on the job. The parameters of learning are different for the two environments. Learning in a formal training program means absorbing knowledge which is presented directly to the student with the important features of the knowledge already emphasized. Learning on the job requires two steps. First, if a relevant event takes place, the worker must recognize the event as significant. Second, the worker must be able to formulate the lesson inherent in the event in such a way as to learn from it. Cognitive ability is critical to the recognition process because the worker must link current information to the knowledge already in memory. Cognitive ability is necessary to learning from the recognition because the information must be restructured to a form relevant to *future* recognition. Thus learning on the job will be more dependent on cognitive ability than learning in a formal program.

According to the classic theory, performance is bounded by learning. If the worker has not learned what to do in a given situation, then the worker cannot respond correctly. Thus there should be a high correlation between learning and performance.

Learning is a necessary but not sufficient condition for performance. Performance may require that the worker go beyond knowledge of the job. Consider a police officer responsible for crowd control. The officer may have mastered the recognized principles of crowd control, but any actual situation will only be approximately like the situation described when the rules were given. Thus the officer must innovate to meet the specific conditions in the actual situation. Crowd control where spectators are enthralled with a fire is different from crowd control when a parade has become out of control which in turn is different from crowd control when a criminal is shooting in the street. Thus the classic theory of performance predicts that cognitive ability will correlate with performance above and beyond the correlation determined by the relationship between cognitive ability and learning.

According to the classic theory, supervisors are mainly observers of performance. However, a supervisor's perceptions of performance will be colored by a variety of nonwork related factors. That is, a supervisor will be influenced by all the factors known to influence person perception; factors such as personal appearance, moral conventionality, etc. Furthermore, the classic theory would predict that supervisor perceptions will be influenced by idiosyncratic factors such as the match or mismatch between the personality of the worker and the personality of the supervisor. The classic theory predicts that supervisor performance ratings will be only an indirect measure of performance. Ratings of the same worker by different supervisors will disagree to the extent that perceptions are influenced by idiosyncratic factors. An average rating across a population of raters would eliminate the idiosyncratic component to ratings, but it would still leave nonwork factors which are common to all raters. Thus even if idiosyncratic factors are eliminated, the purified ratings will still not correlate perfectly with performance.

In summary, the classic theory relating job performance to cognitive ability makes a number of correlational predictions. Because the rate and amount of learning is determined by cognitive ability, the classic theory predicts a high correlation between cognitive ability and learning. Because performance is learned, the classic theory predicts a high correlation between learning and performance. Because innovative adaptation is required by most actual work situations, the classic theory predicts that cognitive ability will be even more highly correlated with performance than would be predicted from the high correlation between ability and learning. Supervisors are predicted to be imperfect measures of performance in two ways: (1) supervisor perceptions will disagree because supervisors are influenced by idiosyncratic nonwork factors such as the personality match or mismatch with the worker, and (2) supervisors will be influenced by common nonwork factors that influence all supervisors.

Testing the classic theory

The predictions of the classic theory can be tested empirically. In order to do this, each factor must be made observable. Cognitive ability was made observable by the testing research of the first forty years of this century (Vernon, 1957; Tyler, 1965). The learning process can be measured after the fact by measuring job knowledge. The greater the worker's job knowledge, the greater the learning which has taken place. Job performance can be measured using work sample methods.

For theoretical purposes, there are at least four key variables to be observed in validation: general cognitive ability, job knowledge, job performance, and performance ratings. For simplicity, abbreviated language for these will be used in the following discussion. The word 'ability' will mean general cognitive ability. The word 'knowledge' will mean job knowledge. The word 'performance' will mean work sample performance; i.e. objective assessment of performance on an content valid work sample. The word 'ratings' will mean supervisor performance ratings. Each variable will be considered to be perfectly measured. Empirical data will be fully corrected for attenuation to provide estimates of the corresponding correlations.

Once the theory has been mapped into observed variables, then the theory can be tested by checking the observed correlations against predictions. The theory predicts a high correlation between ability and knowledge. The theory predicts a high correlation between knowledge and performance. The theory predicts that the correlation between ability and performance will be even higher than the correlation predicted by the high correlation between ability and knowledge. This prediction can be tested using the multiple regression of performance onto ability and knowledge together. The theory predicts that the beta weight for ability will be positive and large for jobs which require a high degree of innovation on the job. Since the supervisor is aware only of the worker's performance and job knowledge and is unaware of the worker's ability, a path model for the four variables should have no direct link between ability and ratings.

The data

Hunter (1983) located 14 studies which measures at least three of four key theoretical variables. He analyzed the correlations between them for an incumbent population because he was interested in performance appraisal where the focal population is incumbents. For purposes of discussing personnel selection, the relevant population is the applicant population. Therefore the correlations considered here will be corrected for range restriction using the average incumbent/applicant standard deviation ratio of 0.67 found for 425 proficiency studies done by the U.S. Employment Service (Hunter, 1980) and using path analytic methods to correct correlations for variables other than ability. These correlations were given in Hunter (1984, 1986). The basic results are presented in Table 17.1. Hunter (1986) presents data for military as well as civilian jobs. The data for military jobs are very similar and will not be reviewed here.

The predictions of the classic learning theory are borne out in the data. The theory predicts a high correlation between ability and knowledge. The correlation between ability and knowledge is 0.80. The classic theory predicts a high correlation between knowledge and performance. The correlation between knowledge and performance is 0.80. The classic theory predicts a high correlation between ability and performance. The correlation between ability and performance is 0.75. The classic theory predicts that ability will be more highly correlated with performance than can be explained solely on the basis of the correlation between ability and knowledge. The beta weight for ability (with knowledge implicitly held constant) is +0.31. The classic theory predicts that ability will be correlated with ratings. The correlation between ability and

Table 17.1   The correlations between general cognitive ability, job knowledge, job performance, and supervisor ratings

---

Definition of variables

A = Ability: General cognitive ability—that factor which explains the high correlations between different cognitive aptitudes (primary factors) and between achievement in diverse areas—estimated by a composite across various aptitudes such as quantitative and verbal aptitude

JK = Job Knowledge—a content valid (based on job analysis) measure of job knowledge

WS = Job Performance—a content valid (based on job analysis) work sample measure of job performance—performance at work stations where performance can be objectively measured

SR = Supervisor Ratings—supervisor ratings of job performance—correlations are corrected for interrater reliability so these ratings are free of both random response error and halo

Correlations (N = 1790)

	A	JK	WS	SR
A	1.00			
JK	0.80	1.00		
WS	0.75	0.80	1.00	
SR	0.47	0.56	0.52	1.00

Multiple correlations

R for WS: 0.82
R for SR: 0.57

---

ratings is 0.47. The classic theory predicts that a path model will fit the data without a direct link between ability and ratings. This, too is true. Thus the classic theory created by learning psychologists and supported by so much other data also fits the validation data. Every major prediction made by the classic theory is verified by the data.

SUMMARY

For purposes of practical validation, it does not matter why cognitive ability correlates with performance. The only practical question for selection is just how high is the validity? This question is answered by the data on work sample performance. However, it is very important to explain why general cognitive ability predicts job performance. The data on job knowledge show that cognitive ability predicts job performance in large part because it predicts learning and job mastery. Table 17.1 shows that ability is highly correlated with job knowledge and that job knowledge is highly correlated with job performance.

The path analysis shows that this indirect causal path accounts for a majority of the effect of ability onto performance.

However, the beta weight for ability net of knowledge is large for civilian jobs and not negligible for military jobs. Thus ability is related to performance itself; not just to job knowledge. This may be because high ability workers are faster at cognitive operations on the job, are better able to prioritize between conflicting rules, are better able to adapt old procedures to altered situations, are better able to innovate to meet unexpected problems, and are better able to learn new procedures quickly as the job changes over time. Content validity is being argued for complex jobs with a high degree of judgement, reasoning, and planning. The positive beta weight for ability supports those linkage analyses.

CONCLUSION

Theory is fueled by facts. Without facts, theory degenerates to empty speculation. But the situation before meta-analysis was even worse. Most comprehensive reviews produced false conclusions about research outcomes. False facts do not just hinder theory building, they kill theory building. The false facts about the relationship between cognitive ability and job performance did not lead to new theories of job performance. The old theories were abandoned and were replaced by a nihilistic anti-theoretical tradition called 'dust-bowl empiricism'. But science based on bad theories leads to false beliefs about facts. This was true in personnel selection. One of the ironies of the dust-bowl position is that meta-analysis has shown all of the 'facts' gathered by that school to be false.

As a method of cumulating research findings, the narrative review was a disaster. The narrative review did not produce accurate assessments of research findings. The vague and ambivalent false conclusions of the narrative review killed theoretical development in most areas and frequently killed subequent empirical research as well. Meta-analysis is now revealing the actual facts produced by the last one hundred years of research. This has led to the first new theoretical work on the determinants of job performance in personnel selection in nearly 30 years. Thus while meta-analysis is not itself a theoretical tool, it is critical to providing the basis of facts from which theories flow.

REFERENCES

Brolyer, C. R., Thorndike, E. L. and Woodyard, E. R. (1927). A second study of mental discipline in high school studies. *Journal of Educational Psychology*, **18**, 377–404.
Glass, G. V. (1976). Primary, secondary, and meta-analysis of research. *Educational Researcher*, **5**, 3–8.

Hunter, J. E. (1979). *Cumulating results across studies.* Paper presented at American Psychological Association, New York.

Hunter, J. E. (1980). *Test validation for 12,000 jobs: an application of synthetic validity and validity generalization to the General Aptitude Test Battery (GATB).* Washington, DC: US Employment Service.

Hunter, J. E. (1983). A causal analysis of cognitive ability, job knowledge, job performance, and supervisor ratings. In F. Landy, S. Zedeck and J. Cleveland (eds), *Performance Measurement Theory.* Hillsdale, NJ: Erlbaum, pp. 257–266.

Hunter, J. E. (1984). *The prediction of job performance in the civilian sector using the ASVAB.* Rockville, Md.: Research Applications.

Hunter, J. E. (1986). Cognitive ability, cognitive aptitudes, job knowledge, and job performance. *Journal of Vocational Behavior,* **29**, 340–362.

Hunter, J. E. and Hirsh, H. R. (1987). Applications of meta-analysis. In C. L. Cooper and I. T. Robertson (eds), *International Review of Industrial and Organizational Psychology, 1987.* New York: John Wiley.

Hunter, J. E. and Hunter, R. F. (1984). Validity and utility of alternate predictors of job performance. *Psychological Bulletin,* **96**, 72–98.

Hunter, J. E. and Schmidt, F. L. (1983). Quantifying the effects of psychological interventions on employee job performance and work force productivity. *American Psychologist,* **38**, 473–478.

Hunter, J. E., Schmidt, F. L. and Jackson, G. B. (1982). *Meta-analysis.* Beverly Hills, CA: Sage.

Hunter, J. E., Schmidt, F. L. and Rauschenberger, J. (1984). Methodological, statistical, and ethical issues in the study of bias in psychological tests. In C. R. Reynolds and R. T. Brown (eds), *Perspective On Bias In Mental Testing.* New York: Plenum Press.

Lent, R. H., Aurbach, H. A. and Levin, L. S. (1971). Research design and validity assessment. *Personnel Psychology,* **24**, 247–274.

Schmidt, F. L. and Hunter, J. E. (1977). Development of a general solution to the problem of validity generalization. *Journal of Applied Psychology,* **62**, 529–540.

Schmidt, F. L. and Hunter, J. E. (1981). Employment testing: old theories and new research findings. *American Psychologist,* **36**, 1128–1137.

Schmidt, F. L. and Hunter, J. E. (1983). Individual differences in productivity: an empirical test of estimates derived from studies of selection procedure utility. *Journal of Applied Psychology,* **68**, 407–414.

Schmidt, F. L., Hunter, J. E., Pearlman, K., and Hirsh, H. R. (1985). Forty questions about validity generalization and meta-analysis. *Personnel Psychology,* **38**, 697–798.

Tyler, L. E. (1965). *The Psychology of Human Differences.* New York: Appleton-Century-Crofts.

Vernon, P. E. (1957). *The Structure of Human Abilities* (Rev. edn). London: Methuen.

18

Comment on Meta-Analysis: Facts and Theories

MARY TENOPYR
AT&T, New Jersey

There is no doubt that the meta-analysis techniques are powerful research tools, which if used properly, can lead to advances both in science and in practice. There are a number of variations of meta-analytic methods which may be applied, depending upon the purposes of the investigator and the characteristics of the particular data set involved (e.g. Callender and Osborn, 1980; Glass, 1976, 1977; Glass, McGaw and Smith, 1981; Hunter, Schmidt and Jackson, 1982; Raju and Burke, 1983; Rosenthal, 1984; Schmidt and Hunter, 1977; Schmidt, Hunter and Pearlman, 1982). Consequently, it would appear that it would be appropriate to speak of the group of meta-analytic techniques rather than a generic meta-analysis.

Although the meta-analytic techniques had their origins in the field of education (Glass, 1976), there is little doubt that Hunter, Schmidt and associates have contributed many significant innovations and been the strongest proponents of the use of meta-analytic procedures in industrial and organizational psychology. The work of these two investigators has been applied widely to study many phenomena of industrial and organizational psychology. Hunter and Schmidt's direct applied work thus far has generally been limited to studies of validity generalization, but now we see in the preceding chapter, that these meta-analytic results are being extended to theory development.

There have been numerous meta-analytic studies other than those of Hunter, Schmidt and associates relevant to the validity of employee selection procedures. In general, the results of these studies have been interpreted to

Advances in Selection and Assessment. Edited by M. Smith and I. T. Robertson

support the concept of wide generalization of validities. However, there are still debates about the mathematics and mechanics of some of the meta-analytic procedures. A particular matter of concern is the susceptibility of applications of the procedures to Type I and Type II error. This area of controversy, which apparently still is far from closure, will not be entered into here. Interested readers can find a plethora of literature on the subject (e.g., Algera, Jansen, Roe and Vjin, 1984; James, Demaree and Muliak, 1986; James, Demaree, Muliak and Mumford, 1988; Kemery, Mossholder and Roth, 1987; Osborn, Callender, Greener and Ashworth, 1983; Paese and Switzer, 1988; Sackett, Harris and Orr, 1986; Sackett, Schmitt, Tenopyr, Kehoe and Zedeck, 1985; Schmidt and Hunter, 1984; Schmidt, Hunter, Pearlman and Hirsh, 1985; Spector and Levine, 1987).

Issue will not be taken with the general proposition that meta-analysis can be useful in building theories. Certainly meta-analysis, properly used, can enhance and integrate the inductive elements of science. In most instances, meta-analytic techniques appear to be superior to the long enshrined critical literature review. However, many meta-analyses are done on such a gross basis and reported in such brevity that the reader who does not have the opportunity to study the source data upon which the meta-analysis was based may be misled. The careful meta-analytic researcher will segregate studies into clear categories, e.g. those which used control groups and those which did not, so that effects of experimental design on results can be readily ascertained. In other words, the meta-analytic researcher should be obligated to follow many of the same procedures as used in an acceptable critical literature review.

This suggestion may seem at odds with the very objectives of meta-analysis and the common tendency to ignore study imperfections in decisions about what studies to include in the meta-analysis. Also, by fractionating data one obviously reduces the number of studies in each analysis and hence alters the dependability of the results. However, unless meta-analytic studies are carefully designed, no conclusions about either theory or practical applications may be made.

One of the major problems in using meta-analysis in developing theory in personnel psychology as it stands today is that in many areas of the field there have been so few studies concerned with theoretical issues. In a large number of instances, data generated for one set of decisions can be useful for other decisions, but more often than not data used for a purpose other than that for which they were collected can only be the basis for hypotheses. In particular, it is very difficult to use data generated for personnel selection purposes for theory building. These data, however, can be an inductive basis for hypotheses which can be supported or not by more refined research. These later studies must be designed carefully so that they will yield results meaningful to the theory being tested. In particular, they must be designed in such a way that alternate hypotheses can be tested.

Much has been said about the need to combine the work of the individual difference researchers and the experimental psychologists. However, despite the pleas for unity, the two disciplines of psychology are far apart even today. Witness the differences between the work of the learning theorists (Bolles, 1979) and cognitive psychologists (Gagne, 1985) and the data Hunter and Schmidt have presented in the preceding chapter. If we are to have meaningful theories, the rather gross predictions of the individual difference psychologists and the mapping of detailed mental processes which are the hallmark of the cognitive psychologists must be reconciled. The combination of the learning theorist's work and that of the individual difference workers is not unknown (e.g. Fleishman and Hempel, 1954); however, recent collaborations appear to be rare.

One key question which needs resolution is how mental abilities relate to the various cognitive systems hypothesized by the cognitive psychologists. For example, how do abilities relate to processing time, short-term memory, problem representative, and application of schemata? An early attempt at resolving these questions was made by Guilford (1965) but apparently the current work in this area is meager. One recent thrust in cognitive research, however, emphasizes that successful problem solving and learning cannot occur without relevant prior knowledge (Chi and Greeno, 1988). Particularly difficult is determining how general cognitive ability, as Hunter and Schmidt follow a line of tradition in describing, relates to the findings of modern cognitive psychology. It is clear that cognitive abilities, as measured by standardized tests, are developed abilities. Can these abilities be conceptualized as nothing more than prior knowledge? Can it be hypothesized that their main function is to form a knowledge base which facilitates the acquisition of new knowledge? Questions like these deserve answers in any comprehensive theory of learning. Such a theory cannot be based on correlational data alone, but must be generated within several lines of investigation.

It is difficult to evaluate the theoretical propositions on learning put forth by Hunter and Schmidt in the preceding chapter. First, they give no reference for what they call the 'classic theory of job performance'. The only referenced research is that by Brolyer, Thorndike and Woodyard (1927), and that yields only research data relevant to the old theory of mental discipline which postulated, for example, that taking geometry would help one learn to think in other areas.

Second, the concept of general cognitive ability has never been universally accepted, although it has a large number of adherents. The meta-analytic work in the area of validity generalization does not appear to provide an appropriate line of support for the concept. In view of the very general nature of the criteria used in most validation studies and the frequent failure of researchers to investigate sufficiently so that they can specify what the criterion is measuring, it is very difficult to draw conclusions about the organization of mental functions from test validation data. With the advent of modern computer monitoring of performance, we may be able to get better criteria, at least with some routine jobs. Early results along these lines involving validation with actual performance data (Sackett, Zedeck and Fogli, 1987) suggest there may have been greater problems than we expected with our traditional criteria.

Third, the implication that cognitive ability tests should predict job learning better than they predict formal classroom learning needs referencing. Dating back to at least Ghiselli (1966, 1973) the research has been clear that classroom performance is more predictable from cognitive tests than is job performance, which should reflect classroom training, as well as on-the-job training and other factors. Furthermore, the implication that the more the job requires innovation, the more likely it is for cognitive tests to be valid needs support, particularly in view of the findings (e.g. Campbell, Dunnette, Lawler and Weick, 1970) that cognitive tests are not highly predictive of success in managerial jobs which should require innovation.

It is difficult to accept the non-referenced premise that supervisors' ratings differ only because of nonwork factors. To the extent that two supervisors may each be familiar with the ratee's performance on only certain aspects of the job, the supervisors' ratings may disagree. Also, when another supervisor other than the immediate superior is available to make a rating, that second supervisor may have his or her ratings shaped by the funneling process, whereby the immediate supervisor gives only certain information about an employee's performance to others, especially higher level supervisors.

Hunter and Schmidt's using work samples as the measure of job performance also is a matter for concern. Those tools which industrial psychologists call 'work samples' and use as criteria in validation studies are, of necessity, usually abstractions. Seldom is it possible to develop an actual work sample. Even the oft-used typing test which is called a work sample is always a simulation. The process of standardization so that the results of the so-called work sample will yield comparable results from all job applicants or incumbents almost always leads to the work sample taking on many of the characteristics of a test. There are also considerations of safety of personnel and protection of equipment. One simply does not allow testing situations in which people can be harmed or allow a possibly partially trained person to operate an expensive piece of equipment. It is usually not economically feasible to allow research endeavors to disrupt, for example, a production line needed full time for the conduct of the company's business. Consequently, often key aspects of performance are eliminated in constructing work samples.

Furthermore, only certain types of jobs, usually the less complex, normally lend themselves well to the development of work samples. Consequently, any generalizations drawn from data on work samples may very well be limited to certain types of jobs. All of the foregoing is not to suggest that work samples, properly conceived and administered, cannot serve well as criteria in the validation studies. However, work samples, as almost all criterion measures, have limitations which make their unqualified use in theory building relative to job performance inadvisable.

Also, the question of method variance needs to be addressed by Schmidt and Hunter. It has been suggested that work samples often take on many of the characteristics of tests; certainly job knowledge tests and cognitive ability tests share method variance. Work samples and cognitive ability tests may well share method variance. Coefficients of correlation among variables which involve measurement by the same methods may be spuriously high and not amenable to broad interpretations, such as those which may be needed for theory building.

SUMMARY

Although the attempt to relate test validation to theory is commendable, its presentation leaves much to be desired. The origins of the theory presented as a classic are not clear. There are questions about the concept of general cognitive ability. Also, there are no indications that alternative explanations such as those which might be based on method variance have been ruled out. What may be involved here is a case of nonidentifiability (Anderson, 1976). In other words, the fact that a certain model fits the data does not mean that other models will not fit the data equally well. Furthermore, the findings may not be generalizable beyond a limited set of jobs. Questions may be asked about using performance on work sample tests as a measure of job performance. In order to judge the adequacy of the performance measures, one would probably have to examine the original data and instrumentation used in studies included in the meta-analysis on which Hunter and Schmidt's theoretical formulations have been made.

There may be many other problems with the data base from which Hunter and Schmidt's theoretical ideas have arisen. Nevertheless, it is refreshing to see innovative attempts to bring theory into industrial and organizational psychology. The authors of the preceding chapter have already stimulated an unprecedented amount of research in the field. Perhaps, more industrial psychologists will take their cues from Schmidt and Hunter and combine the techniques of experimental psychology, cognitive psychology, and industrial psychology to bring us more of the theory which is so very much needed if psychology in the workplace is to take its rightful place in science.

REFERENCES

Algera, J. A., Jansen, P. G., Roe, R. A. and Vijn, P. (1984). Validity generalization: some critical remarks on the Schmidt–Hunter procedure. *Journal of Occupational Psychology*, **57**, 197–210.

Anderson, J. R. (1976). *Language, Memory, and Thought*. Hillsdale, New Jersey: Lawrence Erlbaum Associates.

Bolles, R. C. (1979). *Learning Theory* (2 edn). New York: Holt, Rinehart & Winston.

Brolyer, C. R., Thorndike, E. L. and Woodyard, E. R. (1927). A second study of mental discipline in high school studies. *Journal of Educational Psychology*, **18**, 377–404.

Callender, J. C. and Osborn, H. G. (1980). Development and test of a new model for validity generalization. *Journal of Applied Psychology*, **65**, 543–558.

Campbell, J. P., Dunnette, M. D., Lawler, E. E. III and Weick, K. E. (1970). *Managerial Behavior, Performance, and Effectiveness*. New York: McGraw-Hill.

Chi, M. T. H. and Greeno, J. G. (1988). Cognitive research relevant to education. *Annals of New York Academy of Sciences*, **517** (in press).

Fleishman, E. A. and Hempel, W. E., Jr (1954). Changes in factor structure of a complex psychomotor test as a function of practice. *Psychometrika*, **19**, 239–252.

Gagne, E. D. (1985). *The Cognitive Psychology of School Learning*. Boston: Little, Brown.

Ghiselli, E. E. (1966). *The Validity of Occupational Aptitude Tests*. New York: Wiley.

Ghiselli, E. E. (1973). The validity of aptitude tests in personnel selection. *Personnel Psychology*, **26**, 461–477.

Glass, G. V. (1976). Primary, secondary and meta-analysis of research. *Educational Researcher*, **5**, 3–8.

Glass, G. V. (1977). Integrating findings: the meta-analysis of research. *Review of Research in Education*, **5**, 351–379.

Glass, G. V., McGaw, B. and Smith, M. L. (1981). *Meta-Analysis in Social Research*. Beverly Hills, CA: Sage Publications.

Guilford, J. P. (1965). *Intelligence—1965 model*. Address presented at annual meeting of the American Psychological Association, Chicago, Illinois.

Hunter, J. E., Schmidt, F. L. and Jackson, G. (1982). *Meta-analysis: Cumulating Research Findings across Studies*. Beverly Hills, CA: Sage Publications.

James, L. R., Demaree, R. G. and Muliak, S. A. (1986). A note on validity generalization procedures. *Journal of Applied Psychology*, **71**, 440–450.

James, L. R., Demaree, R. G., Muliak, S. A. and Mumford, M. A. (1988). *Validity generalization: ten years of suspended judgment*. Unpublished manuscript, Georgia Institute of Technology, Atlanta, Georgia.

Kemery, E. R., Mossholder, K. W. and Roth, L. (1987). The power of the Schmidt and Hunter addition model of validity generalization. *Journal of Applied Psychology*, **72**, 30–37.

Osburn, H. G., Callender, J. C., Greener, J. M., Ashworth, S. (1983). Statistical power of tests of the situational specificity hypothesis in validity generalization studies: a cautionary note. *Journal of Applied Psychology*, **68**, 115–122.

Paese, P. and Switzer, F. (1988). Validity generalization and hypothetical reliability distributions: a test of the Schmidt–Hunter procedure. *Journal of Applied Psychology*, **73**, 267–274.

Raju, N. S. and Burke, M. J. (1983). Two new procedures for studying validity generalization. *Journal of Applied Psychology*, **68**, 382–395.

Rosenthal, R. (1984). *Meta-analytic Procedures for Social Research*. Beverly Hills, CA: Sage Publications.

Sackett, P. R., Harris, M. M. and Orr, J. M. (1986). On seeking moderator variables in the meta-analysis of correlational data: a Monte Carlo investigation of statistical power and resistance to type I error. *Journal of Applied Psychology*, **71**, 302–310.

Sackett, P. R., Schmitt, N. W., Tenopyr, M. L., Kehoe, J. F. and Zedeck, S. (1985). Commentary on forty questions about validity generalization and meta-analysis. *Personnel Psychology*, **38**, 697–798.

Sackett, P. R., Zedeck, S. and Fogli, L. (1987). *Relationships between measures of typical and maximum job performance*. Paper presented at the annual meetings of the American Psychological Association, New York, New York.

Schmidt, F. L. and Hunter, J. E. (1977). Development of a general solution to the problem of validity generalization. *Journal of Applied Psychology*, **62**, 529–540.

Schmidt, F. L. and Hunter, J. E. (1984). A within setting empirical test of the situational specificity hypothesis in personnel selection. *Personnel Psychology*, **37**, 317–326.

Schmidt, F. L., Hunter, J. E. and Pearlman, K. (1982). Progress in validity generalization: comments on Callender and Osburn and further developments. *Journal of Applied Psychology*, **67**, 835–845.

Schmidt, F. L., Hunter, J. E., Pearlman, K. and Hirsch, H. R. (1985). Forty questions about validity generalization and meta-analysis, *Personnel Psychology*, **38**, 697–798.

Spector, P. E. and Levine, E. L. (1987). Meta-analysis for integrating study outcomes: a Monte Carlo study of its susceptibility to type I and type II errors. *Journal of Applied Psychology*, **72**, 3–9.

19

A Case Study on Meta-Analysis of Investment Analysts

T. Daniel Coggin
First Union National Bank of North Carolina

Brokerage houses and other investment advisors rely on investment analysts to evaluate the assets in their clients' portfolios. The evaluation of the analysts is usually based on how well they predict the returns on the assets they follow. One such method of evaluation is to compute the correlation between predicted and actual returns. Managers have often noted large differences between such correlations for different analysts and have interpreted these discrepancies as real differences between them.

In a study of US investment analysts, Coggin and Hunter (1983) noted that the number of stocks followed by a given analyst is usually about 30. Hence the correlation for a typical analyst is based on a very small sample and is thus subject to large sampling error. This means that much of the apparent difference in analyst performance is actually sampling error in the correlation coefficient. Coggin and Hunter did a meta-analysis of analyst correlations for a large regional trust company to assess the amount of real difference in analyst performance. They found that once variation due to sampling error was eliminated, there was *no* real difference in analyst correlations. Their results were later replicated by Dimson and Marsh (1984) for a sample of investment analysts in the UK. The fact that there is no difference between analysts in how well they predict return means that there is actually no difference between analysts on that dimension of job performance. This is contrary to findings for job performance in many other areas of human endeavor. How can this be?

There are at least two possible explanations. According to the 'efficient

Advances in Selection and Assessment. Edited by M. Smith and I. T. Robertson

market hypothesis' from financial economics, all relevant information about a given stock at any given moment is known to all market participants and is instantly reflected in the stock price. If this hypothesis were true, all analysts would have the same correlation; but it would be zero. However, the average correlation for analysts is not 0.00 but typically 0.10. Thus analysts *are* able to predict return to some extent, they just do *not* differ in how well they predict. An alternate explanation relies on the fact that analysts do not operate in a vacuum; rather, they are members of a sizable community of analysts. The large brokerage houses employ top analysts to issue reports on the major industry categories and the stocks therein. The remaining vast majority of analysts at smaller firms use those reports as a primary source of information. Thus there is extensive sharing of information among the analysts of a given industry. This sharing implies that there would be little difference in the final predictions made by analysts. Hence there would be little difference in the true correlations between analysts.

These results have important implications for the common practice of compensating investment analysts based upon how well he or she predicts stock returns. If all differences in correlations are attributable to sampling error, then such a compensation scheme amounts to a 'lottery' for analysts' salaries. After the management of the trust company in question reviewed the findings of the study by Coggin and Hunter, the practice of using correlations to make 'between analyst' performance distinctions was discontinued. The trust company then formulated a performance measurement policy which considered the analysts as a single unit rather than as several separate units. The new policy recognizes the fact that comparisons between analysts are meaningless at best and unfair at worst.

REFERENCES

Coggin, T. D. and Hunter, J. E. (1983). Problems in measuring the quality of investment information: the perils of the information coefficient. *Financial Analysts Journal*, **39** (May–June), 25–33.

Dimson, E. and Marsh, P. (1984). An analysis of brokers' and analysts' unpublished forecasts of UK stock returns, *Journal of Finance*, **39**, 1257–1292.

20

Selection Utility Analysis: a Review and Agenda for Future Research

JOHN W. BOUDREAU
New York State School of Industrial & Labor Relations, Cornell University

INTRODUCTION

Whether they are line managers, human resource management staff, or organizational psychologists, managers of human resources must make decisions (e.g. hiring, placement, training, compensation, performance appraisal, feedback, etc.) in which theories of human work behavior play an important role. Industrial/Organizational (I/O) psychologists (and other social scientists) find the organizational environment a rich source of information for advancing knowledge and testing theories about employment relationships, their antecedents and consequences. Applied research articles inevitably discuss 'practical implications', but what is the real value of human resource productivity improvement programs?

The Human Resource Management (HRM) functions of industrial organizations typically lack the influence and visibility of the more 'traditional' management functions (such as marketing, finance, operations and accounting). Journals for HRM professionals routinely lament the slow progress of organizations in implementing programs that have gained wide acceptance by scientists (cf. Jain and Murray, 1984). Journals and books

This research was carried out with support from the U.S. Army Research Institute, contract SFRC # MDA903-87-K-0001. The views, opinions, and/or findings contained in this chapter are those of the author and should not be construed as an Official Department of the Army policy, or decision.

Advances in Selection and Assessment. Edited by M. Smith and I. T. Robertson

routinely admonish and instruct the HRM professionals to 'sell' their programs by emphasizing their effects on organizational goal attainment (Bolda, 1985; Gow, 1985; Sheppeck and Cohen, 1985). Indeed, the question of whether the HRM function contributes to corporate profit is still important enough to merit recent discussion in a widely-cited professional journal (Gow, 1985). It is difficult to imagine such a debate regarding the Finance, Marketing, Accounting, or Engineering departments. Is the contribution of I/O psychology and other social sciences to human resource management really so intangible compared to these other management functions?

Utility analysis involves *describing, predicting and explaining the usefulness or desirability of decision options, and analyzing how that information can be used in decision making.* In I/O psychology, the term utility analysis has become associated with a specific set of models that reflect the consequences (usually performance-related consequences, such as output as sold, sales, net benefits, or reduced costs) of programs (e.g. selection, recruitment, training, performance feedback, goal setting, compensation, internal staffing and turnover control) to enhance workforce productivity. Utility analysis offers a method for better understanding the role of I/O psychology and other social sciences in improving HRM decisions and organizational performance. Moreover, it offers an invitation to I/O psychologists and other social scientists to adopt a truly interdisciplinary approach to important scientific and practical questions.

A CONCEPTUAL FRAMEWORK

Selection utility models can present very complex algebraic and statistical formulas, but their basic concepts are quite logical, simple, and direct.

Selection utility analysis supports decisions

Selection utility models are 'decision aids' (Edwards, 1977; Einhorn and McCoach, 1977; Einhorn, Kleinmuntz and Kleinmuntz, 1979; Fischer, 1976; Huber, 1980; Keeney and Raiffa, 1976), tools for predicting, explaining, describing and analyzing decisions. Decision aids assist decision makers in overcoming limited cognitive capacity ('limits on rationality' according to March and Simon, 1958) by providing a consistent and structured framework within which to compare decision options. Selection utility models offer a consistent structured framework for considering selection consequences, and for communicating those consequences to constituencies in generally-understood units (e.g. dollars).

Applying selection utility analysis models requires: (1) a set of decision options to be considered (e.g. two or more different selection systems); (2) a set of attributes reflecting the characteristics of the options that affect valued outcomes (e.g. validity coefficients, costs, effect sizes, quantity of employees affected), combined with a 'utility scale' that reflects the value of each attribute level to the decision maker (e.g. a scale translating selection validity into dollar-valued performance); and (3) a payoff function, the weighting scheme or other combination rule reflecting the relationships among the attributes in estimating total utility for each option (e.g. an algebraic formula describing the relationship between validity, cost and utility).

Viewing selection utility models as decision tools is quite consistent with their historical development, as will be discussed subsequently. Yet little research has addressed whether they have any effect on actual decisions. Throughout this chapter, I will propose that selection utility research must proceed with a keen awareness of the decisions it is designed to support, and that such an awareness suggests some very different research questions and directions from those currently being pursued.

The unit of analysis: human resource productivity improvement programs

The options considered by utility analysis models are human resource productivity improvement programs. Such programs are combinations of activities (or procedures governing activities) that affect the organizational value of the work force.

Decisions about individuals versus decisions about programs

As Cronbach and Gleser (1965, p. 9) noted, utility analysis is most appropriate for programs that will be applied to many individuals over time. Thus, programs embody procedures, rules or 'strategies' (Cronbach and Gleser, p. 19) intended to be applied to many individuals. Selection utility analysis typically focuses on programs using tests to select new employees. Such programs involve rules indicating how the test is to be applied to applicants, and how the test results are to be used in choosing among applicants.

A distinctive feature of 'programs' is that they affect many hiring decisions about individuals. Selection programs work by providing information that causes certain applicants to be hired who otherwise might have been rejected (and vice versa), resulting in a more productive group of hires than would be possible without the test. The decision about each applicant, however, is not the focus of selection utility analysis. Rather, it is the *decision* to implement a program that will alter the way many applicants are evaluated for hiring. Because such decisions affect many individuals throughout their tenure with the organization, the impact of even a single program decision on future workforce consequences can be quite large, as we shall see.

The organization context

Selection programs 'work' if they increase the correctness of those choices in ways that are important enough to offset the costs of the information. However, each organization or decision maker will define importance differently, depending on the constituents involved, the way it employs employee productivity, and how selection interacts with other programs such as compensation and training. Research has often proceeded as if these factors were held constant, but more integrative future research should examine these relationships more explicitly.

Three basic utility analysis variables: quantity, quality and cost

Selection utility models can be expressed in terms of three basic attributes (Boudreau, 1984, 1987, in press a, b; Boudreau and Berger, 1985a, b): (1) *Quantity*, reflecting the quantity of employees and time periods affected by program consequences; (2) *Quality*, reflecting the consequences (per person, per time period) associated with the program; and (3) *Cost*, reflecting the resources required to implement and maintain the program. The payoff from a selection program can be derived by taking the product of Quantity and Quality, and then subtracting Cost. Generally, the program exhibiting the largest positive difference is preferable.

Selection utility models differ in the manner in which they define each of these three variables, but they all can be understood within this framework.

HISTORICAL DEVELOPMENT

Selection utility analysis models responded to the inadequacies of traditional measurement and test theory in expressing the usefulness of tests. As Cronbach and Gleser stated:

> The traditional theory views the test as a measuring instrument intended to assign accurate numerical values to some quantitative attribute of the individual. It therefore stresses, as the prime value, precision of measurement and estimation. In practical testing, however, a quantitative estimate is not the real desideratum. A choice between two or more discrete treatments must be made. The tester is to allocate each person to the proper category, and accuracy of measurement is valuable only insofar as it aids in this qualitative decision. ... Measurement theory appears suitable without modification when the scale is considered in the abstract, without reference to any particular application. As soon as the scale is intended for use in a restricted context, that context influences our evaluation of the scale. (1965, pp. 135–136)

Therefore, the history of selection utility analysis will be discussed from a decision-making perspective, focusing on each model's definition of 'goodness', and using the concepts of Quantity, Quality and Cost to assess the decision value of each historical development.

Defining payoff with the validity coefficient

Model description

The validity coefficient (the correlation between a predictor measure and some criterion measure of subsequent behavior, usually expressed as $r_{x,y}$) is the attribute of selection that has the longest history. The correlation coefficient and indexes derived from it (e.g. the index of forecasting efficiency and coefficient of determination, see Hull, 1928) lead to the conclusion that only relatively large differences in the validity coefficient produce important differences in the value of a test.

Evaluation from a decision-theory perspective

As indicators of a test's usefulness for decisions, such formulas are quite deficient. First, the implied payoff function is unrealistic. The correlation coefficient measures squared deviations from a predicted linear function, treating any deviation of the predicted value from the linear function as equally undesirable. Overpredicting the best candidate's future performance is treated as equivalent to underpredicting it, yet the former is unlikely to cause serious decision errors, while the latter easily could.

In terms of the three basic program attributes (i.e. quantity, quality and cost), correlation-based models reflect neither the quantity of time periods affected by the selection decisions nor the quantity of employees affected in each time period. They provide only indirect evidence of the predictor's effect on work force quality. Finally, they fail to acknowledge the fact that developing and applying selection programs entails costs.

Defining payoff based on the success ratio

Model description

The 'success ratio' represents the percentage of selected individuals who are successful on the job. According to the Taylor–Russell (1939) tables, when other parameters are held constant: (1) higher validities result in more improved success ratios (because the more linear the relationship, the smaller the area of the distribution lying in the false-positive or false-negative region); (2) lower selection ratios result in more improved success ratios (because the lower the selection ratio, the more 'choosy' is the selection decision, and the predictor scores of selectees lie closer to the upper tail of the predictor distribution); (3) base rates closer to 0.50 result in more improved success ratios because valid selection has less value as you approach a base rate of zero (where none of the applicants can be successful) or as you approach a base rate of 1.0 (where all applicants can succeed even without selection).

Evaluation from a decision-making perspective

Regarding the payoff function, a dichotomous criterion (i.e. selectees are either satisfactory or unsatisfactory) will often lose information because the value of performance is not equal at all points above the satisfactory level, nor at all points below the unsatisfactory level (Cascio, 1982, p. 135; Hunter and Schmidt, 1982, p. 235; Cronbach and Gleser, 1965, pp. 123–124, 138). The more typical (though not uniformly applicable) situation is where performance differences within the two groups exist. Under such situations, a continuous criterion would be more appropriate. Still, the Taylor–Russell model may provide adequate decision support for some situations. Cascio (1982, p. 146) suggests it may be more appropriate for truly dichotomous criteria (e.g. turnover occurrences), or where output differences above the acceptable level do not change benefits (e.g. clerical or technician's tasks), or where such differences are unmeasurable (e.g. nursing, teaching, credit counseling). In terms of the three program attributes (i.e. quantity, quality and cost), the Taylor–Russell model (like its predecessors) ignores both the quantity of employees affected and the number of time periods during which that effect will last. The model does a better job of describing the change in quality produced by the program (in that it provides some idea of increased success probabilities), but this quality measure must be interpreted differently from situation to situation. Finally, the Taylor–Russell model completely ignores costs.

Defining payoff based on the standardized criterion level

Model description

The major criticism of the success ratio was that its dichotomous criterion failed to reflect the true variation in performance. The next version of the selection utility model attempted to remedy this by defining a continuous criterion as the payoff function. Brogden (1946a, b) used the principles of linear regression to demonstrate the relationship between the correlation coefficient and increases in a criterion (measured on a continuous scale).

Assuming a linear relationship between criterion scores and predictor scores, if we derived the best, linear, unbiased estimate of the change in standardized criterion scores (Z_y) corresponding to a change in standardized predictor scores (Z_x) in the applicant population, the linear prediction equation would be:

$$Z_y = (r_{xy})(Z_x) \tag{1}$$

Therefore, if we knew the average standardized predictor score of a selected group of applicants (i.e. $\bar{Z}_x$), our best prediction of the average standardized criterion score of the selected group (i.e. $\bar{Z}_y$) would be the product of the validity coefficient and the standardized predictor score, as shown in Equation (2).

$$\bar{Z}_y = (r_{xy})(\bar{Z}_x) \tag{2}$$

This utility model reflects a continuous criterion (expressed in standardized, Z-score units) as its payoff function, and includes as attributes both the validity coefficient (in the population of applicants to which the predictor will be applied) and the average standardized predictor score of those applicants chosen. The validity coefficient and its derivation were well established, and Naylor and Shine (1965) computed extensive tables showing, for each selection ratio, the corresponding average standardized predictor score (assuming normally distributed predictor scores and top-down applicant selection).

Evaluation from a decision-making perspective

This utility model addresses one shortcoming of the Taylor–Russell model by defining payoff based on a continuous criterion. However, because the criterion is expressed in standard-score units, it is difficult to interpret in units more natural to the decision process (e.g. dollars, units produced, reduced costs, etc.). Also, this payoff function reflects only the *difference* between the average standardized criterion score of those selected using the predictor and the average standardized criterion score that would be obtained through selection without the predictor (the mean of the applicant population which, by definition, has a standard score of zero). The total utility from the program is not computed, only the increment over not using the predictor.

Considering the three basic utility model concepts (i.e. quantity, quality and cost), the quantity of employees and time periods are not reflected, the quality criterion is in statistical rather than tangible units, and the cost of the selection program is still omitted.

Defining payoff in terms of dollar-valued criterion levels

Model description

The most obvious drawback of using standardized criterion levels as the payoff function is that they are difficult to interpret in 'real' units. Selection device development and implementation activities are often expressed as costs (i.e. required uses of resources), usually scaled in dollars. With a standardized criterion scale, one must ask questions such as: 'Is it worth spending $10,000 to select 50 people per year, in order to obtain a criterion level 0.5 standard deviations greater than what we would obtain without the predictor?' Obviously, many HRM managers may not even be familiar with the concept of a standard deviation. Almost certainly, they would find it difficult to attach a dollar value to a 0.5 standard deviation increase in the criterion (especially considering that the decision makers may never actually observe the appropriate population for that standard deviation—the population of applicants to which the predictor would be applied).

Both Brogden (1946a, b, 1949) and Cronbach and Gleser (1965, pp. 308–309) eventually derived their utility formulas in terms of 'payoff', rather than standardized criterion scores. They also both included the concept of costs. Thus, they originated the notion of expressing utility on a dollar-valued scale. To accomplish this, they introduced a scaling factor that translated standardized criterion levels into dollar terms, and they added a term for the costs of the selection program. The scaling factor is simply the dollar value of a one-standard-deviation difference in criterion level (symbolized in various ways, including σ_y, σ_e, and SD_y, the latter being used here). The cost factor is usually expressed as the cost to administer the predictor to a single applicant (usually symbolized as C). Finally, the utility value is symbolized as $\Delta \bar{U}$, to indicate that it represents the *difference* between the dollar payoff from selection without the predictor and the dollar payoff from selection with the predictor (this is usually called the 'incremental' utility of the predictor). The resulting utility equation may be written as Equation (3).

$$\Delta \bar{U} = (SD_y)(r_{x,y})(\bar{Z}_x) - C/SR \qquad (3)$$

The per-applicant cost (C) is divided by the selection ratio (SR) to reflect total cost of obtaining each selectee (e.g. if the selection ratio is 0.50, then one must test two applicants to find each selectee, and the testing cost per selectee is twice the cost per applicant).

Thus, Equation (3) depicts the incremental dollar-valued criterion level of those selected with a predictor (x), in a population of applicants where the validity coefficient is $r_{x,y}$; where a one-standard-deviation difference in criterion levels equals SDy; where the average standardized predictor score of those selected is equal to $\bar{Z}_x$; and the per-selectee cost of using the predictor is (C/SR). To express the total gain from using the predictor to select N_s selectees, we simply multiply the benefits by the number selected, change the symbol for incremental utility from $\Delta \bar{U}$ to ΔU, and multiply the per-applicant cost by the number of applicants (N_{app}) as shown in Equation (4).

$$\Delta U = (N_s)(SD_y)(r_{x,y})(\bar{Z}_x) - (C)(N_{app}) \qquad (4)$$

Cronbach and Gleser (1965, p. 39) also recommended computing the difference in utility between two tests, which simply involves substituting the difference in validities for $r_{x,y}$ and the difference in costs for C in Equations (3) and (4).

Finally, to incorporate the duration of the effects of better-selecting one employee cohort, Schmidt, Hunter, McKenzie and Muldrow (1979) multiplied the benefit component of these models by the expected tenure of the hired cohort (i.e. T).

Evaluation from a decision making perspective

Scaling the per-person, per-time-period incremental criterion level in dollars seems more in keeping with organizational objectives to increase dollar profits. The B-C-G utility model incorporates a scaling factor (SD_y) to translate standardized criterion levels into dollars. Measuring SD_y has proven controversial as will be discussed subsequently.

The B-C-G model incorporates the three basic selection utility analysis components (i.e. quantity, quality and cost). Quantity is incorporated in the number selected and their average tenure. Quality is incorporated in the product of $r_{x,y}$, $\bar{Z}_x$, and SDy (producing the per-person, per-time-period incremental dollar-valued criterion level). Costs to develop and implement the selection program are contained in the cost factor (C).

Encouraging more widespread selection utility analysis applications

The B-C-G utility model remained largely unnoticed by I/O psychologists (at least in terms of published research studies), though this model represented a fundamental and important alternative to traditional measurement theory as a framework for I/O psychology research. The reasons for this lack of attention are unclear. It is likely that the algebraic complexity of these models proved daunting to managers, so researchers may have encountered difficulty communicating the purpose and importance of the models. Moreover, researchers may have incorrectly assumed that all model parameters must be fairly accurately measured to apply the models because the aim was to produce a point estimate of utility. This misconception still exists today, as discussed subsequently.

Hunter and Schmidt (1982) and Schmidt et al. (1979) noted the limited application of the B-C-G models and proposed that three widely-held misconceptions might explain it: (1) the belief that utility equations are of no value unless the data exactly fit the linear homoscedastic model, and all marginal distributions are normal (in fact, the B-C-G model only introduces the normality assumption for 'derivational convenience', see Hunter and Schmidt, 1982, p. 243, as it provides an exact relationship between the selection ratio and the average standard test score of selectees); (2) the belief that test validities are situationally specific, making application of utility analysis possible only when a criterion-related validity study has been performed in the particular situation (in fact, 'validity generalization'—Hunter, Schmidt, and Jackson,

1982, research suggests that much of the variability in validity coefficients observed across studies is due to artifacts of the studies rather than real differences in the predictor-criterion relationship); (3) the belief that the parameter scaling standardized values into dollars (i.e. SD_y) is difficult or impossible to measure. A later section will discuss this measurement issue in detail.

Financial/economic factors: utility analysis as an investment model

The dollar-valued payoff model led to speculation that selection utility could provide a link between Personnel/HRM research and the more traditional management functions (Landy, Farr and Jacobs, 1982, p. 38; Cascio and Silbey, 1979). Recent research suggested enhancements to the traditional selection utility model designed to incorporate financial and economic considerations into the analysis. Boudreau (1983a) suggested that by measuring utility with a payoff function reflecting sales or 'the value of output as sold', researchers were probably overstating HRM program effects on after-tax profit (the payoff scale used for financial investments). He showed how the utility formulas could easily be altered to account for three basic financial/economic concepts: variable costs, taxes and discounting.

First, 'sales (or service) value' (i.e. the change in sales revenue or output as sold) differs from 'service cost' (i.e. the change in organizational costs associated with changed service value), which differs from 'net benefits' (i.e. the difference between service value and service costs) produced by an HRM intervention. HRM programs that improve sales value can require additional support costs (e.g. increased inventories to support higher sales, increased raw materials usage to support higher output volumes, increased salaries/benefits as incentives for improved performance). Moreover, many interventions operate not by increasing sales revenue or output levels, but by reducing costs (e.g. Florin-Thuma and Boudreau, in press). Boudreau (1983a) included the effects of HRM programs on service costs by multiplying the incremantal service value increase by a proportion (V) reflecting the change in net benefits per change in sales value. Second, most organizations pay taxes on income. Boudreau proposed multiplying both the net benefits and the implementation costs (C) by one minus the applicable tax rate (i.e. $1-TAX$) to reflect after-tax effects. Third, returns can often be invested to earn interest. A dollar received in the future is worth less than a dollar received today, because the latter can earn interest in future periods. Boudreau demonstrated how the interest rate earned on program returns (i.e. i) could be incorporated into the selection utility analysis model.

Boudreau proposed that by incorporating these financial adjustments, reported utility values would better reflect the economic realities of organizations, would be more comparable to investment values reported for programs in other management functions, and might be more credible to managers accustomed to working with financial analysis. Cronshaw and Alexander (1985) also argued for HRM programs as financial investments, suggesting that 'a major reason for the differential success of human resource and financial managers in implementing their respective evaluation models is the greater rapprochement of capital budgeting with the everyday language of line managers and with the financial planning needs of the organization' (p. 102).

The employee flows utility model

To move beyond selection utility models reflecting only the consequences of hiring one group of employees, Boudreau (1983b) proposed the 'employee flows' model. Organizations seldom invest in a selection program to use it once and then stop. Rather they can continuously reapply the program as new members enter the workforce. To analyze only the first-cohort effects is tantamount to analyzing an investment in new manufacturing facilities based on only one production run. Clearly, such a focus omits a large part of the decision's effects.

Boudreau proposed that a more accurate approach would reflect the number of 'treated' (i.e. better-selected) employees in the workforce in each future period (i.e. N_k), and the costs incurred to select the employees joining the workforce in each future time period (i.e. C_k). Boudreau acknowledged that any of the utility variables could change over time, and noted that the 'flows' model could reflect such temporal changes. The flows model highlighted the importance of the Quantity concept (the number of employees and time periods affected by the intervention) in explaining the potentially huge effects of human resource management decisions.

To illustrate the effects of employee flows, Boudreau used data from the Schmidt et al. (1979) study. However, whereas the earlier authors had computed quantity by multiplying the size of the first selected cohort (i.e. 618) by its expected tenure (i.e. approximately 10 years), Boudreau assumed that each cohort of 618 selected employees remained on the job for 10 years, and then left to be replaced by a newly-hired cohort. The effect of these assumptions was that the number of better-selected employees in the workforce steadily rose (by 618 per year) during the first 10 years (as new employees were added to the workforce and joined previously-selected employees), until it reached 6180. For the next five years, vacancies created by the separation of systematically-selected employees were filled with systematically-selected employees, so the number of treated employees in the work force remained at 6180. When the program was terminated, the number of treated employees in the work force slowly diminished (by 618 each year) until it reached zero. Boudreau used an analysis period of 25 years (i.e. the program was applied for 15 years and then stopped).

Using the one-cohort model, Schmidt *et al.* proposed that the effects of improved selection would affect 6180 person-years of productivity (i.e. 10 years average tenure times 618 hired employees). Using the employee flows model, Boudreau calculated that the program would affect 92,700 person-years of productivity (i.e. the sum of N_k over all 25 years). This is a critically important point. Repeated application of improved selection programs can affect huge numbers of employee-years of productivity producing massive potential productivity effects. The key to understanding this is to recognize that HRM programs are likely to be re-applied over time, rather than applied only once. Just as one would not attempt to justify a million-dollar investment in a new manufacturing plant based only on the first production run, HRM decision makers should not attempt to justify investments in HRM programs based only on the first cohort affected.

Integrating employee recruitment into selection utility analysis

Boudreau and Rynes (1985) noted that while the early Taylor–Russell selection utility model explicitly included the 'base rate' (i.e. the proportion of applicants whose performance would exceed minimally acceptable levels if randomly selected), the majority of selection utility research was conducted under the implicit or explicit assumption that all selection options would be implemented within the same applicant population.

Two factors may make such assumptions simplistic compared to organizational reality. First, as Boudreau and Rynes (1985) noted, common wisdom in the recruitment literature suggests that more rigorous or intrusive selection methods may affect the size and/or characteristics of applicant pools (though there is little research to support or refute this suggestion). Second, recruitment strategies (e.g. personalized follow-ups, realistic job previews, choices of recruitment sources) are explicitly designed to alter applicant population characteristics, presumably to enhance organizational outcomes.

Boudreau and Rynes proposed that every parameter of the utility model could be affected by recruitment strategies, or could be affected by applicant reactions to selection devices. For example, applicant populations might be more homogeneous (reducing both SD_y and the correlation coefficient) if more stringent standards were applied to recruitment sources. Higher salary offers might increase the size and perhaps the qualifications of the applicant pool (affecting both the selection ratio and the average qualification level of the population). In the Boudreau–Rynes model, utility values are represented on an absolute scale, reflecting both the average and the incremental value of the selectees. They demonstrated how the incremental selection utility model alone may severely understate the combined value of integrated recruitment and selection, and how improved base rates may actually offset reductions in selection effectiveness caused by restrictions in range or smaller applicant pools.

THE STATE OF THE ART IN EMPIRICAL RESEARCH: UTILITY VALUES FOR SELECTION PROGRAMS

I recently reviewed empirical studies through 1986, with utility values for 39 interventions. The unavoidable conclusion is that selection programs pay off handsomely. Virtually every study has produced dollar-valued payoffs that clearly exceeded costs. Studies dealing with many employees and multiple-year tenure can produce utility values as high as $20 to $30 million (e.g. Schmidt et al., 1979; Cascio and Ramos, 1986). The clear positive payoff from selection programs remains evident in studies with relatively small SD_y values as well as in studies with large SD_y values, and with selection ratios as high as 50 percent. As would be expected, the largest utility values result in studies where large numbers of individuals are affected by the program (i.e. where N_s is large). Many of the studies were designed to examine whether substituting a more-valid selection method for a less-valid one (usually in interview) produced greater dollar-valued payoff (Burke and Frederick, 1985; Cascio and Ramos, 1986; Cascio and Silbey, 1979; Ledvinka, Simonet, Neiner and Kruse, 1983; Schmidt et al., 1979; Schmidt, Mack and Hunter, 1984; Rich and Boudreau, 1987). In every case the more valid (and usually more costly) selection procedure produced the greater utility.

Utility values as measured by the B-C-G model appear to be quite high. Moreover, the measured costs of improved selection are usually minuscule compared to the benefits. Such a conclusion seems inconsistent with the ongoing debate over whether human resource management's contribution is ignored, whether HRM issues should be considered in organizational planning, and whether HRM programs represent appropriate uses for organizational resources.

THE STATE OF THE ART IN EMPIRICAL RESEARCH: MEASURING THE STANDARD DEVIATION OF PERFORMANCE IN DOLLARS

The standard deviation of dollar-valued job performance in the applicant population (SD_y) was characterized as the 'Achilles' Heel' of utility analysis by Cronbach and Gleser (1965, p. 121). The large amount of recent research aimed at better estimating this elusive concept suggests that many of today's selection utility researchers agree, and regard accurate measurement of SD_y as a fundamental requirement for useful selection utility analysis research (Burke and Frederick, 1984, 1985; Weekley, O'Connor, Frank and Peters, 1985). I located 26 studies, with over 100 individual SD_y estimates. The trend in research activity is evident, with only 5 studies between 1953 and 1979 and 21 studies between 1979 and 1986.

Effects of setting

A wide variety of occupations has been examined, with the choice of occupation usually determined by whatever research setting presented itself to the researchers. Jobs where workers exercise more discretion regarding the quantity and quality of production and/or where variation in production has large implications for organizational goals should exhibit higher SD_y values than jobs without these characteristics, assuming the same variability in skill and motivation in each workforce. Of course, different jobs probably face different ranges of skill and motivation among job incumbents, which could cause even jobs of high discretion and importance to produce lower observed SD_y values than jobs without those characteristics. Most SD_y studies focused on only one job, making across-job comparisons difficult (because jobs, measurement methods, settings and time periods are confounded). In studies of more than one job (Wroten, 1984; Eaton, Wing and Lau, 1985), results suggested the SD_y estimation method affected whether cross-job differences were observed.

Every SD_y study used job titles to identify employees holding similar job duties and tasks. Such an approach may inadvertently include across-job differences in the SD_y measure. For example, although computer programmers may all hold the same job title, certain programming jobs may involve primarily transcribing flowcharts into computer code, while other programming jobs may involve designing the logic of the program (Rich and Boudreau, 1987). Clearly the latter job has more potential for both valuable positive contributions and/or costly mistakes. If the selection test will be used primarily to select programmers assigned as coders, this will overstate SD_y (and vice versa). Moreover, if jobs with different titles actually share duties, this could explain the lack of consistent job-to-job differences.

Effects of payoff scales

The most general definition of payoff for utility analysis is '*all consequences of a given decision that concern the person making the decision (or the institution he represents)*' (Cronbach and Gleser, 1965, p. 22). Payoff measures should reflect different outcomes (e.g. productivity increases, labor cost reductions, affirmative action goal attainment, improved organization image, consistency with fundamental organizational beliefs, high levels of financial return, etc.) in different decision situations, consistent with the objectives of decision makers (see Cronbach and Gleser, 1965, p. 23). The payoff scales used in selection utility analysis research focus on the consequences of increased labor force quality, so the payoff from improved selection depends heavily upon how the quality enhancements caused by such programs will be used.

Three general uses for improved labor force quality are: (1) raising the quantity of production; (2) raising the quality of production; and (3) reducing production costs. Managers may use labor force quality increases in any or all of these ways, or may combine them. A payoff scale defined in terms of profit can reflect any or all of these uses. Payoff scales reflecting only quantity or quality or cost may fail to reflect the two omitted uses. Payoff scales reflecting revenue enhancements (through higher quality or quantity) and cost reductions dominate the selection utility literature, though profit-based scales are emerging.

Payoff as cost reduction

Most of the earliest selection utility analysis applications focused on *cost reduction* as the salient outcome of improved selection. Doppelt and Bennett (1953) focused on reductions in training costs. Van Naersson (1963) focused on reductions in driving accident and training costs. Lee and Booth (1974) and Schmidt and Hoffman (1973) focused on reduced costs of replacing separations. More recently, Eaton, Wing and Mitchell (1985) measured payoff in terms of the avoided costs of additional tanks, and Schmidt and Hunter (1983) noted that increased workforce productivity might reduce 'payroll costs' by producing the same amount of output with a smaller number of employees (p. 413). Arnold, Rauschenberger, Soubel and Guion (1983) adopted the premise that improved selection would allow hiring fewer employees to do an equivalent amount of work. These payoff functions are also consistent with the 'behavioral costing' approach to HRM program analysis described by Cascio (1982). While cost reductions often offer a highly visible and salient payoff function in situations where cost reduction is the dominant consideration, its deficiencies have led researchers to explore further options.

Payoff as the 'value of output as sold'

Schmidt *et al.* (1979) measured SD_y in terms of the 'yearly value of products and services', and the 'cost of having an outside firm provide these products.' Hunter and Schmidt (1982, pp. 268–269) interpreted the payoff function as the *value of 'output as sold,'* or what the employer 'charges the customer.' Most research has focused on similar payoff scales (Bobko, Karren and Parkington, 1983; Bolda, 1985; Burke and Frederick, 1984, 1985; Cascio, 1982; Cascio and Ramos, 1986; Cascio and Silbey, 1979; Eaton, Wing and Lau, 1985; Eaton, Wing and Mitchell, 1985; Eulberg, O'Connor and Peters, 1985; Ledvinka *et al.*, 1983; Mathieu and Leonard, 1987; Reilly and Smither, 1985; Schmidt *et al.*, 1984; Weekley *et al.*, 1985; Wroten, 1984). The 'sales value' payoff scale reflects the increased revenue generated by employees as a result of the program, but it may be a deficient payoff definition. When organizational investments are evaluated based on profit contribution, evaluating selection investments based only on revenue contribution may artificially inflate selection utility values.

Payoff as increased profits

The initial attention to the payoff function for utility analysis proceeded from the notion that the payoff scale should be applicable to business decisions, and generalizable across business organizations. This suggests defining payoff as the *contribution to organizational profits*. Brogden and Taylor (1950) proposed the 'dollar criterion' reflecting the sales revenue generated when a product is sold, less any production costs. Cronbach and Gleser (1965) provided a very general payoff concept, including all consequences important to decision makers. Thus, their payoff concept is consistent with a 'profit' definition, though it can encompass even broader definitions. Only one study actually adopted a payoff function reflecting profit contribution (Reilly and Smither, 1985), with results suggesting that the graduate students in their simulation differed most in their SD_y estimates when they were asked to consider 'net revenue' rather than 'new sales', or 'overall worth'. Similarly, Bobko *et al.* (1983) found that sales counselor supervisors exhibited much more variable SD_y estimates when attempting to estimate 'yearly value to the company' rather than 'total yearly dollar sales'.

Summary

Although costs, sales and profits have enjoyed some attention as payoff functions, any payoff function should be judged on its ability to improve decision quality or better describe, predict and explain decisions. All existing payoff scales reflect a concern with productivity-based outcomes, virtually ignoring other consequences of selection decisions (e.g. community relations, workforce attitudes, adherence to a code of ethics). Every payoff function will be deficient in some way, so the fundamental consideration is how the organization will use such quality improvements (i.e. increasing revenue versus reducing costs versus increasing profit). The typical research approach of comparing SD_y estimates based on different payoff functions fails to reflect this fundamental decision context. Future research should focus on how productivity improvements are actually used so that the payoff function better reflects the actual decision.

Effects of the focus population

Virtually all SD_y estimates are based on the incumbent population (e.g. Bobko *et al.*, 1983; Burke and Frederick, 1985; Cascio and Silbey, 1979; Eaton, Wing and Mitchell, 1985; Janz and Dunnette, 1977; Schmidt *et al.*, 1979; Schmidt and Hunter, 1983; Wroten, 1984), probably because the incumbent population is most familiar to job supervisors. However, the incumbent population is not technically the appropriate population of interest. For selection utility, the appropriate population is the applicant population to which selection procedures will be applied. This population may differ from the incumbent population for a number of reasons.

First, if certain procedures (for example, promoting out the best performers and dismissing the worst performers) make the incumbent population a restricted sample of applicant job performance (Schmidt et al., 1979), then SD_y estimated on job incumbents will be downward-biased. Second, applicant population changes over time due to different recruitment procedures or labor market influences (Becker, 1985; Boudreau and Rynes, 1985) may operate either to increase or decrease performance variability, and make applicant SD_y levels either higher or lower than SD_y among job incumbents. Third, estimating SD_y on job incumbents encourages estimators to consider all of the incumbents they have had experience with, including incumbents with different tenure levels. If performance varies with tenure, then SD_y estimated on the incumbents will reflect this tenure variability. However, this variability will not be present among cohorts of selectees because each cohort of hired applicants will have equal tenure throughout their employment. Thus, where job tenure and performance are related, an SD_y estimate based on job incumbents may overestimate applicant SD_y. Fourth, as noted earlier, virtually all utility analysis research groups employees with similar job titles to form the focus population. However, if task assignments or work environments differ within the same job the variability of performance may differ as well. SD_y estimates based on incumbent populations may be inaccurate reflections of the actual SD_y in the selection system (Bobko et al., 1983, and Rich and Boudreau, 1987 discuss this issue).

Most authors who discuss this issue adopt the argument that incumbent-based SD_y estimates are conservative due to restricted range. However, there is as yet no evidence regarding the possible biasing effects of variability due to tenure, different recruiting approaches, or different labor market conditions. Indeed, not one study has compared SD_y estimates based on the applicant population to those based on the incumbent population.

Effects of measurement technique

Because SD_y was characterized as the Achilles' Heel of utility analysis by Cronbach and Gleser (1965) and because differences in SD_y can cause such large differences in total utility estimates, many have argued that it is important to develop better SD_y measures. Though variations on each theme are prevalent, it is possible to divide SD_y measurement methods into four categories: (1) Cost accounting, (2) Global estimation, (3) Individualized estimation, and (4) Proportional rules.

Cost accounting

These methods use accounting techniques to attach a value to units of performance or output for each individual, with the standard deviation of these individual performance values representing SD_y (e.g. Roche, 1961; Van Naersson,
1963; Schmidt and Hoffman, 1973; Lee and Booth, 1974). The difficulty and
arbitrariness of cost accounting has frequently been cited as arguing in favor
of simpler methods (e.g. Cascio, 1982; Cascio and Ramos, 1986; Hunter and
Schmidt, 1982; Schmidt et al., 1979).

Global estimation

These methods have experts estimate the total yearly dollar-valued performance at two, three, or four percentiles of an hypothetical performance distribution, with average differences between these percentile estimates representing
SD_y (e.g. Bobko et al., 1983; Bolda, 1985; Burke and Frederick, 1984, 1985;
Cascio and Silbey, 1979; Eaton, Wing and Lau, 1985; Eaton, Wing and
Mitchell, 1985; Hunter and Schmidt, 1982; Mathieu and Leonard, 1986; Rich
and Boudreau, 1987; Schmidt et al., 1979; Schmidt, Mack and Hunter, 1984;
Weekley et al., 1985; Wroten, 1984). Subjects often find the task difficult, refuse
to do it, or produce high inter-rater variance (e.g. Bobko et al., 1983; Mathieu
and Leonard, 1987; Rich and Boudreau, 1987; Reilly and Smither, 1985).
Providing a common 50th percentile anchor can reduce inter-rater variability
as can consensus ratings (Burke and Frederick, 1984; Wroten, 1984) but this
makes SD_y dependent on the anchor (Bobko et al., 1983; Schmidt, Mack and
Hunter, 1984; Wroten, 1984), violating the statistical assumption of independence between the mean and the standard deviation.

Only limited evidence exists on the accuracy of global SD_y estimation, and
tests are usually based on arguably deficient objective performance measures.
Bobko et al. (1983) found that the actual distribution of sales revenue (number
of policies sold times average policy value) for sales counselors was normally
distributed, and that the SD_y estimate based on the averaged difference between
the 85th and 50th and the 50th and 15th percentiles was not significantly
different from the actual sales distribution (although the percentile estimates
were quite different). However, when respondents were asked to consider the
'overall worth of products and services' and 'what you would pay an outside
organization to provide them', the values were only about one-tenth the actual
sales standard deviation, and apparently anchored on pay levels rather than
sales. Burke and Frederick (1984) also found SD_y estimates of overall worth
were lower (about 1 percent of the actual sales standard deviations), and
anchored on various activities including sales. Reilly and Smither (1986) found
that graduate students participating in a business simulation (who had been
provided with data to estimate actual standard deviations) produced global

SD_y estimates slightly higher than the simulation information (for repeat sales and new sales) and much higher than the simulation for net revenue. The SD_y estimate of overall worth was 49 percent of actual repeat sales, 3.45 times actual new sales, and 1.92 times actual net revenue. Thus, the research is sparse and the results are mixed, providing little evidence that global SD_y estimates reflect actual sales or productivity information.

Individualized estimation

This method translates some measurable characteristic of each individual in the sample (e.g. pay, sales activity, performance ratings) into dollars using a scaling factor such as average salary or average sales, with the standard deviation of these values representing SD_y (e.g. Arnold *et al.*, 1982; Bobko *et al.*, 1983; Burke and Frederick, 1984; Cascio and Ramos, 1986; Dunnette, Rosee, Houston, Hough, Toquam, Lammlein, King, Bosshardt and Keyes, 1982; Eulberg, O'Connor and Peters, 1985; Janz and Dunnette, 1974; Ledvinka *et al.*, 1983; Reilly and Smither, 1985). Three individualized estimation techniques have emerged.

First, Cascio (1982) and Cascio and Ramos (1986) used CREPID (Cascio–Ramos Estimate of Performance In Dollars). This method breaks a job into important 'principal activities'. Then, each activity is rated on four dimensions (time/frequency, level of difficulty, importance, and consequence of error), and the ratings multiplied to give an overall weight to the activity. The proportion of total weights becomes the final importance weight assigned to each activity. To assign a dollar value to each activity, average salary for the job is divided among the activities according to the proportional importance weights. After this 'job analysis' phase, supervisors are asked to rate employees' performance on each principal activity, using a 0 to 2 scale. To translate these ratings into dollars, they are multiplied by the dollar value assigned to that activity. After each employee has been assigned a dollar value for each activity, these activity values are summed to provide the total dollar value of yearly performance for that employee.

Janz and Dunnette (1977) proposed a second technique. Their approach also involves identifying critical job activities. However, rather than allocating salary to each activity based on its time/frequency, importance, etc., the Janz and Dunnette procedure requires job experts to estimate the 'relative dollar costs associated with different levels of effectiveness on each of the various job performance dimensions' (p. 120), by tracing the consequences of the various levels of effectiveness to determine their impact on activities to which costs and/or value can be attached.

A third approach to individualized estimation involves having experts simply assign dollar values to individual employees directly. Bobko *et al.* (1983) used this method to derive an SD_y estimate based on sales levels (sales volume times average insurance policy value), with each person's yearly sales representing the individual value estimate. Burke and Frederick (1984) also used individual sales levels. Wroten (1984) adopted a similar approach, but did not have sales data available. He simply asked his supervisors to provide a direct estimate of the yearly dollar value of each employee's performance. Ledvinka et al. (1983) used total payroll plus benefits divided by the number of insurance claims as the value per claim, and then multiplied this value by the actual standard deviation of claims processed.

Individualized estimation has the advantage of assigning a specific value to each employee that can be explicitly examined and analyzed for its appropriateness. Such analysis might be useful in determining which individual attributes contribute to differences in judgments. Methods involving behavioral job analysis (e.g. CREPID or Janz–Dunnette) may be more understandable or credible to those familiar with the job, though absolutely no evidence exists on this issue. Still, each method makes certain basic assumptions regarding the nature of payoff. CREPID is based on the assumption that the average wage equals average productivity, a position not supported by economic theory and clearly violated in organizations with tenure-based pay systems, pay systems based on rank, and many hourly-based pay systems. Sales-based measures are based on the assumption that sales captures sufficient performance differences to be useful (an assumption that may omit important job tasks, such as training, that reduce an individual's sales but increase the group's sales). Janz–Dunnette is based on the assumption that job behavior effects on costs and revenues can be accurately traced by managers. Individualized estimation methods are often more complex, costly and time consuming than other estimation methods, and as yet no evidence suggests whether they improve decisions.

Proportional rules

This measurement approach multiplies some available productivity-related variable (e.g. average wage, average sales, average productivity value) by a proportion to estimate SD_y (e.g. Hunter and Schmidt, 1982; Schmidt and Hunter, 1983; Eaton, Wing and Lau, 1985; Weekley et al., 1985; Cascio and Ramos, 1986; Eulberg et al., 1985; Mathieu and Leonard, 1987). Proportional rules emerged in part from observations concerning the relationship between SD_y estimates and average salary levels, and in part from the desire to provide a straightforward SD_y measurement method that could be used even when the global estimation procedure is not feasible. The method involves multiplying average salary in a job by some proportion (e.g. between 40 and 70 percent) to derive the SD_y estimate for the incumbent employee group.

Hunter and Schmidt (1982, pp. 257–258) reviewed empirical studies and compared their SD_y estimates to reported or derived average salary levels. They discovered that SD_y averaged about 16 percent of average salary. The authors also reviewed two of their own studies (using a global estimation procedure) and noted that SD_y was 60 percent of annual salary in one study of budget analysts and 55 percent of annual salary in another study of computer programmers. They estimated that 'the true average for SD_y falls somewhere in the range of 40 to 70% [of average salary]' (p. 258). They also reviewed empirical data on productivity levels measured in units of output. Their review indicated that for non-piece-rate situations the average ratio of the standard deviation to the mean productivity was 0.185, while in piece-rate situations the average ratio was 0.150, and in uncertain compensation systems the average ratio was 0.215. They concluded that 'researchers examining the utility of personnel programs such as selection and training can estimate the standard deviation of employee output at 20% of mean output without fear of overstatement', and that 'the findings of this study provide support for the practice that we have recommended of estimating SD_y as 40% of mean salary' (p. 412).

The proportional rules proposed by Schmidt and Hunter are intriguing because they suggest that simple SD_y estimation may be quite feasible in virtually all situations. However, this simplification is obtained by assuming that average salary is indeed equal to about half the value of the average value of products 'as sold', which may be violated by tenure-based pay systems, negotiated pay systems, labour market conditions such as unemployment, and internal labor markets (e.g. Becker, 1964). One must also assume that SD_y is equal to about 20 percent of the average value of products 'as sold', which was not the case in a number of the studies reviewed by Schmidt and Hunter (1983).

My review of utility studies through 1986 uncovered 17 SD_y estimates below 40 percent of salary, 18 estimates within the 40 to 70 percent range, and 29 estimates above 70 percent of salary. No SD_y estimates fell below 20 percent of mean output, 9 fell between 23 and 34 percent, and 27 fell above 34 percent (many of these were quite substantially above 34 percent, some as high as 100 percent or more). While these results support the conservatism of this decision rule, it should be noted that a detailed meta-analysis has not been conducted. Moreover, the results suggest that using the Hunter–Schmidt proportional rule may produce such conservative estimates that severely understated utility estimates and rejection of potentially useful HRM programs might result.

Summary

Existing research suggests that differences between SD_y estimates using different methods are often less than 50 percent (and may be less than $5000 in many cases). However, it is tempting to consider the fact that these differences may be multiplied by factors of hundreds or thousands in deriving the final total utility value. Even a small difference multiplied by such large values can imply vast total utility differences, tempting some to conclude that we need substantially more research on SD_y measurement to whittle down such differences and provide more precise total utility estimates. However, carefully considering the role of uncertainty in selection utility tempers this conclusion.

THE ROLE OF UNCERTAINTY AND RISK IN UTILITY ANALYSIS

How is it that selection utility analysis research can simultaneously produce such clear evidence of program payoff (i.e. virtually every study showed positive and often quite large utility values) and such a raging debate on the proper measurement method for one utility parameter (SD_y)? One explanation is that although the expected utility values are quite high, there is also substantial uncertainty associated with these utility estimates, and that uncertainty stems largely from measurement error in SD_y. Properly investigating this issue requires changing the focus of utility analysis from attempting to develop the most accurate estimate of expected utility to attempting to estimate both the expected value and the distribution of values (Boudreau, 1984; Rich and Boudreau, 1987). It focuses attention away from measurement and toward uncertainty and risk in the decision situation.

Four alternative approaches for estimating uncertainty

Rich and Boudreau (1987) provided a conceptual framework for uncertainty in utility analysis and empirically applied four alternative methods to account for uncertainty: (1) sensitivity analysis; (2) break-even analysis; (3) algebraic derivation of utility value distributions; and (4) Monte Carlo simulation analysis.

Sensitivity analysis

Several utility analysis applications have addressed possible variability in utility parameters through sensitivity analysis (e.g. Boudreau, 1983a, b; Boudreau and Berger, 1985a; Cascio and Silbey, 1979; Florin-Thuma and Boudreau, 1987; Schmidt *et al.*, 1979; Schmidt *et al.*, 1984). Sensitivity analysis varies each of the utility parameters from its lowest to its highest value, holding other parameter values constant. The utility estimates resulting from each combination of parameter values are examined to determine which parameters' variability has the greatest effect. A variant of sensitivity analysis involves attempting to be as 'conservative' as possible in making utility estimates. This approach has led researchers to produce clearly understated SD_y values (Arnold *et al.*, 1982), or to estimate the 95 percent confidence interval surrounding the mean SD_y value and use the value at the bottom of this interval in the utility computations (e.g. Schmidt *et al.*, 1979; Hunter and Schmidt, 1982; Schmidt *et al.*, 1984). If resulting utility values remain positive in spite of such conservatism, it is presumed that they will turn out to be positive in the actual application.

Though valuable, sensitivity analysis usually provides no information about the effects of simultaneous changes in several utility parameters (though Boudreau and Berger, 1985a, and Boudreau, 1987, expressed the effects of simultaneous changes in utility parameters) and provides no information regarding the utility value distribution or the probabilities associated with particular parameter value combinations (Hillier, 1963, p. 444). Setting all parameters at their most conservative levels (a statistically unlikely event) risks incorrectly concluding that some programs will not pay off.

Break-even analysis

Boudreau (1984) proposed that a relatively simple uncertainty analysis could be carried out by calculating the lowest value of any individual utility parameter (or parameter combination) that would still yield a positive total utility value. These parameter values were termed 'break-even' values because they represent the values at which the HRM program's benefits are equal ('even with') the program's costs. Any parameter values exceeding the break-even value would produce positive total utility values, and vice versa. Such logic is well-known in microeconomic theory and financial management (i.e. Bierman, Bonini and Hausman, 1981). Boudreau showed that such analysis was useful not only when analyzing a single program, but also when multiple alternatives are involved (with more expensive alternatives offering greater potential payoffs). Boudreau's approach is relatively simple and explicitly focuses on the decision context. Rather than advocating improved measurement in all situations, Boudreau proposed that one should first maximize the knowledge to be gained from existing information (usually the quantity of employees affected and the costs of the program) by estimating the critical values for the unknown parameters, and then determining whether further measurement effort is warranted. Because controversy surrounded the accuracy and validity of SD_y estimates, Boudreau concentrated his analysis on that utility parameter, demonstrating that the break-even SD_y values for the studies by Cascio and Silbey (1979), and Schmidt *et al.* (1979) were substantially lower than the expected SD_y value they derived.

I applied break-even analysis to my more recent review of empirical utility studies. This not only verified the conclusion that selection program utility is uniformly high, but also shed some light on the SD_y controversy. Without exception, the break-even SD_y values fell below 60 percent of the estimated SD_y value. In many cases, the value necessary to break even was less than 1 percent of the estimated value! In fact the break-even SD_y value exceeded 20 percent of the estimated value in only 6 of the 41 analyses. The vast majority of utility analysis applications concluded that the more-valid selection device is worth the extra costs. Break-even analysis supports this conclusion, suggesting that it could probably have been reached without ever actually measuring SD_y (or at least by measuring it in the simplest and most conservative manner possible). The break-even SD_y values often fall several standard deviations below the expected value. Sometimes (e.g. Rich and Boudreau, 1987) the break-even SD_y value falls below the lowest value estimated by any of the subjects. Recent research incorporating Boudreau's break-even analysis approach has reached similar conclusions (e.g. Burke and Frederick, 1985; Cascio and Ramos, 1986; Eaton, Wing and Lau, 1985; Florin-Thuma and Boudreau, 1987; Karren, NKomo and Ramirez, 1985).

Algebraically deriving utility value variability

Recently, statistical formulas for the variance of products of random variables have been adapted to utility analysis. Goodman's (1960) equations for the variance of the product of three or more random variables under conditions of independence were adapted by Alexander and Barrick (1986) to produce a formula for the standard error of utility values associated with a one-cohort selection utility model. Algebraic derivation provides a variance estimate, but it requires assumptions about the distribution shape (e.g. normality) to make strong probabilistic inferences. Existing literature provides no empirical information supporting or refuting the assumption of normality, but Hull (1980) noted that non-normal distributions are likely when: (a) programs can be abandoned or expanded during their life; (b) non-normal components heavily influence the distribution; and (c) there is only a small number of variables.

Monte Carlo analysis of utility value variability

Monte Carlo analysis involves describing each utility model parameter in terms of its expected value and distribution shape. In each trial, a value for each utility parameter is 'chosen' from the distribution for that parameter, and the combination of chosen parameter values is used to calculate the total utility value for that trial. Repeated application of this choosing and calculating procedure (using a computer) produces a sample of trials from which the distribution properties of the utility values can be derived. Thus, unlike the other three methods, simulations can vary many parameters at once, can reflect dependencies among the parameters, can acknowledge possible program expansion or abandonment, and can reflect non-normal distribution assumptions.

  Rich and Boudreau (1987) applied Monte Carlo analysis (and compared it to each of the other three uncertainty estimation methods) using an application of the Programmer Aptitude Test (PAT) to select computer programmers in a mid-size computer manufacturer. They discovered that all of the utility parameters were subject to some degree of uncertainty or variability over time. They also discovered that SD_y variability heavily influenced the utility value distribution and that the distribution of SD_y values was positively skewed as in other studies (Bobko et al., 1983; Burke and Frederick, 1984; Schmidt, Mack and Hunter, 1984; Mathieu and Leonard, 1987). Rich and Boudreau's (1987) findings suggested that the distribution of utility values was greatly affected by the assumptions about the SD_y distribution. They also found that the simulation suggested a greater amount of risk (variability) in utility values than the algebraic derivation because the simulation better reflected dependencies among utility parameters and parameter relationships over time. However, break-even analysis, algebraic derivation and Monte Carlo simulation all led to the same conclusion: positive payoff from the selection program was very likely.

FUTURE RESEARCH IMPLICATIONS

Promising future research directions include integrating selection utility with employee separations and job changes within the organization, extending the payoff function to encompass consequences other than productivity, and studying how selection utility information affects decisions.

The external employee movement utility model

Boudreau and Berger (1985a, b) suggested that there were important analogies between employee acquisitions and employee separations. Selection utility involves choosing a subset of employees to join the workforce from a pool of applicants. Retention utility involves 'choosing' a subset of the previous-period's incumbent workforce to remain with the organization (though retentions are more bilaterally chosen than acquisitions, the analogy for utility purposes is still correct). The utility of both acquisitions and retentions depends on the *quantity* of employees affected (i.e. the number hired and the number retained), on the *quality* of affected employees (i.e. the per-person, per-time period effects of selection strategies; and the per-person, per-time period effects of the retention pattern), and on the *costs* incurred to implement or accommodate the movements (i.e. selection device development/implementation costs and separation costs such as severance pay, relocation assistance, etc.). Boudreau and Berger (1985b, pp. 598–599) concluded that a utility analysis based only upon selection consequences risks not only producing deficient utility values, but also producing values that could lead to faulty decision making. Their results also suggested that selection utility models that ignore retention utility effects may substantially overstate utility values (when less-valuable employees are retained) or understate utility values (when more valuable employees are retained).

Omitting retention utility considerations may severely bias selection utility estimates. When improved selection causes the retention pattern to become less optimal or when the retention pattern is such that the value of improved selection is lost quickly, selection utility values based on simpler models may lead to incorrect decisions. This suggests that employee turnover research and employee selection research should be integrated, with both areas attending to the effects of the other. Moreover, it suggests that studies of employee separations (e.g. 'turnover') that focus only on the costs of separations or on the characteristics of those who leave and stay (e.g. Cascio and McEvoy, 1985; Dalton, Krackhardt and Porter, 1981; McEvoy and Cascio, 1985) must be considered in light of the fact that they fail to consider the effects of those acquired to replace the separations. Thus, the external employee movement utility model provides the framework for integrating and expanding selection utility research.

Integrating selection with internal staffing

Selection programs that appear optimum for a single job may have substantial consequences for internal movement. For example, if improved selection for lower-level jobs also identifies skills and abilities useful in upper-level jobs, then more-valid external acquisition strategies may produce substantially higher benefits than the simple selection utility model can recognize. Conversely, if selection devices are targeted to skills exclusively applicable to a lower-level job, but employees routinely move to upper-level jobs using other skills, then maximizing lower-level job selection utility may simultaneously reduce utility for the upper-level job. These phenomena require an explicit framework integrating the consequences of internal and external employee movement and suggesting the variables likely to determine the utility of such movements—a utility model for internal and external employee movement.

Boudreau (1987) developed such a utility model. His utility model draws upon the analogies between internal and external employee movement. Specifically, Boudreau proposed that each internal employee movement involves a separation from one organizational job and an acquisition by another. Thus, the pattern of internal employee movement can be analyzed using the concepts of selection and retention utility, but must recognize that both types of utility are affected by the same movement. Boudreau's results suggested that decisions based solely on an external selection utility model (or even the external movement utility model including acquisitions and separations/retentions) may produce utility values leading to erroneous conclusions when internal movement patterns offset the apparent positive effects of external selection and retention, and vice versa. Future research should adopt a broader perspective by incorporating internal movement consequences into investigations of productivity-enhancement interventions.

Using selection utility analysis models to examine actual decision processes

While selection utility analysis results are often reported as if they will influence decisions, enhance credibility, and encourage a broader decision focus, existing research has ignored these phenomena. Studies are needed to examine whether the results of selection utility analysis actually affect managerial decisions, whether decision maker's reactions to selection utility results are affected by different estimation techniques, and whether selection utility models accurately reflect the concerns of decision makers. Florin-Thuma and Boudreau (1987) derived the utility of a performance feedback intervention in a small organization, asked decision makers to estimate the parameters of the utility model, and to develop their own decision model. Decision makers underestimated the magnitude of the performance problem and the intervention's effect. Factors considered by decision makers but not included in the utility model (e.g. customer dissatisfaction) argued against the intervention. However, when dollar values were attached to these factors and when the decision maker's assumptions were incorporated into the model, the utility results still suggested substantial payoffs. Apparently, the decision makers had failed to implement the performance feedback intervention because they had simply never considered the performance problem serious enough to warrant systematic consideration. Utility analysis improved their awareness of the problem and their decision.

These results suggest research questions and methodologies to explore more fully the effects of utility analysis on decisions. Such research should draw on the substantial body of knowledge regarding irrationality in decision making (e.g. Kahneman and Tversky, 1972, 1973; March and Simon, 1958). Selection utility analysis models offer detailed frameworks for program analysis. They are normative descriptions of the factors that decision makers 'should' consider in making selection decisions. However, Etzioni (1986) has suggested that rational decision making must be induced because it is contrary to natural inclinations. Selection utility analysis may provide such inducements, but we must first understand how actual decisions depart from selection utility analysis prescriptions, and focus our efforts to induce more rational decision making. Research linking selection utility analysis to actual decisions may discover how selection utility analysis models can be enhanced by better reflecting actual decision considerations.

Selection utility analysis offers vast research potential. Moreover, the results of such research are likely to have very important implications for the ways Human Resource managers (and those who assist them) apply findings from industrial psychology and other social sciences. Future research should emphasize the decisions supported by utility analysis, should incorporate economic information into utility analysis, should adopt a broader and more integrative perspective regarding multiple interventions, and should attend more closely to the effects of utility analysis on managerial decisions. With attention to the research questions noted above, researchers and decision makers will produce decision tools that truly reflect a partnership between applied social science research and managerial decisions regarding human work behavior.

REFERENCES

Alexander, R. A. and Barrick, M. R. (1986). *Estimating the standard error of projected dollar gains in utility analysis.* Working paper, University of Akron.

Arnold, J. D., Rauschenberger, J. M., Soubel, W. and Guion, R. M. (1983). Validation and utility of a strength test for selecting steel workers. *Journal of Applied Psychology,* **67**, 588–604.

Becker, G. (1964). *Human Capital.* New York: National Bureau of Economic Research.

Becker, B. (1985). Utility analysis of human resources programs: Some caveats. Unpublished manuscript.

Bierman, H. Jr, Bonini, C. P. and Hausman, W. H. (1981). *Quantitative Analysis for Business Decisions.* Homewood, Ill: Irwin.

Bobko, P., Karren, R. and Parkington, J. J. (1983). Estimation of standard deviations in utility analysis: an empirical test. *Journal of Applied Psychology,* **68**, 170–176.

Bolda, R. A. (1985). Utility: a productivity planning tool. *Human Resource Planning,* **8**, 111–132.

Boudreau, J. W. (1983a). Economic considerations in estimating the utility of human resource productivity improvement programs. *Personnel Psychology,* **36**, 551–557.

Boudreau, J. W. (1983b). Effects of employee flows on utility analysis of human resource productivity improvement programs. *Journal of Applied Psychology,* **68**, 396–407.

Boudreau, J. W. (1984). Decision theory contributions to HRM research and practice. *Industrial Relations,* **23**, 198–217.

Boudreau, J. W. (1987). *Utility Analysis Applied to Internal and External Employee Movement: an Integrated Theoretical Perspective.* Ithaca, New York: Author.

Boudreau, J. W. (in press, a). Utility analysis: A new perspective on human resource management decisions. In L. D. Dyer and G. Holder (eds), *Human Resource Management: Evolving Roles and Responsibilities.* Vol. 1, ASPA/BNA *Handbook of Human Resource Management.* Washington, D. C.: Bureau of National Affairs.

Boudreau, J. W. (in press, b). Utility analysis for human resource management decisions. In M. D. Dunnette (ed.), *Handbook of Industrial/Organizational Psychology* (2nd edn).

Boudreau, J. W. and Berger, C. J. (1985a). Decision-theoretic utility analysis applied to external employee movement. *Journal of Applied Psychology* [Monograph], **70**, 581–612.

Boudreau, J. W. and Berger, C. J. (1985b). Toward a model of employee movement utility. In K. M. Rowland and G. R. Ferris (eds), *Research in Personnel and Human Resource Management.* Greenwich, Conn.: JAI Press, pp. 31–53.

Boudreau, J. W. and Rynes, S. L. (1985). The role of recruitment in staffing utility analysis. *Journal of Applied Psychology,* **70**, 354–366.

Brogden, H. E. (1946a). On the interpretation of the correlation coefficient as a measure of predictive efficiency. *Journal of Educational Psychology*, **37**, 65–76.

Brogden, H. E. (1946b). An approach to the problem of differential prediction. *Psychometrika*, **14**, 169–182.

Brogden, H. E. (1949). When testing pays off. *Personnel Psychology*, **2**, 171–183.

Brogden, H. E. and Taylor, E. K. (1950). The dollar criterion—applying the cost accounting concept to criterion construction. *Personnel Psychology*, **3**, 133–154.

Burke, M. J. and Frederick, J. T. (1984). Two modified procedures for estimating standard deviations in utility analyses. *Journal of Applied Psychology*, **69**, 482–489.

Burke, M. J. and Frederick, J. T. (1985). *A comparison of economic utility estimates for alternative rational SD_y estimation procedures*. Paper presented at the 45th annual meeting of the Academy of management. San Diego, CA.

Cascio, W. F. (1982). *Costing Human Resources: the Financial Impact of Behavior in Organizations*. Boston, MA: Kent.

Cascio, W. F. and McEvoy, G. M. (1985). Strategies for reducing employee turnover: A meta-analysis. *Journal of Applied Psychology*, **70**, 342–353.

Cascio, W. F. and Ramos, R. (1986). Development and application of a new method for assessing job performance in behavioral/economic terms. *Journal of Applied Psychology*, **1**, 20–28.

Cascio, W. F. and Silbey, V. (1979). Utility of the assessment center as a selection device. *Journal of Applied Psychology*, **64**, 107–118.

Cronbach, L. J. and Gleser, G. C. (1965). *Psychological Tests and Personnel Decisions* (2nd edn). Urbana, IL: University of Illinois Press.

Cronshaw, S. F. and Alexander, R. A. (1985). One answer to the demand for accountability: selection utility as an investment decision. *Organizational Behavior and Human Decision Processes*, **35**, 102–118.

Dalton, D. R., Krackhardt, D. M. and Porter, L. W. (1981). Functional turnover: an empirical assessment. *Journal of Applied Psychology*, **66**, 716–721.

Doppelt, J. E. and Bennett, G. K. (1953). Reducing the cost of training satisfactory workers by using tests. *Personnel Psychology*, **6**, 1–8.

Dunnette, M. D., Rosse, R. L., Houston, J. S., Hough, L. M., Toquam, J., Lammlein, S., King, K. W., Bosshardt, M. J. and Keyes, M. (1982). *Development and validation of an industry-wide electric power plant operator selection system*. Edison Electric Institute.

Eaton, N. K., Wing, H. and Lau, A. (1985). *Utility estimation in five enlisted occupations*. Paper presented at the 1985 Military Testing Association (MTA), San Diego, CA.

Eaton, N. K., Wing, H. and Mitchell, K. J. (1985). Alternate methods of estimating the dollar value of performance. *Personnel Psychology*, **38**, 27–40.

Edwards, W. (1977). Use of multiattribute utility measurement for social decision making. In D. E. Bell, R. L. Keeney, and H. Raiffa (eds), *Conflicting Objectives in Decisions*. New York: Wiley.

Einhorn, H. J. and McCoach, W. P. (1977). A simple multiattribute utility procedure for evaluation. *Behavioral Science*, **22**, 270–282.

Einhorn, H. J., Kleinmuntz, D. N. and Kleinmuntz, B. (1979). Linear regression and process-tracing models of judgment. *Psychological Review*, **86**, 465–485.

Etzioni, A. (1986). Rationality is anti-entropic. *Journal of Economic Psychology*, **7**, 17–36.

Eulberg, J. R., O'Connor, E. J. and Peters, L. H. (1985). *Estimates of the standard deviation of performance in dollars: An investigation of the influence of alternative sources of information*. Paper presented at the 45th Annual Meeting of the Academy of Management, San Diego.

Fischer, G. W. (1976). Multidimensional utility models for risky and riskless choice. *Organizational Behavior and Human Performance*, **17**, 127–146.

Florin-Thuma, B. C. and Boudreau, J. W. (1987). Performance feedback utility in a small organization: effects on organizational outcomes and managerial decision processes. *Personnel Psychology*, **40**, 693–713.

Goodman, L. A. (1960). On the exact variance of products. *Journal of the American Statistical Association*, **55**, 708–713.

Gow, J. F. (1985). Human resource managers must remember the bottom line. *Personnel Journal*, April, 30–32.

Hillier, F. S. (1963). The derivation of probabilistic information for the evaluation of risky investments. *Management Science*, **9**, 443–457.

Huber, G. P. (1980). *Managerial Decision Making*. Glenview, Ill.: Scott, Foresman and Co.

Hull, C. L. (1928). *Aptitude Testing*. Yonkers, New York: World Book.

Hull, J. C. (1980). *The Evaluation of Risk in Business Investment*. Oxford: Pergammon Press.

Hunter, J. E. and Schmidt, F. L. (1982). Fitting people to jobs: the impact of personnel selection on national productivity. In M. D. Dunnette and E. A. Fleishman (eds), *Human Performance and Productivity*, vol. 1. Hillsdale, NJ: Erlbaum, pp. 233–284.

Hunter, J. E., Schmidt, F. L. and Jackson, G. B. (1982). *Meta Analysis: Cumulating Research Findings across Studies*. Beverly Hills, CA: Sage.

Jain, H. and Murray, V. (1984). Why the human resources management function fails. *California Management Review*, **26**, 95–110.

Janz, J. T. and Dunnette, M. D. (1977). An approach to selection decisions: Dollars and sense. In J. R. Hackman *et al.* (eds), *Perspectives on Performance in Organizations*. New York: McGraw-Hill, pp. 119–126.

Kahneman, D. and Tversky, A. (1972). Subjective probability: A judgment of representativeness. *Cognitive Psychology*, **3**, 430–454.

Kahneman, D. and Tversky, A. (1973). On the psychology of prediction. *Psychological Review*, **80**, 237–251.

Karren, R. J., NKomo, S. and Ramirez, D. (1985). *Improving personnel selection decisions: A field survey using decision theory and utility analysis*. Paper presented at the 45th annual meeting of the Academy of Management. San Diego, CA.

Keeney, R. L. and Raiffa, H. (1976). *Decisions with Multiple Objectives: Preferences and Value Tradeoffs*. New York: Wiley.

Landy, F. J., Farr, J. L. and Jacobs, R. R. (1982). Utility concepts in performance measurement. *Organizational Behavior and Human Performance*, **30**, 15–40.

Ledvinka, J., Simonet, J. K., Neiner, A. G. and Kruse, B. (1983). *The dollar value of JEPS at Life of Georgia*. Unpublished technical report.

Lee, R. and Booth, J. M. (1974). A utility analysis of a weighted application blank designed to predict turnover for clerical employees. *Journal of Applied Psychology*, **59**, 516–518.

March, J. G. and Simon, H. G. (1958). *Organizations*. New York: Wiley.

Mathieu, J. E. and Leonard, R. L., Jr (1987). An application of utility concepts to a supervisor skills training program: a time-based approach. *Academy of Management Journal*, **30**, 316–335.

McEvoy, G. M. and Cascio, W. F. (1985). Turnover and employee performance: A meta-analytic review. Presented at the 45th annual meeting of the National Academy of Management. San Diego, August.

Naylor, J. C. and Shine, L. C. (1965). A table for determining the increase in mean criterion score obtained by using a selection device. *Journal of Industrial Psychology*, **3**, 33–42.

Reilly, R. R. and Smither, J. W. (1985). An examination of two alternative techniques to estimate the standard deviation of job performance in dollars. *Journal of Applied Psychology*, **70**, 651–661.

Rich, J. R. and Boudreau, J. W. (1987). The effects of variability and risk on selection utility analysis: an empirical comparison. *Personnel Psychology*, **40**, 55–84.

Roche, U. F. (1961). The Cronbach–Gleser utility function in fixed treatment employee selection. Unpublished doctoral dissertation. Southern Illinois University, 1961. Portions reproduced in L. J. Cronbach and G. C. Gleser (eds), *Psychological Tests and Personnel Decisions*. Urbana. Ill., University of Illinois Press, 1965, pp. 254–266.

Schmidt, F. L. and Hoffman, B. (1973). Empirical comparison of three methods of assessing utility of a selection device. *Journal of Industrial and Organizational Psychology*, **1973**, 13–22.

Schmidt, F. L. and Hunter, J. E. (1983). Individual differences in productivity: an empirical test of estimates derived from studies of selection procedure utility. *Journal of Applied Psychology*, **68**, 407–414.

Schmidt, F. L., Hunter, J. E., McKenzie, R. C. and Muldrow, T. W. (1979). Impact of valid selection procedures on work-force productivity. *Journal of Applied Psychology*, **64**, 609–626.

Schmidt, F. L., Mack, M. J. and Hunter, J. E. (1984). Selection utility in the occupation of U. S. park ranger for three modes of test use. *Journal of Applied Psychology*, **69**, 490–497.

Sheppeck, M. A. and Cohen, S. L. (1985). Put a dollar value on your training programs. *Training and Development Journal*, November, 59–62.

Taylor, H. C. and Russell, J. T. (1939). The relationship of validity coefficients to the practical effectiveness of tests in selection: Discussion and Tables. *Journal of Applied Psychology*, **23**, 565–578.

Van Naersson, R. F. (1963). *Selectie van chauffers*. Groningen: Wolters. Portions reproduced in L. J. Cronbach and G. C. Gleser (eds), *Psychological Tests and Personnel Decisions*. Urbana. Ill., University of Illinois Press, 1965.

Weekley, J. A., O'Connor, E. J., Frank, B. and Peters, L. W. (1985). A comparison of three methods of estimating the standard deviation of performance in dollars. *Journal of Applied Psychology*, **79**, 122–126.

Wroten, S. P. (1984). *Overcoming the futilities of utility applications: measures, models and management*. Presented at the American Psychological Association's 92nd Meeting, Toronto, August.

21

Comment on Selection Utility Analysis

PAUL R. SACKETT
Industrial Relations Center, University of Minnesota

SELECTION UTILITY ANALYSIS IN PRACTICE

The number of research citations in Boudreau's paper makes it clear that selection utility analysis is a subject of considerable interest to researchers. Less apparent is whether and how utility analysis is being implemented in practice. The present author has obtained some data which offer limited insight into this question. Sixteen proposals from psychological consulting firms for the development and validation of selection systems which had been submitted to a number of organizations in response to requests for proposals between the years 1983 and 1986 were examined by this author, who had been retained by the organizations to advise them in the selection of a consultant to develop and validate the systems. In all cases the request for proposals included a request that a utility analysis be conducted, and asked that the proposed approach to utility analysis be specified.

Examination of the utility proposals revealed that 8 of the 16 proposed to use the Brogden–Cronbach–Gleser utility approach and 8 proposed a Taylor–Russell approach (see Boudreau's paper for a description of these approaches). None of those using the Brogden–Cronbach–Gleser approach incorporated any of the more recent amplifications of the model, such as the tax and discounting parameters discussed by Boudreau. Given the recency of these modifications of the model, their exclusion should not be surprising. Of those using the Brogden–Cronbach–Gleser approach, half proposed to estimate SD_y using the Schmidt, Hunter, McKenzie, and Muldrow (1979) subjective estimate

Advances in Selection and Assessment. Edited by M. Smith and I. T. Robertson

approach and half proposed to use the 40 percent of salary rule of thumb as the SD_y estimate.

Thus at least in this limited sampling of the use of selection utility analysis in applied settings, the approaches used were quite simple. While recent research focuses on fine-tuning the Brogden–Cronbach–Gleser model, a number of practitioners are still relying on the Taylor–Russell approach. Whether this represents lack of awareness of the more recent developments or a conscious decision to use a simpler approach could not be determined.

THE ROLE OF 'NUMBER OF TIME PERIODS AFFECTED' IN UTILITY ANALYSIS

Boudreau has done the field a great service by reframing selection utility models as consisting of three basic attributes—quantity, quality, and cost—and in emphasizing the critical role of quantity (number of employees and number of time periods affected) in determining the utility of a human resource program. My sense is that psychology has focused on the 'quality' component because that is where psychological input to the model is obviously reflected: predictor validity, mean predictor score of selected individuals, and standard deviation of performance. The models, as presented to students of psychology, tend to focus on utility per selectee per time period, resulting in the presentation of utility as 'quality minus cost'. Multiplying utility per selectee by number selected and by average tenure to obtain total utility tends to be presented as an afterthought: the quantity component does not receive the attention given to the quality component.

On the surface, this emphasis seems reasonable: obtaining appropriate validity information and performance variability information for input into the model jump out to psychologists as the aspects of the utility model that are not mundane and that require their expertise. I will contend here that incorporating the quantity component of the model, particularly the 'number of time periods affected' variable, makes important assumptions about the stability of performance, the stability of predictor validity, and the relationship between performance and turnover that have not received adequate attention. Each of these will be addressed in turn.

First, multiplying utility per selectee per time period by the average number of time periods an employee will remain on the job assumes that the standard deviation of performance remains constant across these time periods. Conceptually, competing models of performance variability over time are plausible. One possibility is that variability increases over time: while both high and low performers benefit from training and experience, high performers benefit more, thus increasing the standard deviation of performance. A second is that over time variability decreases: high ability individuals reach maximum performance more quickly than low ability individuals, but over time the performance gap closes. Data from the task acquisition literature support this second possibility: Ackerman (1987) shows that performance variability typically declines across trials. However, generalization from short term task performance to long term job performance is questionable. A third possibility is that performance variability remains constant over time. Schmidt, Hunter, Pearlman, and Hirsh (1985) cite a doctoral dissertation by McDaniel (1985) as indicating no change in the standard deviation of job performance with job experience.

Alternatively, under some circumstances performance variability may increase over time and under others it may decrease. Work in the area of cognitive skill acquisition which categorizes tasks as controlled information processing tasks (i.e. tasks continuously involving novel information and thus requiring conscious attention) vs automatic information processing tasks (i.e. tasks invariant in information input and processing demands) (e.g. Shiffrin and Schneider, 1977) may prove relevant. Performance variability may remain constant or increase for jobs involving primarily controlled processing and decrease for jobs involving primarily automatic processing.

No attempt is made here to conduct a thorough search for literature on performance variability over time; the intent is merely to call attention to the implicit assumption that variability is constant. Note that if the true state of affairs is that performance variability increases, treating performance variability as a constant produces a conservative utility estimate. Only if performance variability decreases does treating it as a constant inflate a utility estimate.

The second implicit assumption made in multiplying utility per person per time period by the number of time periods affected is that validity remains constant over time. In other words, if a test correlates 0.35 with first year performance and the average tenure is 10 years, inserting these values in the utility equation is only appropriate if the test were also to correlate 0.35 with performance over the subsequent 9 years. This assumption of constant validity has recently been questioned by Henry and Hulin (1987), who present data on objective performance indices of professional baseball players over a 10 year period: the last year in the minor leagues and 9 years in the major leagues. They examined intercorrelations among these 10 years of performance data and found a systematic pattern of results: performance in adjacent years (e.g. year 1 and year 2; year 6 and year 7) correlates relatively highly (0.51 for batters and 0.67 for pitchers), but as the time interval between measures increases, the correlation between the measures decreases. For example, year 1 and year 10 performance correlate 0.12 for batters and 0.08 for pitchers. Henry and Hulin suggest that one can conceptualize year 1 performance as an ability measure, and thus interpret the data as showing a systematic decrease in ability-performance correlations (i.e. validity coefficients) over time.

Conceptualizing first year performance as an ability measure is troubling, as it is at least mathematically possible for an external predictor (e.g. a paper and pencil ability test) to have a constant correlation with performance over time even though the performance measures show this pattern of decreasing intercorrelations as the time interval increases. However, conceptualizing first year (i.e. minor league) performance as a work sample test does not require the troubling equation of performance with ability. I/O psychologists tend to think highly of job simulations as work sample tests; the more realistic the simulation the better. Therefore, view the minor leagues as a very elaborate simulation and consider minor league performance as a predictor of major league performance. If one followed the relatively common practice of obtaining criterion data for validation purposes after one year on the job (i.e. in the major leagues) and then correlated minor league performance with this criterion, one would obtain a correlation of 0.31 for batters and 0.49 for pitchers. This gives a very different picture of the predictive power of minor league performance than is obtained by averaging the correlations between minor league performance and performance in each of the nine successive years. The average correlation for batters is 0.17; for pitchers it is 0.15. Attempts to determine the utility of this work sample predictor inserting first year validity and multiplying by average tenure would lead to a substantial overestimate.

It can no doubt be argued that professional baseball is an idiosyncratic occupation, differing in many ways (e.g. an extremely low selection ratio) from most other occupations. No argument is made here that these findings must generalize to other jobs or to other predictors. Nonetheless, the presentation of data on one selection situation in which validity decreases over time suggests that consideration of the stability of validity over time is appropriate.

The third implicit assumption made in multiplying utility per selectee per time period by the number of time periods affected is that there is no systematic relationship between turnover and performance. Utility estimates will be in error if the average tenure of high performers is greater than or less than that of low performers. This issue has received considerable attention in the turnover literature; a review by Jackofsky (1984) indicates that empirical findings are mixed, with some showing higher turnover among high performers, other showing higher turnover among low performers, and others showing no difference. Jackofsky presents a conceptual model hypothesizing a positive relationship between performance and voluntary turnover, a negative relationship between performance and involuntary turnover, and a strong negative relationship between job satisfaction and turnover for high performers as a result of ease of movement for high performers. These hypotheses suggest that the performance-turnover relationship can vary from situation to situation and that routinely assuming no relationship in planning a utility analysis may be misleading.

In sum, the above discussion counters the notion that the 'quality' component of the utility model is the sole way in which psychological research contributes to effective use of the model. The assumptions outlined above highlight even more strongly the notion that striving for point estimates of utility should be replaced by analyses incorporating the degree of uncertainty present in most parameters of the model.

POINT ESTIMATES VS BREAK-EVEN ANALYSIS

Boudreau argues compellingly against exerting large amounts of research effort pursuing the SD_y estimation problem. Research comparing SD_y estimation approaches has tended to indicate that different approaches do not converge; which estimate (if any) is correct cannot be determined. Attempts to find an external standard for comparison appear doomed: the presence of an objective performance standard (e.g. sales figures) against which estimates can be compared raises an additional series of concerns. Estimators may simply be using the standard as the basis for their judgments, thus limiting generalizability to jobs for which an objective standard is not available. Also, as Boudreau notes, the standard itself is likely to be deficient as a measure of global performance.

These concerns lead Boudreau to frame the utility question not as 'what is the return on this investment?', but rather as 'can we state with confidence that the return will be above a specific value?'. Thus by focusing first on the 'quantity' and 'cost' components of the utility model, one can determine the value of the 'quality' component needed to reach this specific value—either a break-even point or a specified return on investment. Once this is determined, conservative estimates of the variables entering the quality component are obtained. If inserting these estimates into the equation produces a utility value in excess of the specified return, one can conclude that the proposed investment is worthwhile. If these conservative estimates produce a value short of the specified return, the analysis can be repeated with less conservative values, each with a probability attached, and the risk of failing to produce the specified return can be determined.

While this approach seems eminently reasonable, the implications of moving away from attempting point estimates of utility should be noted. The approach just discussed implies that an organization is making a 'go/no-go' decision about a personnel/human resource program (e.g. should we or should we not establish an assessment center for managerial selection?). However, consider situations in which multiple possible investments are being compared (e.g. should we spend our fixed budget on an assessment center or on a training program?). In such situations both a point estimate of expected utility and an assessment of variability around this estimate are needed.

The above example dealt with comparing very different investments (e.g. a training program vs new computers). There has been some sentiment in the personnel/human resource community that by mastering and using the terminology of the fields and finance and accounting and by applying utility analysis using this language the personnel/human resource function will be able to compete with other functional areas for additional financial support. While this may be of value in the future, perhaps attempts at this type of competition represent overreaching at this point in time: rather than attempting to make a case for the relative value of personnel/human resource programs compared to other investments, we should acknowledge the uncertainty involved in our utility estimates (even if others are not as willing to acknowledge the uncertainty in their estimates) and focus our efforts on showing that a positive return can be expected from human resource investments. Simply having this message received and accepted by the business community would be a major step forward.

UTILITY ANALYSIS: DECISION AID VS SCIENTIFIC TOOL

It may be useful to differentiate between two very different ways of using the utility model. One focuses solely on the model as a decision aid. The user of the model relies on estimates from managers of all components of the model: quality, quantity, and cost. Accuracy of the parameter estimates is not an issue: if the manager believes that the increment in performance per person per time period resulting from a graining program will be $200, that value is inserted in the equation. The value of the model using this approach is simply the formalization of the thought processes and value judgments of the managers involved in the decision. A consultant using this approach says, in essence: 'I don't have expertise in estimating model parameters; what I have to offer is a framework for integrating the various factors that can influence a decision'.

The second way of using the model involves attempting to determine model parameters accurately. Research into model parameters may produce findings at odds with initial managerial expectations; for example, the increment in performance per person per period of time may be greater or less than managers would have expected. A consultant using this approach says, in essence: 'I offer both a framework for integrating the various factors that can influence a decision and expertise in determining model parameters (e.g. the validity of the program under consideration)'.

Thus two consultants offering 'expertise in utility analysis' to organizations may be offering very different things: a decision framework vs the decision framework plus expertise in measuring model parameters. This discussion suggests the need for clarification when a proposal for services simply indicates that 'utility analysis will be conducted'.

TIME PERSPECTIVE OF ORGANIZATIONAL DECISION MAKERS

Boudreau's reframing of utility analysis in terms of the three components of quality, quantity, and cost has effectively pointed out the critical role played by the quantity component. By extending utility computations beyond a single time period for a single cohort and considering that the typical selection system will be applied to multiple cohorts of individuals who will on average remain in the organization for a considerable amount of time one recognizes the leverage value of the quantity component of the model.

While the benefits of a selection system accrue over a substantial period of time, it is not uncommon for the costs to be concentrated at the development stages of the system. A test that may cost virtually nothing to use once developed and validated may require an up-front investment of hundreds of thousands of dollars for development and validation. Data that may be persuasive to a utility researcher taking a long term perspective may be seen as irrelevant by a manager whose reward system emphasizes only short-term payoff. Thus in communicating information about the utility of human resource programs higher level managers seem to be the appropriate target level if higher level managers tend to take a longer time perspective than lower level managers. Changing the time perspective of individual managers may be easier said than done without a change in the organizational reward system to reinforce taking a long term perspective.

DETECTING THE EFFECTS OF SELECTION SYSTEMS

A common skeptical response to claims that selection systems can make huge contributions to productivity is that if the gains were really that large they would be readily detectable: detectable not only to researchers with elaborate techniques, but also to the typical manager. Scientific selection is not new; there has been ample opportunity for the higher performance of organizations or organizational subunits using valid selection programs to manifest itself. Should not performance improvements of the magnitude reported be visible to the naked eye?

This leads to some speculation about the sensitivity of managers to differences in performance. First, Boudreau's point about the leverage value of average tenure and number of cohorts affected is relevant: a very small average performance gain per time period may translate to very large total utility. Second, and related, the average performance gain per employee per time period may be dwarfed by the standard deviation of performance. Managers may take greater note of the extremes in performance; a selection system that increases average performance may only slightly reduce the standard deviation of performance. Managers' attention may focus on dealing with problem performers: that the selection system has not eliminated these may affect perceptions of the effect of the system. Third, the relatively small number of individuals for whom a first line supervisor is responsible may not be a large enough sample for mean performance differences to be readily visible, particularly in situations where hiring is sporadic and done when vacancies arise rather than in large cohorts. If, for example, the first new hire assigned to a supervisor after implementation of the new selection system is a mediocre or substandard performer, this may cloud the supervisor's opinion of the system. Fourth, unless a formal experiment is done in which some employees are hired using the new selection system while others are hired simultaneously using the old, comparisons by supervisors of employees selected using the old and new systems are confounded by memory effects. Inexperienced employees selected under the new system can easily be compared with experienced employees selected under the old system; less readily available, unless historical objective performance data are routinely kept, is information about how those selected under the old system performed as new hires.

This is certainly not a complete list of reasons why performance gains may not readily be perceived by supervisors; nonetheless, it does suggest that the fact that performance gains are not sometimes readily apparent should not be seen as a strong argument that the gains suggested by utility analysis are somehow in error.

CONCLUSION

This chapter has used Boudreau's work as a starting point for a discussion of some issues in the application of utility analysis. Several of the ideas suggest future research directions, such as the discussion of stability of validity over time, the stability of performance variability over time, the relationship between performance and turnover, and the perception of differences in job performance by supervisors. Interest in utility analysis is substantial; continued work on both the measurement of model parameters and on the effective communication of utility analysis results to organizational decision makers is needed.

REFERENCES

Ackerman, P. L. (1987). Individual differences in skill learning: an integration of psychometric and information processing perspectives. *Psychological Bulletin*, **102**, 3–27.

Henry, R. A. and Hulin, C. L. (1987). Stability of skilled performance across time: some generalizations and limitations on utilities. *Journal of Applied Psychology*, **72**, 457–462.

Jackofsky, E. F. (1984). Turnover and job performance: an integrated model. *Academy of Management Review*, **9**, 74–83.

McDaniel, M. A. (1985). *The evaluation of a causal model of job performance: the interrelationships of general mental ability, job experience and job performance.* Doctoral dissertation, George Washington University.

Schmidt, F. L., Hunter, J. E., McKenzie, R. C. and Muldrow, T. W. (1979). Impact of valid selection procedures on work-force productivity. *Journal of Applied Psychology*, **64**, 609–626.

Schmidt, F. L., Hunter, J. E., Pearlman, K. and Hirsh, H. R. (1985). Forty questions about validity generalization and meta-analysis. *Personnel Psychology*, **38**, 697–798.

Shiffrin, R. M. and Schneider, W. (1977). Controlled and automatic human information processing II: perceptual learning, automatic attending, and a general theory. *Psychological Review*, **84**, 127–190.

22

Case Study on Utility: Utility to the Rescue, a Case of Staffing Program Decision Support

Tom Janz
University of Calgary, Alberta

BACKGROUND TO THE ANALYSIS

Specialists in the human resources (HR) department of a large, public telephone utility faced a big problem. Some time ago, they had decided to improve staffing effectiveness by adopting behavior based, patterned interviews founded on formal job analyses (Janz, Hellervik, and Gilmore, 1987; Janz, 1987a). The HR specialists consulted with a firm specializing in behavioral interviewing, and had already spent substantial internal resources to develop the job analyses leading to structured interview questions. But they had proceeded to the point of actually training in-house trainers without obtaining senior executive approval. The executive presentation seeking this approval was less than a week away when the HR specialists became aware of the selection utility formula, and its power to cast the decision as an investment having costs, benefits, net benefits, return on investment, and net present value (Schmidt, Hunter, and Pearlman, 1982; Boudreau and Berger, 1985; Janz and Etherington, 1985).

The HR specialists were particularly concerned since a Vice President had expressed concern over the large time investment already made by his people in the job analysis phase. He was not sure that the further time spent for training line managers was worth while.

Advances in Selection and Assessment. Edited by M. Smith and I. T. Robertson
© 1989 John Wiley & Sons Ltd

UTILITY THEORY AND CALCULATION

The utility theory that guided the selection of parameters and the calculations arises from Cronbach and Gleser's (1965) classic treatment. While the basic formula relating staffing parameters to dollar costs and benefits remains useful over time, it fails to account for the following five practical realities (Boudreau and Berger, 1985; Janz, 1987b).

First, earlier applications of the Cronbach formula relied on analyzing only one year's hiring (Schmidt, Hunter, McKenzie, and Muldrow, 1979). Since an investment in more accurate staffing decisions is likely to affect hiring decisions for more than just one year, forecasts should examine the impact on the projected hiring over a meaningful life of the investment. This calculation analyzes the forecasted selection openings over the next four years.

Second, the probability of the applicant accepting offers was previously assumed to be 1.0. In practice offer acceptance varies substantially from this level, falling as low as 30 percent, lowering forecast utility. This calculation multiplies selection gain by the probability of offer acceptance.

Third, as it stands, the utility formula makes no allowance for the almost universal phenomenon of the short list. After the job opening is posted or advertised, someone faces a pile of applications or resumes. Trimming that pile down to those applicants who will be invited to appear for testing or interviews remains a crucial selection phase. Previous utility formula assumed that all applicants received the same selection treatment. This calculation computes the screening and hiring selection gains as well as selection costs separately, allowing a more realistic portrayal of costs and benefits.

Fourth, utility essentially calculates net benefit or benefit minus costs. To make sound investment decisions, managers often examine net benefit in conjunction with return on investment. Financial managers also understand the time value of money. Net present value reveals the net benefit in today's dollars of the future returns from better employees. This calculation presents Return On Investment (ROI) and net present value for the staffing investment.

Fifth, utility forecasts remain subject to inflation and taxes, yet the Cronbach and Gleser equation leaves them out. For this calculation, tax considerations adjust both the costs and savings for the organization's tax rate. Inflation adjusts costs as well as the standard deviation of performance for annual projected wage inflation.

THE PARAMETERS

The HR specialists from the telephone utility provided estimates of the following parameters. First, openings were forecast for 1987 (388), 88 (300),

89 (200), and 90 (100) for a total 988. As the years progressed, their estimates grew more conservative.

Based on their knowledge of the workforce, the HR specialists set average tenure at 10 years and average salary over all positions coming open at $35000. They agreed that the 40 percent rule applied for setting annual dollar performance spread. Based on their experience with conducting the current staffing system, they currently recruit using postings, ads, and agencies, spending $125500 in 1987 on recruiting and receiving 20 serious applications per opening. Their current screening process is subjective, yielding a validity of 0.1 for a cost of $20 per resume. Offers were accepted 90 percent of the time.

Their current selection method is unstructured interviews and references, with relevant appraisal information for internal moves, yielding a validity of 0.4 for a cost of $300 per applicant (some travel involved). The staffing investment they compared to current practice was structured, behavioral interviewing. Startup costs were $225,000 including the job analyses, pattern development, and training all line managers. An extra $40 per applicant was added for the more intense behavioral interviews. Validity was set conservatively at 0.7 (Janz, 1987b).

Corporate tax rate was 20 percent. They projected wage inflation at 4 percent over the next five years and selected 11 percent at the long term bond rate for the net present value calculation.

UTILITY FORECAST RESULTS

For spending a total of $1.7m on recruitment, screening, and unstructured interviews to fill 988 positions over the next four years, the modified utility formula forecasted a dollar performance saving of $73m compared with random selection.

If the phone company completes its plans to install behavioral interviewing, it will spend a total of $2.1m on recruitment, screening and behavioral interviews to fill the same 988 positions, but the forecasted performance saving rises to $116m compared with random selection.

Directly comparing the costs and the benefits for unstructured vs behavioral interviews after tax adjustments reveals a cost difference of $471,000, and a benefit difference of $45m for a net benefit of $44.8m. This represents a return on investment of 95 times. The net present value analysis over the 19 years that these savings in improved job performance are realized produced a $28.3m net present value.

PRACTICAL RESULTS

The utility forecasts were completed in one hour using the program cited (Janz, 1987b) and the results were faxed to the head office. They were included in the executive presentation the next day. According to the HR contacts, the utility forecasts were the hit of the presentation. The President was astonished to see how quickly this investment in better people paid off. He commented that with returns such as these, the company could not afford not to proceed with the remaining stages of the training. The skeptical VP was not at this meeting, and the President did not want things to fall between the cracks. He read a directive that 'behavioral interview training will receive priority' into the minutes of the meeting, ensuring a clear understanding of its importance.

REFERENCES

Boudreau, J. W. and Berger, C. J. (1985). Decision-theoretic utility analysis applied to employee separations and acquisitions. *Journal of Applied Psychology*, **70**, 581–612.

Cronbach, L. J. and Gleser, G. (1965). *Psychological Tests and Personnel Decisions*, (2nd edn). Urbana, IL: University of Illinois Press.

Janz, J. T. (1987a). The selection interview: the received wisdom versus recent research. In Dolan and Schuler (eds), *Canadian Readings in Personnel and Human Resource Management*. St. Paul, Minn: West.

Janz, J. T. (1987b). *Utility Analysis for Practical Settings: the Staffing Cash Flow PC Program and Manual*. Calgary, Alberta: Human Performance Systems, Inc.

Janz, J. T. and Etherington, L. E. (1985). Using forecasted net benefits in designing improved recruitment and selection systems. *International Journal of Forecasting*, **1**, 287–296.

Janz, J. T., Hellervik, L. and Gilmore, D. C. (1987). *Behavior Description Interviewing: New, Accurate, Cost Effective*. Newton, Mass: Allyn and Bacon.

Schmidt, F. L., Hunter, J. E., McKenzie, R. C. and Muldrow, T. W. (1979). Impact of valid selection procedures on workforce productivity. *Journal of Applied Psychology*, **64**, 609–626.

Schmidt, F. L., Hunter, J. E. and Pearlman, K. (1982). Assessing the economic impact of personnel programs on work-force productivity. *Personnel Psychology*, **35**, 333–347.

Index